DOROTHY L. SAYERS

CHILD AND WOMAN OF HER TIME

DOROTHY L. SAYERS

CHILD AND WOMAN
OF HER TIME

A supplement to
The Letters of Dorothy L. Sayers

VOLUME FIVE

CHOSEN AND EDITED BY

BARBARA REYNOLDS

WITH A PREFACE BY
CHRISTOPHER DEAN

THE DOROTHY L. SAYERS SOCIETY

Introduction and Notes Copyright © 2002 by Barbara Reynolds
Preface Copyright © 2002 by Christopher Dean

First published in Great Britain by The Dorothy L. Sayers Society
Carole Green Publishing 2–4 Station Road, Swavesey, Cambridge CB4 5QJ

ISBN 0 95180 07 8

British Library Cataloguing-in-Publication Data
A catalogue record of this book is available from the British Library

Designed and produced by Geoff Green
at Geoff Green Book Design, Swavesey, Cambridge CB4 5RA
Typeset in Baskerville
Printed in Great Britain by
St Edmundsbury Press
Bury St Edmunds, Suffolk

Frontispiece:
Johanna Lloyd Portrait by Sir Joshua Reynolds.

Contents

ഏഏഏ

Preface

ᘓᘔᘓᘔᘓᘔ

To this day Dorothy L. Sayers remains full of surprises. She left so many unsolved mysteries in her works and in her life, but great detective writer that she was, she left clues for those who know where to look. What a treat it is to have these two incomplete texts or sketches introduced for the first time, faithfully edited by Barbara Reynolds, who does know where to look.

After the success of the first volume of *The Letters of Dorothy L. Sayers* seven years ago it seemed right that the Dorothy L. Sayers Society should take on the responsibility for the publication of further volumes, and I feel more than justified in this decision when I see the extent to which all four volumes have become not just a delight to those who read for pleasure but a valuable source of research for scholars into Sayers' works as well as her life. Look at the insight into her plays, her concern for every detail of production as well as structure, her views on other writers and artists. See the extent of her search into biblical and theological exactitude, her concern for truth in the case of Robert Graves and Lucan, and her passionate love affair with Dante. All of these are interwoven with minute details of her life with family and friends. Anyone wishing to study her as a critic of drama (1909–1957) has a wealth of material to hand.

This book is very different from its predecessors because it shows us the writer at work, it presents the process of building up a novel from raw material, *The Letters*, through the first draft, *My Edwardian Childhood*, to the second, *Cat O'Mary*. It contains those parts which the author would have eliminated in the final version and in this sense we are greatly privileged. They are different, too, in that the raw material and the first draft are written in the first person singular while the second draft, which begins to turn into the novel, is in the third person. This can be clearly seen by comparing the description in *My Edwardian Childhood* with that in *Cat O'Mary* of the family's arrival at Bluntisham/Fentisham. Or again when comparing the enthusiasm in *The Letters* of Dorothy, Molly and Violet at Godolphin for acting and reading with the emotional feel for words which Rose and Kate experience in *Cat O'Mary* when reading Marlowe: "One can get quite giddy on Marlowe. [...] Words, words, words. [...] Words to be chanted, shouted, bawled aloud to the winds! 'Shut up, you ass! Everybody'll think you're crazy'. Well, let them [...]...Come and stay with us one holidays and we will act it together." The first phrase reminds one of Harriet's question to Peter in the punt in *Gaudy Night*: "Do you find it easy to get drunk on words?"

The third section of the novel would be disappointing were it not for the help of a recently discovered notebook and Barbara Reynolds' careful piecing together of other, external, evidence. On its own it is insubstantial and uneven, dissimilar to the first two parts, but it was a very proper decision to include it because it shows the early attempts to express ideas which are later fully developed in ways we might not have expected. As a writer, proud of her craftsmanship, Dorothy L. Sayers would surely have approved of showing the way in which her work was structured.

The Introduction is the fascinating key to this book. It is integral to the texts because Barbara Reynolds conducts and concludes her investigation into the genesis and completion of this apparently incomplete book; *apparently* incomplete because Dorothy L. Sayers never published *Cat O'Mary*. Barbara Reynolds lays before us the chronology of these two drafts; by remarkable good fortune she is able to link these to the notebook which was in use in 1934, and she makes her deductions. She doesn't treat the question *Why* Dorothy Sayers never completed the much advertised "straight novel" but she proposes a convincing case to prove *How* she did finish it.

The notes not only explain allusions and concepts from a past age but they relate to Sayers' own life and her other works. Most helpful are the appendices explaining Euclid's Tennis Court, the French translations and the genealogical tree. The illustrations are superb. They range from 18th century portraits by Sir Joshua Reynolds and Charles Willson Peale to early and modern photographs and Norah Lambourne's delicate reconstruction of the Sayers family walking up the drive to Bluntisham rectory.

When we thanked Barbara Reynolds for her magnificent work in completing four volumes of *The Letters of Dorothy L. Sayers* we had every reason to believe that she had finished her task. But we didn't read her Introduction to Volume four carefully enough, for she wrote only that it was "the last of my selection of the letters"; we should have remembered what Dorothy Sayers herself wrote in a different context: "I can now see no end to Peter this side of the grave". This could indeed be applied to the extent of Sayers scholarship throughout the world, the many different themes which it encompasses and the byways into which she leads us, all of which are put into perspective by Barbara Reynolds' continued devotion to her work.

Christopher Dean
Chairman, The Dorothy L. Sayers Society. 2002

Introduction

ↄↄↄↄↄↄ

This volume serves as a supplement to the *Letters of Dorothy L. Sayers*, not only to those of her childhood but also to the period of her life when she was working on what she called a "straight novel". Although unfinished, the two texts which are published here for the first time reveal a number of unknown aspects of Dorothy L. Sayers, the child and woman of her time.

*

On 19 January 1932 Dorothy Sayers wrote to her cousin Ivy Shrimpton:

> In a spasm of middle-agedness the other day, I started to write memoirs of my childhood – but I find I don't remember much about it, really![1]

A month later, on 17 February, writing again to Ivy, she said:

> I have for the moment abandoned my "Memoirs", as I shall have to get on with a new book – which is to be all about a big church in the Fens, and a grave which is suddenly found to have an extra body in it!![2]

The "Memoirs", as she calls them, were entitled *My Edwardian Childhood* and this is the earliest known mention of them.

The "new book" was *The Nine Tailors*, which was published on 8 January 1934. She was under contract to her publisher Victor Gollancz to produce one detective novel a year. *Have His Carcase*, published on 11 April 1932, was to have been followed immediately by *The Nine Tailors* but work on the bell-ringing which plays a crucial part in that novel took her so long that, in order to fulfil her obligation, she was compelled to write another novel quickly on a subject that was familiar to her. This was *Murder Must Advertise*, based on her experience as a copy-writer at Benson's, published on

---

1 See Volume I, p. 319.
2 Ibid. p. 320.

6 February 1933. She told Gollancz that she hated it because it was not the book she wanted to write,[3] but despite her own feelings about it *Murder Must Advertise* was an immediate success and has remained one of the most popular of her novels ever since.

Between finishing *Have His Carcase* and the date of its publication she had been ill. This is shown in a letter to Professor Donald Tovey dated 18 January 1934, in which, apologising for an error, she said:

> …being very unwell at the time, [I] was unable to correct my own proofs. I'm very sorry.[4]

It is not known what the illness was, but "very unwell" suggests something more serious than a bad cold or influenza. It may be that she occupied her convalescence jotting down her early memories, a relatively undemanding task and one which evidently gave her pleasure, as can be seen from the happy tone of the text. Her son John Anthony was by then eight years old and perhaps her observation of his childhood had put her in mind of her own. Her letter to Ivy Shrimpton of 19 January 1932 in fact begins:

> I enjoyed John's letter – I fear he is a bit of a prig – but so was I at his age.

There are two interesting connections here: one, between her childhood and that of her son's, and two, with the sub-title of the second text, also based on her childhood, *Cat O'Mary: The Biography of a Prig*.

Two years separate the writing of *My Edwardian Childhood* and *Cat O' Mary*. During that interval several events occurred which partly explain why both works were left unfinished. On 19 November 1932, her preparatory work on bell-ringing completed, she told Ivy Shrimpton that she had begun writing *The Nine Tailors*.[5] She also told her that she had written for the *Radio Times* "a nice, bright, Christmas murder dealing with refined persons in high society".[6] Early in 1933, as though she had not enough to do, she entered into a lengthy, detailed and time-consuming discussion of Sherlock Holmes studies with the American scholar Harold W. Bell.[7] By June of that year she had put even more pressure on herself. Writing to Ivy on the 21st, she said:

3   Ibid. p. 322.
4   Ibid. p. 340.
5   Ibid. p. 324.
6   i.e. "The Queen's Square", published later in *Hangman's Holiday*, Gollancz, 1 May 1933.
7   See *Baker-Street Studies*, edited by H. W. Bell, "Holmes' College Career", pp. 1–34. See also Volume I for letters to H. W. Bell, pp. 325–328, 329–334. "Holmes' College Career" and three other studies on Holmes were later published in *Unpopular Opinions*, Gollancz, 1946; now reprinted in *Sayers on Holmes* (with Introduction by Alzina Stone Dale), the Mythopoeic Press, 2001.

I have been tremendously hard at work this last week, or I'd have written sooner. I've taken on some reviewing work[8] in addition to my other jobs, which has meant reading two novels a day or thereabouts – rather strenuous. However, I've got well ahead with the thing now and it won't be so bad in future.[9]

It may be that she took on this extra burden in order to be able to afford to send her son to boarding-school, a plan she mentions to Ivy in the same letter. She also tells her that her husband Mac has been having "a long series of sessions with a doctor". Such consultations cost a good deal of money. Furthermore, it was not only Mac's health that was causing problems; their relationship was becoming more and more difficult, to the point that she was considering a separation. On 11 November she scribbled a harassed note to Ivy:

> So sorry; life has been full of all sorts of bother — financial, domestic and otherwise. But I shall be passing through Oxford about Nov. 25th and will look you up then, as I've got a bit of business to discuss with you. ...[10]

The "bit of business" concerned preparatory measures for the adoption of John Anthony by herself and Mac. A legal document to this effect, dated 3 November 1933, was signed by Ivy Shrimpton later that month.

She was, not surprisingly, on the verge of a nervous breakdown and had been ordered by her doctor to take three weeks' complete rest. She followed his advice and arranged to go on a motoring holiday with her friend Muriel St Clare Byrne, who later said that she noticed at the time that Dorothy seemed very depressed.[11]

The Nine Tailors, soon to be published, was about to bring her the greatest acclaim of her career to date. Charles Williams, who had seen an advance copy, wrote in ecstatic praise of it to Victor Gollancz:

> It's a marvellous book; it is high imagination. ...You won't do a greater book in all your serious novels this year. The end is unsurpassable.

Writing to Gollancz herself on 31 December 1933, she said:

---

8   For the *Sunday Times*. She continued this work until August 1935. See Ralph E. Hone, "Dorothy L. Sayers: Critic of Detective Fiction", *SEVEN: An Anglo-American Literary Review*, volume 6, 1985, pp. 45–69. See also Mike Ripley, "Reviewing the Reviewer: Dorothy L. Sayers as Crime Critic 1933–1935", *The Proceedings of the Dorothy L. Sayers Society Convention 1999*.

9   See Volume I, pp. 334–335.

10 Ibid. p. 339.

11 See Barbara Reynolds, *Dorothy L. Sayers: Her Life and Soul*, Hodder and Stoughton, 1993, chapter 17, p. 244.

> Thank you so much for your letter with Mr Williams' lyrical appreciation of *The Nine Tailors*. I only hope he isn't pulling my leg – it sounds too good to be true![12]

It is possible that recalling memories of Bluntisham had given her the idea of setting her next novel in the Fens. If so, we have *My Edwardian Childhood* to thank for what is regarded as the first of her masterpieces, the second being *Gaudy Night*. On the other hand, it could be that, having chosen that setting, her personal memories were revived and she felt the impulse during her "spasm of middle-agedness", induced perhaps by convalescence from her mysterious ailment, to get them down on paper.

Whatever the circumstances in which she wrote it, *My Edwardian Childhood* is a vivid and detailed recall of her earliest years, written straight off in under a month, with only a few corrections. The title is strange, for her first eight years were passed in the Victorian era, not the Edwardian. Perhaps she intended to give greater emphasis to the years which followed. This she did in *Cat O'Mary*, the title she gave to her intended "straight novel".

It is evident that she had begun thinking about this in 1933 at the latest, for in her letter to Gollancz of 31 December of that year she had added: "I must get on with that straight novel of mine!" She later described her plans for it in her article entitled "Gaudy Night".[13] She says there that while looking about for some means of putting Harriet on an equal footing with Peter, and so enabling her to accept him as a husband, she was at the same time

> …playing with the idea of a "straight" novel about an Oxford woman graduate who found, in middle life, and after a reasonably satisfactory experience of marriage and motherhood, that her real vocation and full emotional fulfilment were to be found in the creative life of the intellect.

Since it was to be a departure from the Lord Peter Wimsey series, she had decided to publish it under a pseudonym. For this purpose she assumed the name of an 18th-century cousin on her mother's side,[14] Johanna (or Joanna) Leigh, a romantic figure whose portrait was painted by Sir Joshua Reynolds between 1775 and 1776. She is represented attired in one of Reynolds' "classical" gowns, leaning gracefully towards a tree on which she is inscribing her first husband's name. Born on 6 October 1758, she was the third daughter and co-heiress (with her several sisters) of John Leigh of North Court House in the Isle of Wight. In 1775 she married Richard Bennett Lloyd, a colonial from Maryland, by whom she had four children.

12 See Volume I, p. 339.
13 Published in *Titles to Fame*, edited by Kilham Roberts, 1937, pp. 73–95.
14 See Appendix D for diagram showing the genealogy.

The portrait was evidently painted to celebrate the marriage. Richard
Bennett Lloyd was commissioned as an Ensign in the Coldstream Guards
in 1773 and resigned in 1775. The Lloyds were a wealthy family, well known
in political circles in Maryland. In 1780 Richard and Johanna, with the
children, went to America and became involved in the social life which
centred around George Washington and his wife. In 1788 Johanna, by
then "the relict of Richard Bennett Lloyd, Esquire", married Francis Love
Beckford of Basing Park, Hampshire (a cousin of William Beckford of
Fonthill),[15] by whom she had seven children. The date of her death was
1814. Dorothy Sayers possessed a black and white photograph of the portrait by Reynolds, torn from a journal. The original is now owned by Lord
Rothschild.[16]

The "straight novel" was advertised as forthcoming by Gollancz in 1933
and again as late as July 1935 in a new edition of *Whose Body?*. It was also
announced as being in preparation in the *New York Times Review of Books* of
14 October 1934. No attempt was made in these advance notices to conceal
the identity of the author. It amused her Oxford friend, Maurice Roy
Ridley, to address her as "Joanna" in his letters to her.

Cat O' Mary is divided into two parts which are strangely unequal in the
quality of the writing. The first and more extensive portion consists of a
development and enrichment of *My Edwardian Childhood*, beginning again
with her earliest years and continuing with her schooldays. This section is
even more vivid and detailed than the earlier text and seems to have been
written without interruption, probably in the first three months of 1934.
The second part consists of brief, disconnected sketches, which indicate
roughly how the novel was to have continued. A reference towards the end
of one of these to A. P. Herbert's novel *Holy Deadlock*, published by
Methuen in April 1934, establishes the earliest date by which this section
could have been written. From the context it would seem that it was
written a year or so later.

There exists also a small notebook containing brief jottings in pencil and
two sections of narrative written in ink which are early drafts and ideas for
the novel. A few of the pages contain brief suggestions of plots for short
stories, some of which were carried out. On one page a reference to *The
Corpse on the Mat*, a detective novel by Milward Kennedy, indicates that she
was planning to mention it in one of her reviews for the *Sunday Times*, as she
in fact did in the issue published on 8 April 1934.

The perplexing title, *Cat O'Mary*, is explained by the epigraph which

15   William Beckford (1759–1844), remembered chiefly as the author of the fantastic oriental
     story *Vathek, An Arabian Tale*, 1786.
16   It is reproduced as a Frontispiece to this volume by kind permission of Lord Rothschild.
     Designated "Mrs Lloyd inscribing a tree, Sir Joshua Reynolds, c. 1776", it hangs in
     Waddesdon Manor, Buckinghamshire.

stands below it in the manuscript, an adaptation of two lines of a poem by
Rudyard Kipling, of which the originals are:

> The sons o' Mary seldom bother; they have inherited that good part;
> But the sons o' Martha favour their mother of the careful soul and the
> troubled heart.

In the epigraph Dorothy Sayers ("Johanna Leigh") has altered "sons" to
"cats", in keeping with her chief character's name, Katherine; the earliest
section of the work is sub-entitled "Kitten into Cat". An allusion to the
detached self-interestedness of both children and cats explains the author's
choice of Christian name. Katherine's surname, Lammas, is perhaps
intended to suggest a late harvest (which is what the word "lammas"
means). Like Mary in the New Testament, Katherine had chosen the way
of contemplation and like Hilary Thorpe in *The Nine Tailors* she was destined to reach creative and intellectual fulfilment late in life. In choosing
her married name, Somers, Dorothy Sayers was perhaps continuing the
underlying meaning of Katherine's autumnal flowering after her marriage
was dissolved.

In one of the jottings in the notebook there is a reference to the story of
Martha and Mary:

> What our Lord meant was, never try to alter anybody – did not so much
> blame Martha for being domestic as for trying to make Mary domestic too
> – Mary is one of the lucky ones – don't envy her, don't badger her. We
> mostly admire Mary on Sundays and Martha on weekdays. Nobody but
> Jesus really likes Mary.

The account of Katherine's school-days tallies closely with the letters
which Dorothy wrote home from the Godolphin School in Salisbury.
Names of places and people are transparently disguised. Bluntisham
becomes Fentisham, the Godolphin becomes the Beaufort in the fictitious
cathedral city of Carisbury, her cousin Ivy becomes Myrtle, her school-
friend Violet becomes Rose, her mathematics teacher Miss Hancock
becomes Miss Peacock and her beloved Miss White who taught her French
becomes Miss Greene. Her piano teacher, Fräulein Fehmer, reappears as
Fräulein Heyser and a few details are added to what we already know of
her from the letters. Whether the portrait of Miss Dando is a faithful repre-
sentation of Miss Douglas, Headmistress of the Godolphin, we can now
only guess.

One intriguing character eludes identification. This is Great-aunt
Agatha, said to be her mother's aunt. A forthright, independent-minded
woman, she wins Katherine's trust, for she never asks embarrassing questions and can be relied upon to make sensible comments in difficult situations. She appears also in the later section of the work, when Katherine,
grown up and married, is about to have a baby. To escape the tiresome

fussing of her mother and husband, Katherine goes to stay with her. Later, when her husband asks for a divorce, it is Great-aunt Agatha to whom again she turns for the bracing effect of her unsentimental and realistic out-look. The figure of a brusque, matter-of-fact elderly lady, with the sugges-tion of a racy past, is a minor character in more than one of Dorothy Sayers' short stories. There is even a trace of her in one of her last works, an unfinished novel about Dante and his daughter. The notebook contains an intriguing intention to saddle the unmarried Great-aunt Agatha with a son. The jotting is headed "Aunt Agatha's love-affair" and continues:

> "But didn't you find it all very awkward?"
>
> "There were some awkwardnesses, of course", admitted Aunt Agatha, "but take it all in all it wasn't nearly as troublesome as Uncle Fred's dia-betes, for example."
>
> "The baby?"
>
> "He did very well as a button-manufacturer in Bradford. I met him a few times, but we had nothing in common. He died early – 59– did himself too well…"[17]
>
> K. wonders – how about her girl? Nothing in common – she would hate to part from boy – but strong conviction she wd. have liked boy even if she hadn't been his mother.

Detachment and emotional honesty are among the themes explored in *Cat O'Mary*. It appears that Dorothy Sayers intended to develop them oblique-ly, attributing to a fictitious character, in this case Great-aunt Agatha, what she discerned in herself. This is confirmed by her letter to Ivy Shrimpton, dated 10 December 1928, when her own son was nearly five years of age:

> Very many thanks for your letters and photos. J.A. looks quite a credit to us! I must really try to feel thrilled about him – but I don't believe I ever should about *any* child under whatever circumstances! It's funny, but I don't think "family ties" have ever meant anything at all to me. I only like people as individuals, apart from who they are. Indeed, I actively dislike nearly all my Sayers relations, or at most, tepidly tolerate them. I like the Leighs – and of course, my dear, I'm damned fond of you – but because you are you – not because you happen to be a cousin. Same with J.A. He seems to be turning out a good sort of kid, and I'm disposed to like him – but for no other reason.[18]

One of the chief characteristics of Dorothy Sayers, which she gives also to Katherine, was a fierce resistance to having feelings which she did not pos-sess foisted upon her. This resistance was all the stronger because she

---

17 It is a strange coincidence that D. L. S.' own illegitimate son, John Anthony Fleming, was to die at the age of 60, in 1984.

18 See Volume I, p. 290.

realised, looking back on her childhood, that she had assumed feelings which were not always genuine. In the notebook she drew up a list of what she headed "Succession of worked-up emotions":

1. the governess
2. ? music
3. the schoolmistress
4. the don
5. the lover
6. the children

From this it appears that she knew in later life that her affections for a governess and for her favourite teacher at the Godolphin had been exaggerated and dramatised, "worked up" for effect. It appears that she intended to provide Katherine Lammas with exaggerated emotions regarding a don at Oxford (Sir Hugh Allen?), a lover (Eric Whelpton or John Cournos?) and later, in marriage, her children. The question mark before "music" is interesting, conveying that she recognised a distinction between herself and Katherine in this connection.

Such assumed feelings were closely connected in her mind with the stereotyped role imposed on women, from which both she and Katherine Lammas try to break free. They were also connected with her sense of embarrassment relating to religious piety, which she rejected with vigour. There is a jotting about this in the notebook:

> Religion: something of that did remain – the hard intellectual core.

This is what she later defined, in her letter to John Wren Lewis,[19] as "the passionate intellect", asserting vigorously that she could arrive at faith by no other means.

Almost all the events in the life of the young Katherine are described exactly as they occurred in the life of the author. There are two deviations, however, one of less importance than the other. Unlike her creator, Katherine gives up her violin lessons, realizing when she arrives at school that she has been poorly taught and that she is not herself interested enough in music to try to improve. In real life Dorothy did continue with the violin, even learning the viola as well, and kept up her playing long into adulthood, both at Oxford when she returned there in 1917 to work for Basil Blackwell, and at L'Ecole des Roches in Normandy, where she worked as assistant to Eric Whelpton from 1919 to 1920. The music master there told her she would be able to earn her living as an orchestral violinist if she wished.

The second deviation is of greater importance. It concerns her feelings

19   See Volume IV, pp. 135–145.

North Court House, Isle of Wight. Home of Johanna Leigh

Richard Bennett Lloyd. Portrait by Charles Willson Peale

Miniatures of Richard and Johanna Lloyd

Basing Park, Froxfield, Hants. Home of Johanna and Francis Beckford

about her Confirmation. Her letters about this to her parents and her account of it in *Cat O'Mary* are strikingly at variance. On 15 April 1930, she wrote to Ivy who had asked whether she had any objection to her son being baptized. He was then six years old.

> Personally, I am all against making sacraments into conveniences, but if you feel very strongly about it, do as you like. Being baptised without one's will is certainly not so harmful as being confirmed against one's will, which is what happened to me, and gave me a resentment against religion in general which lasted a long time. My people (weakly) thought it would "be better" to have it "done" at school – and it was the worst possible school for the purpose, being Low Church and sentimental – and I (still more weakly) gave in because I didn't want to be conspicuous and fight it out. Afterwards, when I became High Church, I wished I hadn't done it, because then I could have undertaken it properly, without fury and resentment, and without having the dreariest associations connected with the Communion Service. What sort of bloke is the parson? Is he Catholic-minded or Evangelical? Or merely "Established"? If he is a High Churchman with a sound theology, well and good; but the cultivation of religious emotion without philosophic basis is thoroughly pernicious – in my opinion.[20]

This important statement coincides closely with Katherine's feelings about her Confirmation as she describes them in *Cat O' Mary*, written four years later. The letters Dorothy wrote about it in 1910, however, give a very different impression. Some of the discrepancies can be explained by a desire not to distress or embarrass her parents, but not all. Her expressions of admiration and affection for the Dean of Salisbury, for example, go beyond tactful restraint: "our beloved Dean" , "the darling...the angel".[21] Canon Myers of St Martin's, who prepared the Godolphin girls for Confirmation, is described as "jolly nice":

> I went in the other day to tell him about my besetting sins and we ended by discussing Oxford and my future career. Phoebe wondered what on earth I was making such a terrific long confession about.[22]

And in her letter of 23 March she wrote:

> I had a small talk with Canon Myers last night – he is ripping.

The veils which the girls wore for the ceremony, described in *Cat O'Mary* as being of "an excessive ugliness", are on the contrary warmly approved of in the same letter:

20 See Volume I, p. 306.
21 Letters dated 27 February and 6 March 1910 (not included in Volume I).
22 See Volume I, p. 38, 40.

> Our veils were most awfully nice – chiffon – very simple with just a litle ruche at the top. I thought they looked nicer than any of the others, and people who could see better than I could say the same – I think nothing is more horrid than a skimpy little tail of net with a vast bunch or bunches on top – I suppose one ought not to think about such things, but I *do* like to see things in really good taste – ours most certainly were that.

Strange to say, the weather conditions on the great day changed completely between 1910 and 1934! In *Cat O' Mary* the scene is described as follows:

> The day was wet, and the candidates went down to the Cathedral in three moth-eaten fourwheelers, smelling like damp and ill-ventilated loose-boxes.

But on 23 March 1910, the very day of the Confirmation, Dorothy wrote to her parents:

> We drove down to Cath. – it was a glorious day – I was quite hot in my muslin frock.[23]

And on 9 April she wrote to her cousin Ivy:

> I told you, I think, that I was going to be confirmed. It was a lovely day, and it all went off beautifully. It was a huge ceremony – about 220 candidates, I think – and the Cathedral was simply *packed*.[24]

It would seem that whatever misgivings and reluctance Dorothy Sayers felt, and suppressed, about the ceremony when she was a girl of sixteen gathered force with the years, and by the time she was a woman in her forties she looked back on the occasion with loathing.

Her view of the child she is portraying has also grown surprisingly hostile. She had already expressed this feeling in a letter to Charis Frankenburg, dated 5 March 1929.[25] She says there that she loathed school and thoroughly disliked all retrospect, probably because her "present vanity despises and dislikes [her] former self".

There is a marked difference in this respect between *My Edwardian Childhood* and *Cat O' Mary*. All the first-person recollections of herself in the earlier text are tolerant, amused and affectionate. In the two years that elapsed between the texts she seems to have taken a violent dislike to the child she once was:

> She liked correcting other people, but didn't like being corrected herself, and would argue a point with obstinacy. She had a great opinion of her own cleverness, and to be proved wrong was humiliating. … As time went

23　Ibid. p. 40.
24　Ibid. p. 41.
25　Ibid. p. 291.

on, Katherine developed all the faults and peculiarities of an only child whose entire life is spent among grown-up people. She was self-absorbed, egotistical, timid, priggish, and, in a mild sort of way, disobedient.

The self-disgust expressed in the following paragraph is startling:

> If egotism, greed, covetousness, cruelty and sloth are sins, then children possess that original sinfulness in high degree. …When Katherine in later years looked back on the childish figure that had been herself, it was with a hatred of anything so lacking in those common virtues which were to be attained in after years at so much cost and with such desperate difficulty. She saw through no rosy mist of illusion; she must, she knew, have been a disagreeable child. Strangers rightly considered her a prig.

This was written at the very time when Dorothy L. Sayers, the novelist, suddenly a best-seller and hugely admired, was being sought after and lionized. She was interviewed by the national press, she lunched with celebrities, she was elected a charter member of the newly founded Sherlock Holmes Society, she was a leading light of the Detection Club; in other words, she had "arrived".

Two or three months previously her personal life had reached a crisis and she was facing the realization that her marriage was a failure. The contrast between the two situations was a puzzling challenge. Why was she so successful creatively and so unsuccessful in her sexual life? As she looked back, a series of failed relationships confronted her: unrequited love for Eric Whelpton, unconsummated passion for John Cournos, a disastrous affair with Bill White resulting in an illegitimate son, and now the threatened break-up of her marriage. Was there something lacking in her?

The "straight" novel she had been contemplating in 1933 provided an opportunity to examine her shortcomings. That she thought of it in such terms is shown by jottings in the notebook:

> Get in strongly the feeling that "inside me I don't *really* care" – childhood (Fanny Maud)[26] – and make it *recur*. Note real respect for Maths mistress, which *lasts*. …

Katherine, hearing that a woman has killed herself on being deserted by a man, is shown (in the notebook) to have a sudden revelation about her feelings concerning her divorce: that she isn't and couldn't be hurt to that point. It is not worth it. Her vanity is more hurt than anything else. Again in the notebook, thinking of the possibility of committing suicide by putting her head in the gas oven, Katherine says to herself:

---

26 The nickname for Miss White, the teacher at the Godolphin School for whom she worked up what she later recognized as spurious emotions.

> I am trying to pretend it doesn't matter because it has beaten me – I have
> made a muck of all my emotional relations and I hate being beaten, so I
> pretend not to care. … But it has NOT beaten me, because I haven't done
> this and never could. It isn't that I have failed and therefore pretend not to
> care. I DON'T CARE and that is why I have failed.

The direction which the "straight novel" was taking in her mind gave her
the idea that an objective analysis of herself as a child might throw light on
her failures as an adult. She decided therefore to develop *My Edwardian
Childhood* and use it as a beginning for the new project.

The scheme, however, did not work. A novel about a woman who "after
a reasonably satisfactory experience of marriage and motherhood [finds]
that her real vocation and full emotional fulfilment were to be found in the
creative life of the intellect" (as she later described her original intention)
does not develop convincingly from a hostile account of a child described
as a prig. The Katherine Lammas of the early section is scarcely recogniz-
able in the later. The truth of the matter is that Dorothy Sayers became
entangled in writing two different works with two different aims, and lost
her direction. This is the main reason why *Cat O' Mary* was never completed as a novel.

Another reason, which led to a productive and fortunate result, was that
on 13 June 1934, her forty-first birthday, she attended a gaudy at
Somerville College. The purpose of the occasion was to celebrate the
appointment of her old tutor Mildred Pope to the chair of French at
Manchester University. Dorothy Sayers was invited to propose a toast to
the University of Oxford. In her article "Gaudy Night" she relates what
happened:

> While investigating the possibilities of [a novel about the intellectual life]…
> I had to ask myself exactly what it was for which one had to thank a
> university education, and came to the conclusion that it was, before every-
> thing, that habit of intellectual integrity which is at once the foundation
> and the result of scholarship.

She realized at the same time that she had hit on the solution to the problem of Peter and Harriet:

> On the intellectual platform, alone of all others, Harriet could stand free
> and equal with Peter, since in that sphere she had never been false to her
> own standards.

This impersonal goal had been trenchantly expressed in the notebook in
the following important jotting:

> THE ONLY THING THAT IS AN END IN ITSELF – UNBOUGHT,
> NOT CALCULATED, NOT PERISHABLE, requiring no lies, no emo-
> tion – with this there can be no trifling and never has been. Without know-

ing it, this is the one thing that I have never been false to, never indifferent
to, never emotional about but it has *lasted*.

From a jotting in the notebook, it is apparent that she intended that her last
chapter should be headed "Nothing Else Matters".

Her discovery of how to bring Harriet and Peter together in a shared
impersonal devotion to the pursuit of truth led to the writing of *Gaudy Night*.
Everything that she originally intended to say in her "straight novel" about
intellectual fulfilment and scholarly integrity, her love for Oxford, for
learning for its own sake, went instead into the second of her two masterpieces. She had found a solution not only to the problem of Peter and
Harriet but to her own.

Thus the "straight novel", or rather, the later sections of it, were trans-
formed into *Gaudy Night*. The stronger creation, Harriet Vane, took over
from the shadowy adult Katherine Lammas, absorbing some of her characteristics, becoming strengthened thereby into the figure of a modern
woman.

The two reconstructions of childhood and schooldays of the late
Victorian and Edwardian periods, however, are anything but shadowy.
They provide a glimpse of social history as vivid and intimate as a family
album. We know what people wore; what their furnishings and ornaments
were like; how a large rectory was managed, without labour-saving devices
but with the devoted help of uncomplaining servants. The description of
Mrs Appleton ironing with old-fashioned flat irons heated on a range and
squeezing woollen garments through a mangle is so immediate as to make
the reader feel the heat as she holds an iron near her cheek and smell the
soapy fragrance of the wet woollens as they emerge flat from the rollers.
Few people nowadays have seen such things. Those who have recognize
the scene instantly and are magically transported back to childhood. The
drive in a dog-cart to St Ives on market-day, watching "the long bay back
of Jenny the mare and the solemn jerking of her tail"; the difference
between a "put up", when Jenny was taken out and left in a loose-box (for
sixpence) and a "tie-up", when her reins were fastened to a post (for threepence); the visit to the house of Mrs Welbeck, the brewer's wife, one's footsteps echoing beneath a flagged archway, filled with empty beer barrels
and the sour-sweet smell of beer, the garden overhanging the river where
one could fish for minnows; a governess mincing along the muddy Fen
roads, dressed like a fashion plate in a "lovely afternoon costume of purple
cloth, the front and sleeves of which were filled with a delicate pink and
white floral chiffon, a hat crowned with cock's feathers and a boa and muff
of silver fox" – such pictorial writing as this, not to be found in any of her
other works, gives the reader an inkling of an unknown Dorothy Sayers
who might have become a novelist of a quite different kind.

The account of Katherine's experience of boarding-school is a brilliant re-creation of adolescent fears, embarrassments, resentments, emotional attachments and intellectual excitement. We hear the chattering voices of schoolgirls, the repressive rebukes of mistresses, the clatter and bustle of a day regulated relentlessly by the ringing of bells. This is an experience of school life which was familiar to many girls until recent times but would scarcely be recognized now. The range of reading in English, French and German literature is also far beyond present-day expectations and opportunities. Dorothy Sayers was well advanced in these subjects by the time she went to boarding-school at the age of fifteen, but she was not exceptional among her peers in that respect, nor was the high standard of teaching unusual at the best English public schools of that time, whether for boys or girls. What was exceptional was Dorothy's enraptured surrender to the power of words, particularly of poetry. This is something which remained with her all her life. Her vivid and joyful recollection of it at the age of forty-one brings her creative mind more intimately within our understanding than ever before.

The disconnected sketches of the later part of the novel provide nothing so substantial but from them the following can be pieced together. There are three lists of dates within which the action is imagined as taking place. The one eventually adopted gives the birth of Katherine as 1890, but Sayers had not quite made up her mind and the time-scheme vacillates. Like herself Katherine first goes to school at the age of 15. She is at Oxford from 1909 to 1913; she marries in 1915, aged 25. In 1916 her daughter Molly is born, followed by her son Stephen in 1919. Her daughter marries in 1933. In 1934, she divorces her husband for desertion and adultery and resumes academic research as a historian. One of the first things she does when she is free (according to an entry in the notebook) is to qualify for her Oxford M.A. and take it (as Dorothy Sayers herself had done in 1920, when Oxford University officially conferred degrees on women).

Her husband, Geoffrey Somers, is a well-to-do man who works in the City. They have a large house in the country, called Ridings, with an extensive garden. There is a butler, a cook, several maids, and a chauffeur. There is a billiard-room. During her marriage Katherine has lived the comfortable, upper middle-class life of wife and mother, with no demands upon her intellect, meeting and talking with her neighbours and entertaining guests. An example of the inane conversation in which she is trapped is found in the dialogue with Mrs Halliday. The First World War is mentioned but seems to make no difference to their lives, except that fruit and fresh vegetables are hard to obtain, but this will scarcely affect them with their large garden. Geoffrey appears to have served in the army but to have been invalided out with a wound in the leg. In the notebook there is a jotting to show that the role of housewife does not really interest her:

She worries about household and family things because she is always being told she ought to. Every so often gets sense that it *really* doesn't matter. Profoundly indifferent.

After eighteen years of marriage Geoffrey confesses to his wife that he is having an affair with a secretary, named Lilias, who works for his firm in London. Katherine agrees to divorce him and they discuss the matter calmly, without acrimony. In this they reflect the married couple in A. P. Herbert's novel *Holy Deadlock*, already mentioned, in which John and Mary Adam continue to express mutual affection and are eager to do what is best in each other's welfare. This novel had brought the question of divorce into general discussion and was to prove influential in bringing about a reform in English law. At that period adultery had to be proved by the petitioner. The legal procedure was divided into two stages: a decree nisi, followed later, if no subsequent intercourse could be proved to have been committed by the petitioner, by a decree absolute. In order to spare the wife unpleasant publicity, it was usual for the husband, whether he was the guilty party or not, to do what was called "the gentlemanly thing", namely to provide spurious evidence by arranging for a chambermaid at a hotel to discover him in bed with a woman hired to act the part of his adulterous partner. The divorce court judge usually accepted the fake evidence, but not always. Sometimes it was necessary to repeat the procedure in the hope that the case would come up before a more compliant judge.

Dorothy Sayers refers satirically to this situation in her novel *Busman's Honeymoon*, where Mirabelle, Countess of Severn and Thames, writing to the Dowager Duchess of Denver, says:

> I can't see Peter exhibiting himself in the Divorce Courts for his own amusement, though, no doubt, if asked to oblige, he would carry it through with an air. (Which reminds me that my idiot great-nephew, Hughie, has bungled matters as usual. Having undertaken to do the thing like a gentleman, he sneaked off to Brighton with a hired nobody, and the Judge wouldn't believe either the hotel bills or the chambermaid – knowing them all too well by sight. So it means starting all over again from the beginning.)[27]

This is a clear echo of a passage in *Holy Deadlock*, in which the presiding judge listens to the opening speech:

> At the fatal word "hotel" he looked up from the pleadings before him and looked down at Mr Ransom.
> "A hotel? At Brighton?", he said. "All this sounds very familiar. And now you are going to tell me, I suppose, that the respondent and the

---

27 Prothalamion, first letter.

woman Myrtle spent two nights at this hotel and were seen in bed by a chambermaid, and the respondent sent the bill to his wife – and so on?"[28]

Thus it is that Katherine warns Geoffrey to be careful about the evidence he will have to provide, reminding him of the situation in A. P. Herbert's novel. In order to spare the reputation of Lilias, both Katherine and Geoffrey are prepared to commit what was then called "collusion" and to deceive the court. If this were discovered no divorce would have been granted.

Geoffrey is disconcerted by Katherine's composure and off-hand, practical approach to the divorce and especially by her independent spirit in refusing to accept alimony. This reflects Dorothy Sayers' own attitude regarding the economic dependence of women upon men. In a *curriculum vitae* which she drew up in 1928, when she had been married for two years, under the section headed "Views" she wrote:

> Women and Marriage: Consider that the chief difficulties in most cases are economic. Extremely keen that all women, married or not, should be able to make money for themselves and take their share in the upkeep of the house. Consider that it will soon be thought as degrading to be "kept" by a husband as "kept" in any other way. Would welcome legislation to abolish husband's liability for wife's income-tax, personal debts and other unfair distinctions.

In the notebook, under the heading "Alimony" she jotted the following piece of dialogue for Katherine:

> "I won't take it, why should I? Children provided for, etc. Why live on man who doesn't want me?"

Katherine's sexual relations with Geoffrey had been only moderately satisfying. The notebook hints at this:

> They tell K. that she is "romantic". Geoffrey has the reputation for being solid and practical. She accepts this. Actually, *he* is the romantic – when the spur of romance ceases to function, he loses the impulse to physical love. When romance gets hold of him again, his body responds. K. is realist and passionate but not romantic. She suffers from the withdrawal of the physical intimacy. G. is shocked and horrified at the idea that he has any duty to his wife in this matter.

There are glimpses throughout the work of what would eventually appear in *Gaudy Night*. In the account of her school-days she had already chosen Shrewsbury as the name for a fictitious Oxford college. In the notebook,

28   *Holy Deadlock*, Hutchinson Library Services Edition, 1972, pp. 99–100.

Katherine, released from marriage, finds a line of verse floating into her mind:

> We whom the years cannot darken, nor death make dumb…
>
> For a moment she could not place the line's origin – she was surprised to discover that it had spun itself unexpectedly out of her own brain. Here was a miracle, appropriate to this astonishing day. Her singing voice, which Geoffrey's first kiss had exiled, had come hoarsely and haltingly back to her.

Here is the first note of Harriet's "singing voice", which would be heard later in *Gaudy Night*, when a detached pentameter and a half came into her mind and she wrote the octave of a sonnet.[29]

From *My Edwardian Childhood* arose *The Nine Tailors*, the novel she called "a labour of love". From *Cat O'Mary* arose *Gaudy Night*, the book in which

> …by choosing a plot which should exhibit intellectual integrity as the one great permanent value in an emotionally unstable world I should be saying the thing that, in a confused way, I had been wanting to say all my life.[30]

The direction of all her later writing now lay before her. After wandering briefly in a maze of unhappiness and self-rejection, she had emerged upon her future path.

But Katherine Lammas did not totally disappear. She came to life again, disguised as Edith Daybrook/alias Janet Reed, in a comedy entitled *Love All*,[31] written by Dorothy Sayers in 1937(or 1938) while on holiday in Venice.[32] "I wrote it", she said, "just for fun".

By then a change had come over her life. Her play *Busman's Honeymoon*,[33] written in collaboration with Muriel St Clare Byrne, had been a resounding success in the London West End and on tour. It had been followed immediately by yet another exhilarating achievement: *The Zeal of Thy House*, her first drama for Canterbury Cathedral. She had now entered a period of quite new fulfilment. The company of actors, the creative exuberance of the theatrical world filled her with joy and a sense of personal liberation.

It was in this mood, and with the beauty of Venice surrounding her, that she wondered lightheartedly what became of Katherine, Geoffrey and Lilias. Did Geoffrey manage, at the first attempt, to provide convinc-

---

29 "The singing voice, stifled long ago by the pressure of the struggle for existence, and throttled into dumbness by that queer, unhappy contact with physical passion, began to stammer a few uncertain notes." (Chapter XI)

30 From her article, "Gaudy Night".

31 Kent State University Press, 1984, edited by Alzina Stone Dale.

32 She visited Venice two years in succession.

33 First published by Gollancz, 1937. Republished in the same volume as *Love All*, 1984. See Note 31.

ing evidence of adultery? Did he and Lilias marry and did they remain together?

Slightly altering two of their names (Geoffrey becomes Godfrey and Lilias becomes Lydia) and at first entitling the comedy *Cat's Cradle*,[34] she recreated their situation but removed it to an entirely different world.

In *Love All* Godfrey Daybrook, a successful author of sentimental novels, is married to Edith, a virtuous but uninspiring wife. They have lived for ten years in a stultifying town called Little Wookham and have one son. Godfrey is fond of Edith and grateful to her, but he falls in love with a glamorous actress, Lydia Hillington, who he believes will bring romance to his life and inspiration to his work. Edith agrees to divorce him and he and Lydia go off together to Venice to await proceedings.

When the play opens eighteen months have passed and Edith has taken no action. The divorce laws of the period make it impossible for Godfrey and Lydia to marry until Edith takes the initiative and serves divorce papers on him. This she has neglected to do and they cannot understand why.

In the meantime, Edith, under the assumed name of Janet Reed, has been enjoying a sensational success as a playwright. She has been so caught up in the whirl of this activity that she has found no opportunity to attend to legal proceedings and has even from time to time forgotten all about her husband. In this she resembles Katherine Lammas who, to her astonishment, finds it easy to forget Geoffrey in the absorbing interest of her historical research.

In Venice, Lydia and Godfrey, unaware that Edith is Janet Reed, discuss their unsatisfactory situation. Lydia has tired of Venice and longs to return to London to resume her profession, to be, as she says, "a real person, to be alive". She decides to leave, in order to apply for the leading role in a new play by Janet Reed. Godfrey also returns to London to see why his wife has not proceeded with the legal arrangements which will set him free.

To his astonishment and indignation, he discovers that his wife has become the celebrated Janet Reed. Like Geoffrey Somers, he has conventional ideas about women. He also believes (again like Geoffrey) that both his wife and his mistress, not to mention his secretary, are devoted to him and find complete fulfilment in ministering to him and to his work.

When Godfrey and Edith meet in London, the dialogue between them bears many similarities to that between Geoffrey and Katherine in *Cat O' Mary* when they discuss the break-up of their marriage. Edith, like Katherine, maintains her composure and explains that she has found fulfilment in her work:

"A job's the real thing. Something one's *made*."

34   Later changed to *Love All*.

Godfrey had shattered her faith in romance but she has built it up again for herself:

> "I found it in my work…for the first time in my life, really making good."

Godfrey replies:

> "I don't believe it. No woman feels like that."

Edith tries to convince him that women, like all human beings, do feel like that and Godfrey (like Geoffrey, in another situation), calls her hysterical, which both men believe all women tend to become from time to time.

There is even a similar conversation on the subject of alimony. Edith says:

> "I'm doing pretty well with all this, and I don't really need so much money from you. I'll tell my lawyers to refund you my personal allowance for this year, and the Court can take my earnings into account when they settle the alimony."

Godfrey (like Geoffrey) is indignant:

> "They will do nothing of the kind. Are you trying to insult me?"

Godfrey (like Geoffrey) resents her detachment:

> "I'm in the wrong. I admit it. I left you for another woman, and – well, there it is, and I'm very sorry for it. But need you make this pretence of not caring a damn?"

*

The themes of the two works are identical: the liberation of a woman from an imposed and passively accepted role which hampers her fulfilment as a human being; the lasting importance of an impersonal job; the spuriousness of stereotyped romance. In mood and tone, however, the two works are very different. *Love All* is a farce, elegantly constructed, hinged on situational paradox, full of laughter. Beneath the merriment, however, can be heard the echoes of the serious concerns of *Cat O'Mary*.

Poor Godfrey (and by implication Geoffrey) ends up as a figure of fun, abandoned by three women he believed were devoted to him, his wife, his mistress and his secretary, all of whom find fulfilment without him.

"Damn!" is his last utterance as the curtain falls.

*

On 26 February 1948, Hatchards, Booksellers to Their Majesties The King, The Queen and to Queen Mary, wrote to Dorothy L. Sayers as follows:

Dear Madam,

We have an inquiry from one of our customers for a book written by you entitled CAT O' MARY under the pen name of J. Leigh, but we regret that we are unable to trace the publication. We wonder whether you would be so kind as to send us a card with any details which would help us.

Assuring you of our best attention,
We are, Madam,
Yours faithfully
A. Kerr
Manager of Order Dept.

At the foot of the letter, Dorothy Sayers' secretary typed:

POSTCARD. In reply to your letter of 26th Feb., Miss Dorothy L. Sayers desires me to say that the book you mention was never written or published.

By then she was deep in her work on Dante, in which she was to find her most joyful intellectual and creative fulfilment.

BARBARA REYNOLDS
13 June 2002

List of illustrations

ᢒᢙᢒᢙᢒᢙ

Frontispiece: Mrs Lloyd inscribing a tree, Sir Joshua Reynolds, c. 1776 (courtesy of Waddesdon Manor, Rothschild family Trusts)

Acknowledgements

ↃↄↃↄↃↄ

My first thanks are due to the Marion E. Wade Center at Wheaton College, Illinois and to Wheaton College Board of Trustees for permission to publish Dorothy L. Sayers' memoirs of her childhood, *My Edwardian Childhood*, and her unfinished novel, based on those memoirs, *Cat O'Mary*. Mrs Marjorie Lamp Mead, Associate Director of the Wade Center, and members of the staff have been tireless in their assistance. I also thank Mr Dan Drake of California for allowing me to consult a notebook in his possession which contains notes for the continuation of *Cat O'Mary* in Dorothy Sayers' handwriting. I also thank the executors of the estate of Anthony Fleming and Mr Bruce Hunter of David Higham Associates for authorising me to publish this volume under the aegis of the Dorothy L. Sayers Society. In this connection I am much indebted to the Chairman of the Society, Mr Christopher Dean, for his advice and help, as well as for his Preface.

This volume contains many illustrations and for these I have many people to thank. Lord Rothschild has most kindly permitted me to use as a frontispiece a reproduction of Sir Joshua Reynolds' portrait of Johanna Lloyd, an eighteenth-century cousin of Dorothy Sayers, whose name she assumed for her novel *Cat O'Mary*. The reproduction of the portrait of her husband, Richard Lloyd Bennett, by the American artist, Charles Willson Peale, I owe in the first instance to information provided by Mrs Maggie Noll and subsequently to the courtesy of the Henry Francis du Pont Winterthur Museum, Delaware. The reproduction of miniatures of Richard Lloyd and his wife, as well as of the painting of Basing Park, I owe to Mr Robin Merton, that of North Court Manor to Major Adrian H. Beckford, all four of these last items having been traced by Mr Christopher Dean.

For photographs relating to Bluntisham, taken specially by Mr Paul Whitehead of Michael Manni Photographic of Cambridge, I have to thank Mrs Sandra Little, who now resides at the Rectory, and Mr Tom Youd, the owner of the charming reconstruction of Bluntisham station. For photographs of St Mary's Church and of Canon John Rumpf and the Rev. Henry Sayers, I thank the Rev.Colin Backhouse for his courtesy and time. The water-colour of the little group arriving at the Rectory in January 1897 was painted specially by the artist Miss Norah Lambourne, who worked with Dorothy Sayers in the production of several of her plays. The painting of the hall of the Rectory, unsigned but probably the work of Dorothy in her teens, I owe to the courtesy of Mrs Fortuna Fleming. Photographs of Dorothy in her childhood and of an example of her handwriting at the age of five were kindly supplied to me by the Marion E. Wade Center, by whose permission I reproduce them here. Photographs of the Godolphin School, Salisbury (represented as the Beaufort School, Carisbury in the novel) I owe to Mr Stephen Lycett, whom I thank for his helpful researches, as also Mr Mark Dunning for his lovely colour photograph of the school in winter.

Both texts contain numerous quotations and several people have traced to their origin those which eluded me or have provided explanations. They are Mr Christopher Dean, Mr Andrew Entecott, Professor Andrew Lewis, the Rev. John G. Simmons, Canon John A. Thurmer and Dr J. Cameron Wilson.

I also thank Mr Christopher Dean for the genealogical table, reproduced in an Appendix, showing the relation between Dorothy L. Sayers and her distant cousin, Johanna Leigh. The explanation and diagrams of Euclid's Tennis Court, also in an Appendix, I owe to my daughter Mrs Kerstin Lewis, whom I here thank formally.

Finally I thank Mr Geoff Green for designing this volume and for much practical help and advice. I am grateful also to Mr Pat Mills for his expert proof-reading.

BARBARA REYNOLDS

My Edwardian Childhood

My Edwardian Childhood

ᏇᏇᏇ

I

I am a citizen of no mean city, for I was born at Oxford, almost under the shadow of Tom Tower.[1] My father was then Headmaster of the Cathedral Choir School, so that I had the honour of a Cathedral christening.[2] I did not appreciate this at the time, but I got my moment of pride out of it later, when, one of the gawkiest of a row of gawky schoolgirls, I waited while the good man who was preparing us for Confirmation took down the particulars of his candidates.[3] When my turn came I was ready for it. Full name? Dorothy Leigh Sayers. When born? June 13, 1893. Where christened? Christ Church Cathedral. He started, gratifyingly, and his pen hovered above the paper. "Are you sure?" Yes, I was sure of that, all right. Like Sherlock Holmes, I never could resist a touch of the dramatic, and my schoolfellows disliked me for my swank; but this time there was nothing to be said. I had been asked a plain question and had given a plain answer. I adduced my evidence, and the recorder was satisfied; and wrote down the noble words. I was confirmed in a cathedral, too;[4] but later, I came down in the world. I was married in a registrar's office in the Clerkenwell Road;[5] I hope I may not be buried in a gaol.[6]

---

1 D. L. S. was born in the Old Choir House, 1 Brewer Street, opposite Christ Church, near the bell known as Old Tom. The house was marked with a plaque in 1993, the hundredth anniversary of her birth.
2 Christ Church is not strictly a College, having been intended as a Cathedral by Cardinal Wolsey, who founded it, and a Cathedral it still is. Its original name was Aedes Christi (the House of Christ) and it is known colloquially as "the House". The Head is a Dean, its disciplinary authorities are Censors and its Fellows are Students.
3 D. L. S. was confirmed while a pupil of Godolphin School, Salisbury, in Easter Week, 1910.
4 i.e. Salisbury Cathedral.
5 On 13 April 1926, at 53 Clerkenwell Road, London, to Atherton Fleming.
6 D. L. S. died on 17 December 1957. Her body was cremated and her ashes are interred beneath the floor of St Anne's Tower, Dean Street, Soho.

Dorothy aged about two

I was born, then, in the Old Choir House, but shortly after this event, the New Choir House was built [7], and we removed to it. I do not remember it very well, except that there was a beam in the ceiling of the night-nursery and that the day-nursery had one of those window blinds made of little pieces of bamboo and beads threaded together on strings. I remember my nurse cutting off one of these pieces of bamboo to make a whistle for me; I wondered at the time how she dared. But that was my third and best-remembered nurse. The first, "Old Nannie", I do not remember at all. The second, Nurse Ashby, was memorable because she wore proper dark-blue uniform, with bonnet and veil. My only clear recollection of her is of being heartily spanked by her on some occasion or other. We were about to go out with the pram, for she had her bonnet and cloak on at the time, and I was rolling on the ground near the nursery door and yelling lustily. This must be my earliest distinct memory, and if that means anything to the psychoanalysts, I make them a present of it.

There was, I know, a pram, but I can see the "mail-cart"[8] more distinctly

7   i.e. 3 Brewer Street.
8   A light vehicle for a child, like the modern push-chair.

in my mind's eye. It was yellowish, with a brown hood, and had some kind of screw or gadget somewhere for locking or fixing something. I think it must have been for locking the wheels, so that it would not run away on its own when left unattended. At any rate, my nurse once left me outside a shop without properly manipulating this device, and in consequence the mail-cart tipped over and shot me out on to the pavement. No harm was done, but I think Nurse Ashby must have been the culprit, and possibly this episode was the cause of her retirement in favour of Nurse Godfrey – always called "Nurse" *par excellence.*

Or, was the real reason connected with "the bold, bad man"? I do not know who this person was, but he was so referred to by my parents, because he came round courting one of the servants. This must have been a little touch of Victorian humour, but to me it had a sinister sound.

I believe it was some relation of Nurse's who was a sailor and brought home a parrot for us. Polly was a great figure throughout my childhood. I remember his being brought into the nursery and allowed to walk about there, until, to my horror, he "dropped a card" on the carpet, and was removed to a cage. The Freudians may make what they like of this memory also, but I think I am right in saying that it was the exaggerated excitement of the grown-ups which impressed the incident so forcibly on my memory. Polly was a grey African bird with a red tail and excellent speaking voice, but I fancy he was kept in the kitchen at the Choir House, for, beyond his first dramatic appearance, he forms no part of my Oxford memories.

The dining-room at the Choir House is rather a dim memory; I know that it had rather low, mullioned windows, but then I know this from having seen it later, and from photographs. My principal recollections of that room are being occasionally present at some meal or other and disliking bacon fat. Also, of having, in that room, bitten a piece out of a wine-glass, to everybody's consternation. It was a pure accident, and I cannot imagine why I was given anything so frangible to drink from, or what could have been in it. By some miracle I did not cut myself, and was only surprised not to be scolded for so obvious a misdemeanour.

There is one other memory – that of my Aunt Gertrude, who had come to visit us after some illness or operation affecting one of her legs – lying upon the sofa with a crutch. She was a very entertaining aunt at all times, and at that period was good enough to give me the run of her workbasket, which contained, among other things, a small wooden cylinder, whose top, on being unscrewed, revealed it to be full of needles.

The drawing-room also is dim to my mind, but I know that it contained many little tables, covered with an assortment of small knick-knacks with which, when I was good, I was allowed to play before being carried off to bed. There were dogs and cats in china and bronze, and a little green Chinese gentleman holding a fan who, for some reason, was known to me

The Rev. Henry Sayers when Rector of Bluntisham

as the Prince of Wales.[9] There was also a white skin rug with a stuffed head and real teeth, open to show a pink composition[10] tongue. The lamps had silk and lace shades on them, and the standard lamp was adorned by a paper snake twisted round it from top to bottom.[11] There were two plates on the wall, framed in crimson plush, and two fans, sewn with iridescent beetle-wings; I think it was here that the window-sills were overlaid with yellow "art muslin" rucked into folds, on which lay frogs made of cotton-wool and wire.

It was also in this room that I remember being told to suck my big toe for the benefit of visitors and also to walk under the great arch formed by my father's legs. My father was a tall man – 6 foot 2 in those days, before age stooped his shoulders – with a fine nose and forehead, the latter being the more noticeable because he was almost entirely bald at a very early age.

9   The Prince of Wales at this time was the future King Edward VII.
10   Unbreakable material used for dolls' heads, among other things.
11   At this period lighting would have been by oil lamps or candles.

Mrs Helen Sayers

The lower part of the face was less powerful than the upper, and his mouth I never really saw at any time, for he wore the rather full and drooping moustache of his period. His eyes, like those of all the Sayers family, were blue, and, whatever the professors of heredity may say, these blue eyes must be a dominant factor, for, in any Sayers cross that I have ever seen, no matter what the colour of the eyes of the mate, the Sayers blue eye has appeared in the offspring.[12] This is the case with myself, for example, though my mother's eyes were brown, and it is also the case with all my Sayers cousins. I attribute it to the fact that both my grandfather Sayers and his wife, my grandmother, were blue-eyed, thus introducing a double dose of blue-eyedness into the family. My grandmother, who probably had not heard of Mendel, assumed, however, no credit in the matter.

This grandmother had a family of nine or ten children, and it is record-ed that on one occasion a photographer was sent for to take a "group" of the entire family in the patriarchal manner of the time. That was before the

12   It did so in the case of her own son, as she must have thought when writing this.

days of the panchromatic plate, and blue, of whatever shade, was apt to "come out" white. Having arranged his subject to his satisfaction the "operator", as he was then called, emerged from beneath his black cloth and called upon the family to "look at the camera". Obediently, some four-and-twenty eyes focused their steely gaze upon him and his machine. "Why!" exclaimed the photographer, aghast, "Why, you've all got the light-blue heye!" My grandmother, much affronted, replied in an icy tone: "We must take what Nature gave us" and the incident was closed.

My mother, whose brown eyes have been mentioned, had also an abundance of bright brown hair and was a very vivacious and attractive woman. I suppose her long upper lip, strong nose and wide mouth made her face too decided for actual beauty, in a day when regularity of feature was more highly esteemed than it is now, but her broad, intelligent forehead, speaking eyes and liveliness of expression must have made her admired at any period. She was a woman of exceptional intellect, which, unfortunately, never got the education which it deserved. If she could have had the advantage of being her own daughter, she would undoubtedly have made remarkable use of the opportunities she would have given herself, and would probably have made her mark as a writer, for her letters show her to have had a great gift for humorous narration.

She began my education early, and her methods were enlightened. My recollection shows me to myself being carried down to her bedroom regularly every morning to sit at her side in bed while she read aloud to me. I followed the words in the book as she read them and in this manner learned to read without difficulty and without knowing what learning was. I am positive (and have since been assured that I am correct in asserting) that I could read fluently before I was four years old and long before I knew my alphabet. This last statement sounds incredible, but as it happens I can prove it. When, later – at, I suppose, the age of five or six, – I was taken to church, I read the rubric "A General Confession" printed at the head of the prayer "Almighty and most merciful Father", as "A General Confusion", and supposed it to be a stage direction, referring to the noise made by the congregation in settling down on their kneelers for this devotional exercise. It was not until later that I was able to spell the mysterious word letter by letter and correct this picturesque impression. I conclude, therefore, that I originally learned to read by memorising the general outline of the words and not the component letters. After this, it would only seem natural to add that I found spelling a great difficulty in later life. The exact contrary is the case. I have never had the slightest difficulty in spelling correctly, except for a childish tendency, which I distinctly remember, to spell "John" "Jhon". My method with this perplexing name was to write the rival forms side by side, when my eye immediately spotted the correct outline; and this, I take it, is a further proof that I learned to read by words and not by letters. I do not know whether all this throws any light on educational problems, except in so far as it goes to prove that scientific methods are an unnecessary nuisance and that my mother was worth a dozen certificated teachers – which I am very willing to believe.

My mother's bedroom was a fascinating place. The bed had brass knobs – large ones at the four corners, and a row of little ones along the rails at head and foot. Some of these could be twiddled round, but some were stiff. The wardrobe had brass handles which hung down, and these could be made to stand attractively upright, except the top pair, which were out of reach, and for which grown-up assistance had to be invoked.

It was in this room that I lay in state when I had "bronchitis and pneumonia" at an early age,[13] due – I was told – to my having been taken out in a November fog. The illness itself has left no impression on me, but I remember being given a set of dolls' furniture, upholstered in blue and white stripes, to aid convalescence. There was also the episode of the pneumonia jacket. This was made of cotton wool, and my nurse was instructed to remove it only gradually, one piece one day and a little more the next. After a day or two, however, she lost patience and, exclaiming, "I don't think you want this old thing any more", threw the whole garment into the fire.[14] I was horrified, expecting to drop dead instantly after such flagrant defiance of the doctor's orders; but nothing of the sort took place.

That is all I remember of the inside of the Choir House, except that on one occasion I penetrated into "the boys'" part of the building with my father for the purpose of borrowing the *Alice* books. A boy took the two red volumes from the bookshelf and slapped the covers together once or twice to expel the dust. From this circumstance I can safely assert that I knew "Alice" before I was four-and-a-half, at which age I left the Choir House.[15] I possessed my own copies later on, but these were the green edition.

There is one more Choir House memory – "Scruggs" – a grey, hairy mass of indeterminate shape, whom later knowledge enables me to place as an Old English sheepdog.[16] I think he must have belonged to the school, as I do not remember that he ever came for walks with the pram.

Stay! another scene dimly arises – a scene of great splendour – the Christmas tree and the boys' Christmas dinner. The choristers, poor lads, having their Cathedral duties to fulfil, were obliged to spend Christmas at school, and these festivities were meant, no doubt, to console them. A great blaze of candles on an enormous tree, and then myself, seated on my moth-

13 It is touching to find that Mrs Sayers, like so many mothers, moved her sick child into her own bed.

14 There was an open fire in the bedroom. Bedroom fires in Victorian, and later, times were lit only when someone was ill.

15 Her father was appointed to the living of Bluntisham-cum-Earith in the Fen district of East Anglia. The family moved into the Rectory in January 1898.

16 She gives this name to a dog in *Five Red Herrings*, first published in 1931.

er's knee at the head of a long table filled with boys, and being allowed "just to taste" the turkey – no more, and the curtain falls again.

What do I remember of Oxford? Nothing of her spires or her colleges, though later I came to know them well. But the gold-fish swimming in the green glass tank in a shop window, and another shop window with the pictures of the dogs in it, one called "A Disgrace to His Family" and the other, "A Credit to His Family", and, in the chemist's window, a terra-cotta statuette advertising Pear's Soap and called "You Dirty Boy!" And the dentist's show case, in which a lifelike set of dentures opened and shut, opened and shut entrancingly, actuated by machinery.[17] Dentists are not now permitted to display these attractions, which seems a sheer loss to mankind. Then there was a shop where one bought cracknel biscuits. I do not know what has happened to cracknels in these days – they do not seem to have as many knobs as they used to have. When I was a child they always had knobs, and the only proper way to eat them was knob by knob, till only the centre remained.

We often walked in Christ Church meadows, the great elms of the Broad Walk being excellent for playing hide-and seek with. In these mead-ows we sometimes met a man who walked queerly, with a stick, holding his right arm straight down by his side. He was known to Nurse and me as "the poor, paralysed gentleman", and we liked him. One day when he met us, he threw down his stick and, with his only living hand, drew from his pock-et a bright red apple, which he gave me. I never knew who he was, and I fear he must now have left Oxford for the city of pearl,[18] but if he is still alive I should like him to know that his bright red apple is not forgotten.

It was in Magdalen Walks,[19] I think, that there was so much of the little brown-leaved creeping ivy; I cannot now see this kind of ivy without shrinking to pigmy stature and recapturing my childhood. And it was, of course, in Magdalen that we fed the fallow deer, but the ducks were at Worcester, very handy to the Choir House, and we often took them bread. Bread, too, was our alms for the great fat goldfish in "Mercury"[20] – enor-mous fish, stately as abbots, and quite unperturbed by the then frequent duckings of freshers in their pond. There has lately been an outcry against the ducking of House men in "Mercury" – another instance of foolish revolt against tradition. Why should Cardinal Wolsey have placed so con-

---

17 She described this later in a sketch entitled "The Tooth of Time". See Barbara Reynolds, *Dorothy L. Sayers: Her Life and Soul*, chapter 1, p. 5.

18 See *Cat O' Mary*, Note 13.

19 These are a complete circuit of an island meadow. The northern section is known as Addison's Walk, named after Joseph Addison who was a Fellow of Magdalen in the reign of Queen Anne.

20 The pond in Tom Quad at Christ Church, so called from the figure of Mercury in the cen-tre. See *Gaudy Night*, chapter 8.

venient a pond in the quad if not for the ducking of unpopular persons? In my childhood, undergraduates were expected to frolic a little, and I was often told of the famous night when the Christ Church men tied the rope of Great Tom up out of reach by way of protest against the Dean's refusal to let them attend the Duke of Marlborough's ball. This was said to have been the only occasion on which Tom had failed to ring out his curfew of 101 strokes at 9 o'clock every night, and it took the European War to silence him again.[21] Tom and his curfew were a sore puzzle to my childhood, for I had been told that no clock ever struck more than twelve, yet he would toll on and on till I had long lost count.

In Oxford I saw my first magic-lantern show, at a children's party given by a don's wife. There was a picture of a clown falling off a donkey, but I was frightened and had to be ignominiously taken out. In general, I did not suffer from terrors as a child and, in particular, never knew what it was to be afraid of the dark. I again owe this to my mother, who had forbidden my nurses, under the most dreadful penalties, ever to alarm me with threats of hobgoblins or bogey-men. In consequence, I always had a robust taste for literary horrors, pleading for the most murderous tales of ogres and the bloodiest parts of *Robinson Crusoe*. It was explained to me that all these stories were make-believe and that nothing of that kind could possibly ever happen to *me* – consequently, I was always readily able to distinguish between fact and fiction and to thrill pleasantly with a purely literary horror. Later in my childhood, I was asked by a cousin of an analytical turn of mind "whether I had ever believed in fairy-tales". I replied, after consideration, that I always believed these things to have happened, "but a long time ago, and in some quite different place – not this world at all". I interpret this saying, now, to mean that I was always able to give imaginative assent to what I knew to be fiction; in which respect I have not changed at all. I cannot remember at any time to have experienced that difficulty in disentangling imagination from fact which is said to beset many children. I never, so far as I know, came home and said that I had seen a fairy in the garden. If I ever had said so, I should have said it as an entirely self-conscious literary effort. I dramatised myself, and have at all periods of my life continued to dramatise myself, into a great number of egotistical impersonations of a very common type, making myself the heroine (or, more often, the hero) of countless dramatic situations; but at all times, with a perfect realisation that I was the creator and not the subject of these fantasies. I am particular about this, because I am aware of the enormous structure of psycho-analytical theory which it is the present fashion to erect upon these childish self-dramatisations. While, in the "cases" recorded by the

21. D. L. S. is referring here to World War I. Great Tom was silenced also during World War II. When the bell was first hung at Christ Church there were 101 scholars. In their memory every evening at five minutes past nine it rings 101 strokes.

psycho-analysts, I recognise many of my own fantasies, and while I am ready to agree that such fantasies may and do in fact often represent an "escape" from the humiliating world of reality, I must and will assert that in my particular case there was never at any moment any blurring of the conscious personality. They were and are the fantasies of a person whose job in life was to be the making of fictions; in any other sense than this there can never have been a child with less imagination than I. To me a tree was a tree; a stone, a stone; and I myself, a child in a white pinafore with a big frill round the neck; nor had any creative fancy the least influence to disturb facts so solidly and obviously concrete. To repeat my original phrase: my imagination is purely literary; my fantasies are, and have always been, deliberate literary creation. I do not know whether this type of imagination is fully understood by those who make a science of the subject; I rather think not.[22] The fantasies of Loeb and Leopold,[23] for example, as baldly described by the psycho-analysts at their trial, sound to me exactly like those in which I indulged in my own childhood; but in the case of the two boys, they led to the actual killing of a victim, whereas in mine they led merely to the writing of detective stories. No doubt there is a common factor (e.g. bloodshed) in the two results, but on the other hand, there appears also to be a differentiating factor of some kind. The point at which confusion is, I think, liable to occur is when people fail to distinguish between the literary imagination and another kind of imagination which I do not understand at all, and which apparently carries with it the liability to believe and live one's own fantasies. When I say I do not understand this latter kind of imagination at all, I am speaking of the understanding of experience; I can imaginatively understand it all right, of course – but that is where the literary imagination comes in. I can imagine it; I can even imagine having it; but I cannot possibly imagine that I have got it, because my imagination is not that kind of imagination.

I have wandered aside into this discussion because I think a great deal of nonsense is often talked about imagination, owing to a confused application of the term to two quite different faculties. This has, for example, a bearing on that rather foolish question whether an author "contains in himself" the potential qualities of all his characters. He must, of course, do so in the sense that he must be able to imagine himself into their skins or, rather, imagine their qualities into his own skin. But this does not necessar-

---

22   See her development of this subject in *The Mind of the Maker*, chapter 9, Note A, Gollancz, 1941, pp. 116–117.

23   Richard Loeb and Nathan Leopold, two teenage youths from prominent Chicago families, murdered 14-year-old Bobby Franks, whose body was found on waste ground near Chicago on 22 May 1924. They were defended by Clarence Darrow, who pleaded reduced responsibility and mental illness, and they were sentenced to life imprisonment. At the time there was much discussion about their youthful fantasies.

ily mean that he has it in him to behave or even feel as they do. In fact it is likely that the mere act of creating the character expels that particular self-dramatisation for ever from the author's imaginative system – a more thorough kind of catharsis than the Aristotelian purge. The better the author as a creator, the more efficient the purge – which possibly explains why those who look for Hamlet in Shakespeare find only the successful business man who produced his stuff and retired on a competency.

To return from Shakespeare to my own insignificance: this fundamental lack of the unselfconscious kind of imagination was apt to trouble my childhood. It seemed rather wrong to me that I could not, like the children I read of in books, see fairies in the flowers and lions under every bush. I have made earnest efforts to frighten myself into fits with hobgoblins or work up a sense of supernatural awe in the contemplation of the sunset, but it was never any good. I could appreciate the picturesqueness of the situation, but I knew clearly enough that it was all mere fiction. The only real fear that I can remember was of a much more practical kind. I had heard of people being struck with blindness, and was possessed with the idea that this might happen to myself. This fear seized hold of me much later than my Oxford period, in consequence of a story told me by my governess. She told me that a lady with whom she had lived had one day actually discovered herself to be blind of one eye, and indeed to have been so for some time without knowing it. This impressed me, and I would wake up at night with the conviction that the same thing might have happened to me and lie anxiously staring, first with one eye and then with the other, at the crack in the shutters, always with the fear that, some time or other, the friendly streak of light would desert me.

In this sense only I was afraid of the dark, and to this day, all my fears are of this strictly practical kind. I am physically extremely timid, and can visualise such practical accidents as sickness, fire, assault and bankruptcy only too vividly. But this is mere visualisation, or imagination in the etymological sense and is, [I] think, really nothing more than an extremely quick linking together of a chain of possible causes and consequences.

Of the other kind of imagination – the purely literary and creative – I never had any lack, nor can I recall ever having been at a loss to amuse myself with such dramatic fancies. The ordinary doll I never cared for, but for a family of toy monkeys, Jacko and Jocko (and later, Micko and Mocko, but they were never such favourites), I constructed endless adventures. Jacko was the eldest monkey; he was originally white and brown and, I suppose, had long fur; but, since the first use I made of a pair of scissors was to clip Jacko, he soon became almost entirely bald, particularly about the face and chest. He must have been a repulsive object, his nose reduced to the bare skin by much sucking (I can taste the pleasant flavour to this day) and his original glass eyes replaced by brown buttons, but he was dear to my heart. Not that he was always the hero of the tales I wove about him –

Jocko, brown and furrier, was the Harry Sandford[24] of my nursery family – but somehow, good or naughty, Jacko had the most character. The bad boy was a rag doll which, for some reason, I called "Frenchman". He had a body gaily embroidered in blue and red wool, and wore a kind of pointed cap, and his black hair and eyes were also stitched upon him in wool. I think he also had bells upon him somewhere. He was the necessary villain in all my plots, and his rôle was to be soundly thumped and thwacked on all occasions. I cannot actually say that I loved him, but I could not have done without him.

Of the stories that came in books, I loved Grimm's *Fairy-Tales* and *Robinson Crusoe* and *Alice*.[25] It was my father's task to read and explain the Alice books, and the fact that I remember these books being fetched from the boys' library thus enables [me] to date my first acquaintance with the meaning of a pun, though the philosophical beauties of the Looking-Glass world were not fully clear to me till a very late period. The sheer gorgeousness of "Jabberwocky"[26] as a sequence of entrancing sounds was early revealed to me, and indeed, many things that I could only dimly understand were delightful by reason of rhyme and rhythm. Lewis Carroll was living in Tom Quad,[27] but I never saw him;[28] I do not think my parents were ever personally acquainted with him.

Another book that it was my father's pleasure to read to me was *Uncle Remus*,[29] in the abridgement published in "Books for the Bairns". I loved Brer Rabbit, and almost wept over his adventure with the Tar-Baby, and I rejoiced over the tale in which Brer Fox, pretending to be dead, is persuaded to "lift up his left leg and holler Wa-hoo!".

I was also read to by my Aunt Mabel, whenever she came and stayed with us – but what were her special books at this period I have forgotten. She was my mother's elder sister, and at this date would be about forty years old. She lived to the age of 83,[30] and my remembrance of her is overlaid by my later knowledge. I can, however, be positive that she was a very entertaining aunt at all times, in a prim, quiet, humorous way. She had not the glamour of my Aunt Gertrude, but the flavour of her games and conversation was always excellent. I will also record for the benefit of a curious posterity that, when at Oxford, she wore a grey stuff[31] dress with a stiff

24 A virtuous character in *The History of Sandford and Merton* by Thomas Day (1748–1789), who is contrasted with the disagreeable Tommy Merton.

25 D. L. S. told me that she had always disliked the stories of Hans Christian Andersen. [Ed.]

26 The' poem in Lewis Carroll's *Through the Looking-Glass*, in invented language, beginning " 'Twas brillig and the slithy toves..."

27 The quadrangle of Christ Church where Great Tom stands.

28 D. L. S. told me that Lewis Carroll had seen her in her perambulator. [Ed.]

29 Folk-lore stories by Joel Chandler Harris, an American author (1848–1908), of which a rabbit and a fox are the main characters, told by a negro to a little boy.

30. With D. L. S. and her husband at 24 Newland Street, Witham, Essex, where she died in 1930.

31 A woollen fabric.

buckram collar, and that in the front of the dress was a kind of bright red waistcoat, adorned with a row of small bone buttons, extending from the throat to the base of the stomacher – for in those days the bodice was always boned, and was worn, of course, outside the skirt. Leg-of-mutton sleeves were fashionable, and the skirt was gathered simply into the belt, after a style known as the "housemaid skirt".

I believe that my Grandmother and Grandfather (on the Sayers side) once came to see me at Oxford, but I do not call my Grandfather to mind at all. My Grandmother (she of the "light-blue heye") certainly came, and impressed herself rather fearfully upon my childish imagination by inviting me to inspect her gold tooth. She meant this to be a treat for me, but I then thought, and still think, the exhibition a rather disagreeable one.

Another Oxford figure that I faintly recall is that of Mrs Slater, the Cathedral verger's wife. She lived near us in Brewer Street, and her greeting for me was "Oh, the little lamb, then" – an expression which my Father often used to quote, mimicking her manner of speech. I liked Mrs Slater, and she gave me a china dog, which stood for many years on the nursery mantelpiece and was a beloved companion in my bath, till one day it fell into the grate and was broken. It was hollow, and there was a small hole in its base by which the water slowly entered, causing it to swim in a fascinating, lop-sided manner. It was a very small hole, and the conflict between the entering water and the outgoing air made a curious and entertaining thin singing and bubbling. Then, too, there was the fun of seeing Nurse shake the water out again at the end of bath-time. I had other things that swam in the bath, notably a green china frog. This, however, got broken easily; it lost a fore-foot, and thereafter would not swim.

I must have met other children at Oxford, but I do not at all remember them. There is a glimpse of my younger cousin, Margaret,[32] who lived with her father and mother in an old house in Holywell. Holywell, like many other Oxford streets, was then paved with cobbles, and I have heard my mother say that the noise made by passing traffic was such that one could not sit in the front rooms of my uncle's house with the windows open. People who complain today of traffic-noises are mostly those who have never heard the noise of an iron-tyred wheel rattling over cobbles.

I have also a faint memory of some children visiting me one day at tea and shyly presenting me with a box of picture-bricks, but who they were I do not know. Indeed, I never cared at all for children, nor have I, at any time of my life, liked the company of people younger than myself. Perhaps this comes of being an only child.

---

32. Margaret Leigh, daughter of Maud and Henry Leigh (1894–1973). See article by G. A. Lee, "Dorothy's Forgotten Cousin: Margaret Mary Leigh – Scholar, Farmer, Author", published by the Dorothy L. Sayers Society, 1988.

Dorothy at the seaside, aged about three

I think I was three-and-a-half when I first saw the sea. I was taken to Broadstairs by my Mother and Nurse, and I still have a tin-type[33] of myself at that period – a very solemn child with a fringe, wearing a sun-bonnet and a pair of striped bathing-drawers, into which my frock is bundled out of the way. Behind me sit Mother and Nurse beneath a large Japanese umbrella. My Mother wears a hideous linen blouse with a stiff collar, a hard sailor hat, and a most appalling thick white veil, made of very close net, which must have been as hot and stuffy as it was unbecoming. My Nurse is dressed somewhat similarly, but without a veil.

Was it on this visit or the following year that I displayed the first signs of a vulgar tendency to pick up stray acquaintances by attaching myself to a total stranger whom I found peacefully sitting at the foot of the cliff? He obligingly waded into the sea with me on his shoulder, and eventually carried me back to my startled Mother, whom I hailed with the gleeful cry: "Mummy! Mummy! I've found a new uncle!" As my Mother used to say

33. A photograph taken as a positive on a thin tin plate.

Arrival at the Rectory. Water-colour by Norah Lambourne

Bluntisham Rectory

The Porch and the Monogram

The Rectory Hall. Water-colour possibly by Dorothy L. Sayers

afterwards, with a twinkle, "He might have been *anybody*" (and in those days, ladies did not speak to "anybody"), but she always admitted that he turned out to be "a very nice fellow", and my own impression is that he was one of the most delightful and satisfactory uncles ever created.

It was certainly in the summer of 1897 that I was again at Broadstairs and saw part of a procession in honour of the Diamond Jubilee.[34] My Aunt Gertrude in this year presented me with a much-loved "Jubilee cup and saucer", adorned with a portrait of the Queen and the flags of Great Britain. It was only used occasionally, as a treat – not like my silver christening knife, fork and spoon, which passed into everyday use as soon as I was of age to handle them.

Towards the end of 1897, I became aware that a great change was impending. There was talk of "the country", and of "the new house", and an enormous book filled with patterns of wall-paper appeared upon the scene, and was anxiously turned over by my parents.

In fact, a living had been offered to my Father, and he, knowing that it was one of the best livings in the gift[35] of Christ Church, had accepted it. The living was that of Bluntisham-cum-Earith, situated, very unexpectedly, in the heart of the Fen-country. It was, I believe, a living that had been received by Christ Church in exchange for a number of smaller livings – and thus it came about that we went from Oxford to a parish only about 16 miles [36] from the sister-university of Cambridge. It was a great wrench for my Mother to leave the town for this remote country place. She had always loved society and civilisation, and she hated the idea of parish duties, for which she had neither training nor desire. But my Father pointed out that an opportunity as good as this would probably not recur, and that the duties of a cathedral chaplain, with the continuous strain which they entailed upon the voice, might in time become too much for him. I fancy, also, though I never heard him say so, that schoolmastering was not altogether congenial to him.

However that may be, the decision was taken. The time for departure

---

34.   The celebration of the sixtieth anniversary of Queen Victoria's accession to the throne.

35.   This expression means that Christ Church was the patron of the parish with the right and duty of appointing the parish priest. The patron was (and is) the descendant or legal successor of the lord or landowner who first built and endowed the parish church, and the priest he appointed was the *rector* (Latin for ruler) who had rights and duties overseen by the bishop. From Norman times the patron could assign the parish in perpetuity to an ecclesiastical institution (usually a monastery or college) which then received the rector's emoluments (notably tithe) but appointed a deputy or *vicar* (Latin *vicarius*) paid a proportion of the income to do the parish priest's work. At the Reformation the laymen who acquired monastic property acquired also the monasteries' parish obligations and emoluments, so becoming lay rectors. Tithe was phased out in the twentieth century, and the distinction between rectors and vicars is now little more than a historical curiosity.

36.   By modern roads, nearer 13 miles than 16.

drew near. Furniture was packed up. Objects belonging to the Choir House were labelled neatly by my Nurse with little tabs "NOT TO BE TAKEN". I was told that my Aunt Mabel and my Grandmother, now a widow, were to come and live with us at Bluntisham. Nurse went with us, of course, and – an immense tribute to my Mother's character – our whole staff of servants. My Mother used to speak of this later. "I told them", she said, "that we were going right away into the country, where they would find the work much harder and the life much duller, without proper shops or amusements, and I said that they must feel quite free, either to come with us or leave us. I should quite understand if they did not want to go. They consulted together and then came back and said they would all go with me." I think my Mother was greatly touched by this; but indeed, she always had the trick of keeping her servants, and to the end of her days she was served with great devotion. And so, on this occasion, we went out patriarchally into the wilderness with our manservant and our maidservants and everything that was ours. Except Scruggs. He did not come with us. Perhaps he belonged to the school, or perhaps he had already taken a longer journey.

The last days came. I think my Father and Mother must have gone ahead with the staff, leaving the rest of us to follow, for I am sure that I was left alone on the last night or two with Nurse in the old house. I remember seeing a little wooden cart belonging to Jacko and Jocko taken down from the top of a cupboard and packed away under my anxious eye. Jacko remained with me. I spent my last day cutting out for him an elegant cap and jacket from some stiff blue material. He looked very smart in it. The nurseries looked dark and empty without their accustomed furniture and litter of toys. It was all rather exciting, but rather solemn.

Curiously enough, I do not in the least remember our departure, nor the long journey by train. When I again wake to consciousness, we are walking up from Bluntisham station to find our new home.

II

The station was about ten minutes' walk from the house.[37] My Aunt Mabel and my Grandmother must have joined us either in Oxford or at some point on the journey,[38] for they are walking ahead of us – my Grandmother in her widow's weeds[39] and my Aunt carrying Polly in a travelling cage. I am walking beside Nurse. I am wearing a brown pelisse and little close bonnet to match, both trimmed with a feathery brown-and-

37   There is now no station at Bluntisham. See colour plates between pp. 32 and 33.
38   Perhaps at Huntingdon, where they could have changed trains for Bluntisham.
39   The black mourning apparel of a widow, which included a becoming bonnet and veil. Widows continued to wear this garment long after the period of mourning.

Canon Rumpf. "The Rectory will last my time"

white trimming which must have been a kind of marabout.[40] The time of year is early January, and as we pass in at the gate, I see, for the first time, winter aconites flowering at each side of the drive, from which I conclude that the winter was a mild one.

Bluntisham Rectory was a big place, with an imposing frontage, added to the quainter older parts behind it. It was, and is, one of those huge country rectories which are now white elephants to an over-taxed and impoverished clergy; but it was none too large for us in later years, when our establishment became greatly increased. Even in [1898][41], with my parents and myself, my Grandmother and Aunt, my Nurse, four maidservants and the manservant, we were not lost in it.

I believe that when we came to it, it was not in very good repair. The aged canon who was my Father's predecessor[42] had had a cheerful habit of saying, when confronted by tales of tumbling walls and decaying woodwork, that "it would last his time". He was quite right. It did last his time; and he contrived to decease conveniently just before dilapidations became due. Fortunately, shortly before we took over, my Mother had come into a

40 Plumes taken from under the wings or tail of a marabout. See photographs p. 31.
41 D. L. S. wrote 1897 but the removal took place in January 1898.
42 Canon John Rumpf, who was Rector at Bluntisham from 1859 to 1897.

small legacy of some kind, and this was spent on re-decorating the house. The job was done (rather to the annoyance of the local tradesmen) by a first-class Oxford firm and no doubt represented the high-water mark of what the 'nineties thought decoration should be.

Let me describe the house as I remember it, for these things are social history.

The hall was an attractive feature of the house – very long, squareish in the middle and tapering to a narrow passage at either end, through round arches draped with heavy dark-blue patterned curtains, looped up with thick cords and tassels. The floor was of stone, but – whether to make less work or for greater warmth – its beauty was obfuscated in these early days by a brown linoleum, lined with black squares to imitate parquet.[43] From the centre part of the hall the staircase wound shallowly up – "a poor staircase", my Mother always called it, with frail Victorian banisters, painted white and surmounted by a mahogany handrail. One of these banisters was individual and exciting, for from time to time it exuded a thick, gummy tear of resin. I am afraid it was not a well-seasoned banister, but there is no doubt that it possessed great personal charm.

Under the staircase stood a large tortoise stove, to warm the hall; I liked to be held up to look at the tortoise on the top and to spell out the mysterious legend "Slow but Sure Combustion".

The dining-room, on the south side, was the finest room in the house, deriving its peculiar character from two fat white fluted pillars which supported a beam at one end. These marked, I think, the place where a part of the next room had been taken into the dining-room, for this next room was but a narrow slip of a place, called, at this time, the "morning-room". There were three large windows to the dining-room, secured at night on the inside by heavy shutters, such as I had never seen before. The exterior of one of these windows (the central window of the house) was framed in a handsome old pillared doorway, said to have been brought from Oliver Cromwell's house at Huntingdon. It gave great dignity to our frontage and presented an agreeable mystery of its own, in the shape of an intricate knot or monogram sculpted in low relief upon the lintel. We often tried to resolve it into letters, but without success. It was perfectly symmetrical and probably a purely formal ornament, but it gave us much food for thought.

The dining-room presented itself to me at first with a wonderful glamour about it, due to the presence of all the drawing-room ornaments, heaped in a glittering mass upon the sideboard, which stood in the "ante-chapel", as we called it, behind the pillars. Thus my first view of it suggested a kind of Aladdin's cave of colour and splendour. When the

---

43 There exists a painting, perhaps by D. L. S. in her 'teens, showing the hall, in which these details are portrayed. It is reproduced between pp. 16 and 17 by kind permission of Mrs Fortuna Fleming.

ornaments went, the glamour went also, but I think I always knew that it was a beautiful room. It was papered, I am almost sure, in blue, with a meandering pattern, and photogravures of seascapes by Peter Graham[44] hung upon the walls, and the paint was blue, with the panels picked out in white. The table was of mahogany, made to an oval shape to my Father's special order, he having been greatly attracted by a similarly-shaped table in the house of a friend at Oxford. Later on, this shape was found to have its disadvantages when seating large parties of people, and an extension was made for each end by the carpenter. These extensions allowed two more people to be placed at either end, but involved the unhappy guests in such a confusion of table-legs that they must have eaten in the very greatest discomfort.

On one side of the dining-room was my Father's study, papered in blue with a self-pattern of large poppies. The American organ, on which he was fond of playing, stood originally in the dining-room, but was later removed to the study. There was no very special feature about the study, except bookshelves and a writing-table, and the fact that one had to knock at the door before entering. I am not sure whether it was here, or in the drawing-room chiffonier, a mysterious and lovely box was to be found (but only by very special permission) containing my Father's Masonic regalia.[45] It was, no doubt, very irregular of him to allow me to be dressed up in these; but it only happened very occasionally and was a particularly solemn treat.

On the other side of the dining-room was the morning-room before-mentioned, papered in a light-green pattern and wainscotted in black. In this room the fireplace and door had not been repainted, but preserved the artistic efforts of the former owners. On either side of the hearth appeared yellow irises on a black ground, while across the chimney-piece ran the legend "Cheerful Hearts Make Cheerful Hearths" in Old English lettering. Designs of birds and flowers were painted on the panels of the door, and when, later, I read *The Moonstone*,[46] I always thought of Franklin Blake and Rachel Verinder as engaged in painting this particular door with the "special quick-drying vehicle" which played so great a part in Sergeant Cuff's detective investigations. My Aunt and Grandmother, and any visiting aunts, sat in this room in the morning and after dinner. Later on, my Mother took it for her own "den", and they sat in the dining-room, which I think they preferred, as being larger and lighter.

At the extreme end of the hall was the drawing-room – seldom entered,

44. Peter Graham, born in Edinburgh in 1836, specialised in Scottish views which also included coastal scenes with wave-dashed rocks and sea birds.
45. Henry Sayers was initiated as a Mason at St Michael's Lodge in Tenbury, where he became Worshipful Master in 1883. In 1885, after taking up his post at Oxford, he joined the Apollo University Lodge, of which he became Worshipful Master in 1889.
46. The novel by Wilkie Collins (1824–1889).

except on "At Home" days or when important visitors were present. At this time it was a dark, rather gloomy room, in spite of its three windows at the farther end. In later years, we opened the fourth window (blocked up, no doubt, in the days of the window-tax). This greatly improved the room and also the front of the house. The drawing-room wall-paper was a deep yellow, and the carpet was yellow too. The curtains were green, and the fireplace was draped with stately green curtains that ran on rods at each side beneath the mantel-shelf. Here all the little tables, the innumerable small ornaments, the art muslin and the paper frogs and snakes reappeared, together with the white wolf rug and the silk lampshades. When visitors came to tea, it was here that I made my appearance. I had a mauve velvet frock and a red plush frock – both trimmed with a deep falling collar of lace.

On the left-hand side of the hall was the day-nursery, to which I shall come back later, and a swing-door leading to a long passage, from which one entered the "boot-hole", the pantry, the "servants' hall" (an extremely small, dark sitting-room with no right to such a pretentious name), a lavatory, the back-stairs and the kitchen; beyond the kitchen were the larder, scullery and laundry. All these (except the lavatory and the servants' hall) were floored with stone or brick, and when I think of the appalling amount of scrubbing there must have been to do, I often wonder what our Oxford servants thought of their bargain. Still, they stayed with us, so I suppose they did not mind.

The ceiling of the passage and the kitchen was thickly starred with iron hooks – relics of an age that cured its own hams and bacon; and the kitchen range was a cavernous affair, given to "eating coal".

Every drop of water for domestic use had to be pumped up by hand. Every morning, at a quarter to eight precisely, the "ker-plonk, ker-plonk" of the hand-pump resounded through the house. About fifteen minutes' exercise on this machine sufficed, if I remember rightly, to fill the cistern for the day, unless the house was especially full, in which case the pumping was renewed in the evening. Even so, the boiler arrangements were extremely inadequate, and eventually a larger tank was put in to supply hot water – still, however, having to be kept full by pumping. As the natural result, my Mother always lived in terror of the water's running short and of our all being blown up. Bath-room, naturally, there was none; our bathing was done in hip-baths and all the water, hot and cold, had to be carried up to the bedrooms in immense brown cans. Strangely enough, my Mother used to say, she never had a servant complain of this colossal labour, in all the twenty years we lived at Bluntisham.

[The manuscript of this section breaks off here.]

Cat O'Mary
The Biography of a Prig
by Johanna Leigh
ഗ᠍ഗ᠍ഗ

The cats o'Mary seldom bother; they have inherited that good part;
But the cats o'Martha favour their mother of the anxious brow and the
troubled heart.

Kipling, as adapted by Somebody

BOOK ONE

Kitten into Cat

ↄ℈ↄ℈ↄ℈

I

"Is it all right?" inquired Mrs Lammas, faintly.

"Right as rain", replied the nurse. "A dear little girl."

And in case the information should not prove sufficiently reassuring as it stood, she added quickly:

"She's got a *splendid* head."

Mrs Lammas was quite satisfied. She had always prayed that, whatever it was, it might have brains.

II

Katherine Lammas was born, very characteristically, at Oxford. All her life she remained exceedingly proud of this achievement, which was due to no exertion of her own, but merely to the fact that her father was headmaster of the choir school at Wolsey College.[1] Her first datable recollection – of which psychologists may make what they like – was of being heartily spanked by Nurse Williams between the ages of two and three years. Before that, there had been "Old Nannie", but a dim impression of dark hair and a white apron is almost too vague to be called a recollection. Nurse Williams was a trained nurse and wore a uniform. It was she who, somehow or other, contrived to keep Katherine out too long in a November fog, thus causing her to contract bronchial pneumonia; after which Nurse Williams left and "Nurse" – the final and only true owner of the title – reigned in her stead. Katherine remembered nothing of the illness, except a pneumonia-jacket of cotton-wool, worn during convalescence. This the doctor had ordered to be removed gradually, a handful at a time; but one day somebody (Nurse? Mother? the Hospital Nurse?) had

---

1   A fictional name for Christ Church, founded by Cardinal Wolsey.

lost patience and flung it bodily into the fire, saying, "I don't think you need this any more". This rebellion of the individual judgment against constituted authority made a very awful impression upon Katherine.

Other early recollections, less painful, were: sucking her own big toe for the gratification of visitors; walking beneath the colossus-arch of her father's straddled legs; and being carried shoulder-high round the draw-ing-room to identify the picture of the Infant Handel Surprised by his Parents.[2] It was probably rather later than this that she began to be taken down to her mother's bedroom each morning, to be read aloud to. From looking over the book during this entertainment, Katherine learnt to read by the time she was three years old, though it was not for some years after that, that she was able to recite the alphabet or infallibly recognise any individual letter. Mrs Lammas was thus an unconscious pioneer of the "Look-and-Say" method,[3] which was not due to become famous till twenty years later. It is said to make children bad spellers, but Katherine always spelt remarkably well.

How far the dreaming spires of Oxford made any impression upon young Katherine it is hard to say; for childish memory became drowned and lost in later knowledge. But the great trout in Mercury,[4] the swans at Worcester, the deer in Magdalen Park, the goldfish that swam in a tank in a shop-window, and Scruggs,[5] the sheepdog attached to the Choir School, always remained with her as pictures viewed from a standpoint three feet from the ground. Nor, in after years, could she ever see the small, brown, creeping, star-leaved ivy without shrinking to dwarf stature and retreading Magdalen Walk; and the same shrinkage took place whenever she smelt the sharp, aromatic scent of fallen yellow poplar leaves.

Other fascinating things presented themselves at eye-level also. In the High Street there lived a dentist, whose door was adorned by a case full of artificial dentures. These, actuated by some fascinating contrivance, opened and shut with a slow, rhythmical motion, and to be wheeled past this spot in her mail-cart was one of Katherine's recognised "treats". There was bitter disappointment on the days, when, owing to Sabbath obser-vance, or neglect to wind the machine, the pink-and-white jaws failed to gnash themselves.[6] Another occasional excitement was the purchase of cracknel biscuits. These had a dry and unrelishable flavour, and their charm was purely ritualistic. It was necessary that each knob should be bit-ten off and consumed separately before the centre was attacked. Then

---

2 Handel, forbidden to play the clavichord, was found doing so secretly in the attic.
3 The Look and Say Method: made popular by the teaching reforms of the American educator John Dewey (1859–1952).
4 The pond in Christ Church, so called from the statue of Mercury in the centre.
5 See *My Edwardian Childhood*, Note 16.
6 Ibid. Note 17.

there was the Post-Office, whose grey metal letter-box bore the initials "V.R." It was explained that these stood for "Victoria Regina", and this was Katherine's first introduction to English history and the dead languages.

The Broad Walk at Christ Church was memorable also, not only because one could play peep-bo behind the elm boles, but because of the Poor Paralysed Gentleman. This kindly person, who walked oddly and stiffly because he could not move his left arm, [7] took a fancy to Katherine and would stop to say good-day to her when he met the pram. One day, he threw down the stick with which he always walked, thus freeing his service-able hand to plunge into his pocket and produce a large, red apple as a gift for Katherine. She never knew who he was, but she always bore about with her that picture of the fallen stick, the red apple under the arching elms.

Apart from the close circle of Mummy, Daddy and Nurse, Katherine's Oxford life was not rich in personal contacts. Of other children, she saw lit-tle and remembered less. She was taken to a children's party given by a don's wife, cried at the magic lantern and was taken out. She was present one year when there was a Christmas tree for the choir-boys and retained a hazy memory of its glitter, and of sitting on her mother's lap at the head of a long table crowded with boys and being given a taste of the turkey. Once, a shadowy child-form invaded the nursery and presented her with a box of bricks. The grown-ups were more distinct. There was Aunt Millicent, who paid several visits, and wore a gown of thick grey stuff[8] with a smart scarlet waistcoat, all little buttons down the front, and Aunt Emily, who had hurt her leg and lay on the sofa, and had a most fascinating work-box in which Katherine was allowed to rummage. Both of these aunts were good with children. A more awful apparition was that of Grannie, who alarmed Katherine by offering a gold tooth for her inspection. This, and the being required to imprint a kiss on Grannie's cheek – withered and unlike the cheeks to which she was accustomed – gave Katherine a curious physical aversion from her grandmother, which no later intimacy and no sense of gratitude for kindness ever quite dispelled. It led her into cruelties which she was ashamed of, but could not explain or control.

An artist-friend, who painted a miniature of her; Nurse's brother, who made a fleeting appearance one day, leaving a grey African parrot behind him; Great-aunt Agatha, a tall, sharp-featured lady, who mercifully took no notice of her, and Cousin Somebody, who tried to endear himself by making nasty faces – these phantoms flitted in and out and were gone. But Katherine had other friends, more important and abiding.

These fell into two groups. The first was headed by Jacko, Jocko and Frenchman. Jacko was the doyen of the nursery cupboard. He had once

7   In *My Edwardian Childhood* it is his right arm that is paralysed!
8   Ibid. Note 31.

Dorothy and her favourite toys

been a white furry monkey, with glass eyes and a tail; but Katherine could
never remember him in full coat. He emerges[9] from the mist of ages with
the hair worn off his chest by constant cuddling, his tail gone, his nose
sucked into shapelessness, his eyes plucked out. Then Nurse had the brilliant idea of refitting his eye-sockets with brown buttons, and thus
renewed, his face took on a pleasing individuality. In the endless dramas
which he was made to enact on the nursery floor, he developed a distinct
character – he was puckish, mischievous, enterprising, always in disgrace,
but enduringly beloved. It was for Jacko that the most fantastic suits of

9   This verb is in the present tense, an indication that she is still thinking of herself, as in *My
Edwardian Childhood.*

clothing were devised; it was Jacko who slept with Katherine in the night-nursery cot. Jocko was larger and furrier and brown; he kept his tail for many years, and his eyes beamed with red and black glass. His character was utterly virtuous and amiable; he was the Harry Sandford[10] of the establishment. Frenchman was a rag doll, curiously attired in a sort of harlequin costume embroidered upon his body in red and blue losenges of woolwork. He had a white face and black hair and was evidently intended by nature to play the villain's part. In this rôle he was indispensable. Less adaptable in composition, but useful, were Jumbo, the beautiful real-skin elephant, Tommy, the wooden horse, and Ajax, the railway engine. For dolls of the accepted kind, Katherine never had any love; Gladys, who was marvellously jointed and possessed a trunkful of exquisite hand-made garments, was admired and respected, but no more.

The second group of friends came out of books. Brer Fox and Brer Rabbit, Robinson Crusoe, all the fairy-tale characters. Most of them belonged to the early-morning readings in bed, but the Uncle Remus stories[11] were Daddy's peculiar property. He read them aloud in the evenings, with Katherine curled up on his knee, and he was fond of bringing them out in casual conversations.

"What do dead folks do, Kitty?"

"They lifts up their left legs and hollers, Wa-hoo!"[12]

One day, Mr Lammas observed to his wife:

"I think Kitty could understand *Alice* now, don't you?"

Mrs Lammas, to whom her daughter's ready understanding was a source of pleasure, agreed, and Mr Lammas said, "Come along, Kitty".

They went down the long passage, seldom traversed by Kitty, which led from the house to the school side of the building. A door was opened and displayed a large, bare room, surrounded by bookshelves. A boy in an Eton suit detached himself from a group by the table.

"Have you got a copy of *Alice?*" inquired Mr Lammas.

"Yes, sir", said the boy. He selected two red volumes from the shelf, expelled the dust by clapping the covers together, and handed them over to Mr Lammas. On that day, Katherine was made free of Looking-Glass House, and learned the nature of a pun.

When Katherine was about four years old, she became aware of a mysterious bustling about the house. There were going to be changes. Enormous books, made up of patterns of wall-paper, made their appearance in the drawing-room among the little tables full of knick-knacks, and were discussed with animation.

Then Katherine was told that they were all going away to live in the

---

10   See *My Edwardian Childhood*, Note 24.
11   Ibid. Note 29.
12   As Brer Fox did when pretending to be dead.

country, and that Grannie and Aunt Millicent were coming to live there too. Nurse was coming, of course, and Jane the parlour-maid and all the other servants. It was all very exciting.

Mother and Daddy disappeared, reappeared, disappeared again. The rooms were dismantled; familiar objects vanished, leaving a dusty emptiness behind. The nurseries were left to the last, and Nurse became very busy, writing labels in her neat handwriting "Not to be Taken Away", and tying them on to all those pieces of furniture which were the property of the college. Daddy and Mother vanished finally, and Aunt Millicent came up from Bognor and took their place for a day or two. There came a night when she and Nurse and Katherine reigned alone in the deserted house, attended only by Jacko. All the other animals had been packed up, but to pack Jacko was unthinkable. He was wearing a smart new suit, made of bright blue glazed book-linen, and this occupied Katherine's mind almost to the exclusion of the new adventure. The next day, they left Oxford behind them and went out into the wilderness.

III

The little country station of Fentisham, Hunts,[13] was about ten minutes' walk from the Rectory. Grannie must have joined the party in London, for they all walked up the roadside path together: Grannie, in her black widow's bonnet and mantle, then Nurse, Katherine and Jacko, then Aunt Millicent, in a long tight coat, feather boa and veil, carrying the parrot's cage. Katherine wore a brown pelisse and little round bonnet, edged with marabout.[14] It was January, and as they turned in at the drive gate, there were winter aconites on both sides of the path.

Fentisham Rectory was a large, ivy-covered house with a great expanse of up-and-down, old-fashioned roofing, masked by an impressive Georgian frontage. It had two acres of garden and a paddock. Its two wide lawns were ornamented with thick shrubberies and many handsome old trees. Behind it lay a cobbled yard with ample stabling. It stood, solid and solitary, fronting the high road with an air of leisured dignity. A remark made by a visiting missionary became proverbial in the family. This person, who had been expected to arrive by the 11.45 train and left to find his own way up from the station, presented himself at the door half an hour after the train had passed, and when every one was wondering what on earth had become of him. He explained that he had walked up the road as far as the church and, not finding the Rectory there, had been obliged to

13   Fentisham is a pseudonym for Bluntisham; Hunts. is an abbreviation of Huntingdonshire. The station no longer exists, but see colour plates between pp. 32 and 33 and photographs on p. 33.
14   See *My Edwardian Childhood*, Note 39.

Dorothy in her bonnet

make an enquiry and retrace his steps. "But you must have passed the Rectory", said Mr Lammas. "Oh, yes", replied the missionary, "I passed the Rectory, but I took it for a gentleman's house." "Well", said Mr Lammas, with a certain mild stateliness, which was habitual to him, "I hope it is."

A gentleman's house it might be, but to Mrs Lammas, coming from the civilisation of Oxford, it was a nightmare. It was a waste of stone passages and frosty corridors. There was no lighting except by candles and paraffin lamps and every drop of water had to be pumped up. The kitchen range was a vast, gloomy monster, lurking in its huge chimney as in a lair and avid of coal at the terrific price of eighteen shillings a ton. Most of the inside walls were of lath and plaster, within which the mice rushed and rattled with a noise like the trampling of armies, and into which driven nails vanished suddenly up to the head to the sound of falling plaster. There was also a lack of outside amenities. The local butcher killed only one day a week and his victims were large, coarse animals, which never seemed to possess any kidneys or sweetbreads. Having one day returned some chops which did not come up to her exacting standard, Mrs Lammas learned to her surprise that there was nothing that could be sent in their place, all the

portions of the carcase having already been apportioned among the customers. The village possessed a small linen-draper's, a small general shop
and a post-office which sold sweets, tops and liquorice laces; any com-
modities which these could not supply had to come from the next town,
four miles off.[15]

There was no society of any kind, except that of the neighbouring par-
sons' wives, the nearest of whom was separated from Fentisham by three
miles of open fenland road. The whole situation was made the more awful
to Mrs Lammas by the problem of a parish of close on a thousand souls.
She was a lively, intelligent woman, unaccustomed to the performance of
good works; and in marrying an Oxford school-master, she had never con-
templated performing the duties of [a] parson's wife in a country parish.
Nor was her sister Millicent going to be much help in coping with the situation. She possessed an almost supernatural power of self-detachment
from all forms of responsibility, and in later years Mrs Lammas was wont
to say with a smile that Millie had contrived to live seventy years in the
world without ever being present at a birth, a death or a house-moving. In
fact, Miss Millicent Warwick had the instinct of self-protection very highly
developed.

Old Mrs Lammas, on the other hand, was delighted with the new situation. A clergyman's widow, and the mother of two clergymen, the church
was in her bones. She had always longed to see dear John with a church
and rectory of his own: it surrounded him with the dignity she felt to be his
due. She was a tall, handsome old woman, immensely active and intelligent, ready to do all she could to help him in taking Sunday School, dis-
tributing the Parish Magazine and visiting the sick. Though she may have
felt that John had made an unexpected choice, she liked and respected her
daughter-in-law – probably all the more because Mrs John Lammas (who
had a pretty spirit of her own) had made it clear from the start that there
could be only one mistress in her house. During the first year at Fentisham
there was occasional friction – for the Lammas family had developed
interference to almost as fine an art as Miss Warwick had developed non-
interference – but in the end the elder lady realised that she was beaten,
and submitted with a good grace.

Of the delicate adjustments arising from this joining of the family for-
tunes, Katherine was allowed to feel and know nothing, and this in itself
speaks volumes for the behaviour of both parties. Her early impressions of
the new home were exciting and pleasurable. The most striking of them
was her first view of the dining-room – larger and lighter than the one at
Oxford, and looking like an Aladdin's treasure-cave, with all the drawing-
room ornaments piled in a rich confusion upon the sideboard. Big, black
early-Victorian fireplaces surprised her by their contrast to those she had

15   In reality, probably St Ives.

The little country station of Bluntisham (rear), in 2002

The little country station of Bluntisham (front), in 2002

Bluntisham station abandoned (ca. 1970)

left, for the Oxford house had been built in the taste of the late eighties.
The new day-nursery had a big window, opening nearly to the ground; on
one side were shelves from floor to ceiling; on the other, a large cupboard,
filled excitingly with china belonging to Grannie. In the hall stood a tor-
toise-stove – a surprising object; Mr Lammas lifted her up to see the tortoise stamped upon the top, and to spell out the cabalistic legend
surrounding it: "Slow but Sure Combustion". Upstairs there was a landing, at the end of which there was the new night-nursery; it had a blue-and-
white floral paper amid whose intricacies Katherine (though nobody else)
could clearly distinguish the forms of two fiery, galloping horses. From this
landing ran a long, dark passage with two precipitous steps at its darkest
part. Here were Aunt Millicent's room and Grannie's room, on the door of
which some former owner had painted a large group of scarlet poppies and
blue cornflowers. One of the downstairs rooms had a painted door, too,
with gaily coloured panels of birds and flowers, and a fireplace adorned
with sprays of yellow iris and a slogan running across it in Old English lettering: Cheerful Hearts Make Cheerful Hearths. Katherine read this out
slowly, under Grannie's guidance, and came to the conclusion that the
phrase was in the nature of a pun, though not so satisfactory as the ones in
the *Alice* books.

Gradually, the household settled down to an established routine. Family
prayers were held in the dining-room before breakfast. Mr Lammas sat at
the head of the table with Bible and Prayer-book; the family grouped
themselves upon their chairs; punctually at half-past eight, the bell was
rung and the servants filed in: Cook, Jane, the housemaid, the kitchen-
maid and the Man. (The Man, being a kind of house–stable amphibian,
appeared in a blue-and-white striped house-coat hastily assumed over his
outdoor nether-garments, and was subsequently banished from Christian
society on the ground that his boots smelt strongly of horse-manure. In the
end he disappeared altogether, and his household duties were performed
by the gardener's boy.) After prayers, there was a pause, during which Mr
Lammas would look sternly at his watch. Breakfast followed, in dining-
room and nursery respectively. In those days, the nursery was the proper
place for little girls, and Katherine always found it a pleasant one. In the
evening, she visited the grown-ups, in the room with the bird-door and the
Cheerful Hearth, and here she slowly advanced from floor-romping to
spillikins[16] and Beggar-my-Neighbour[17] as her understanding developed.
At the proper time she had blancmange and jam for her supper and was
marched off to bed.

The bed-time ritual also became fixed and was in every way character-

---

16   A game played with thin rods of wood or bone, piled in a heap, the object being to pull off
     one at a time with a hook without disturbing the others.
17   A children's card game.

istic of Katherine. In some way or other, she had learnt to sing a childish song, which ran, waggishly:

> Good-night, Mamma, good-night Papa,
> Good-night to all the rest;
> Good-night, Mamma, good-night, Papa,
> I must love Dolly best.

Probably Mr Lammas had found it in a nursery-book and taught it to her, for he was musical (all Lammases were musical) and he was glad, though not at all surprised, to find that Katherine "had an ear". One evening, the fancy came to Katherine to sing this ditty as she passed upstairs to bed – substituting, of course, the name of Jacko or some other temporary favourite for "Dolly", dolls finding no favour in her eyes.

The performance had an immense success. Next evening it was repeated. Thereafter, it became stereotyped. As soon as the nursery door opened, the family gathered in the hall and waited, with pride, amusement and a certain nervousness, to hear whose name would be chosen for the place of honour in the last line. The song became a barometer of Katherine's fluctuating affections. "Mummy", "Daddy", "Nursie", "Auntie" all had their turns, according as they had indulged a caprice or presented a gift; on one occasion Grannie, being unexpectedly promoted, was touched almost to tears. Occasionally a wandering whim or a thirst for novelty would prompt such eccentric variations as "Cookie", "Janey", "Polly" (the parrot) or the name of the butcher or baker. Persons who had offended Katherine were punished by being excluded from the evening chant for weeks together. It was an embarrassing business and to Katherine it eventually became extremely wearisome. It was, however, expected of her. Casual visitors were herded into the hall to listen to it, and if Katherine was in the mood to do the proper thing, their names were duly celebrated in song. Tedious as the duty became, it never occurred to Katherine to shirk it – unless the evening had been a stormy one; and even then the rite would be eventually performed, amid hiccups of distress, after suitable pressure had been applied. Eventually, some circumstance or other intervened to release her from the self-appointed task; nor did the grown-ups ever learn what a burden it had grown to be.

There is a great deal of Katherine in that good-night story: the self-dramatisation, the self-importance, the deference to public opinion, the inability to say No, the pleasure of getting her own back, the occasional sentimentalities and the impatience with the outgrown. It is chastening to reflect that the family became, in all probability, as much bored by the business as she did, and only persisted in it for fear of hurting her feelings.

As time went on, Katherine developed all the faults and peculiarities of an only child whose entire life is spent among grown-up people. She was self-absorbed, egotistical, timid, priggish and, in a mild sort of way, disobedient. With the exception of occasional fits of screaming temper, she was not a naughty child, and her disobedience was almost entirely of the passive kind. She disliked a direct order and obeyed it slowly and reluctantly; but her timidity, partly constitutional and partly acquired, held her closely within the confines of conventional behaviour. She never ran away, or climbed trees, or set herself on fire, or indulged in dangerous experiments. It had been so strongly impressed upon her that her life and safety were the most important things in the world that she avoided all risks – less because she was physically afraid than because she dreaded to hear the words: "I told you what would happen". In fact, in a broad sense, she was not disobedient at all. She believed what everybody told her and conformed to everything that was expected of her. Everybody had decided that she was "clever" (indeed, it was beyond dispute), and she lived up to the reputation cheerfully. She instructed her friends and relations on every subject about which she knew anything, repeating opinions that she had heard and read with a sublime faith in their infallibility. She harangued the gardener (a morose man) about the beneficent habits of "they peafinches", which ate his seedlings and which he tried to trap and slay. Having absorbed from Grannie (who was an old-fashioned High-Churchwoman) decided opinions about the Liturgy, she passed them on to her Aunt Millicent (who had no love for church-going). Her mother told her that a college education was to be desired above all things, and she saw herself, consistently, as one destined for academic honours.

Her father, on the other hand, had made up his mind that she was to be musical; this opinion she also adopted with fervour and held in rather incongruous combination with the academic theory. When she was six years old, a lady called Miss Martin came to teach her to play the violin. A quarter-size violin was the largest that her small hands could cope with. She gave her family a good deal of information about the structure of the violin and the proper method of playing it, and visualised herself as a great musician. It was, perhaps, a sinister indication that she hated practising and shirked it whenever she could, but that was held to be a natural manifestation of the Old Adam. She herself had no doubts whatever of her musical predestination.

But her whole life was a deliberate self-dramatisation. She never had the least difficulty in entertaining herself. When she was not reading, she was playing out interminable dramas with Jacko and Jocko, acting all their parts as well as her own if no grown-up help could be secured. If a grown-up was available – and her grown-ups displayed an unlimited capacity for self-sacrifice in this direction – she preferred the greater realism of having the animals' parts spoken for her, but only in accordance with her precise instructions.

"Auntie, make him say: 'I won't learn my lessons'."

"I won't learn my lessons."

"You're a bad boy, Frenchman. You'll have to be spanked, Auntie make him say: 'Oh, please don't spank me. I will be good.'

"Why don't you make him say it yourself?"

"Oh, no, Auntie. *You* make him say it. *Please*, Auntie, make him say it."

"He says: 'I don't care if I'm spanked or not.'

"Oh, *no*, Auntie, *do* say it right."

"Oh, please don't spank me. I will be good."

"No, Frenchman, you've got to be spanked. Auntie make him yell." Whack! Whack! "Make him yell, Auntie."

And so on, endlessly, tyrannically.

At other times, Katherine lost her identity in that of some beloved character in a book. For a period which must be counted by months, she was Charlotte M. Yonge's[18] "Little Duke". Her father, who had read the book aloud to her, was allowed to be the faithful Osmond, and other subordinate positions were allotted to the rest of the family. The intrusions of the Little Duke upon private life became rather intolerable.

"You mustn't talk like that to me. I'm Duke Richard of Normandy."

"I don't think you ought ever to have read that book", said Mrs Lammas, exasperated at last. "I shall take it away from you. It is making you very rude and pert."

Katherine was hurt. Surely people ought to see that her behaviour had nothing to do with herself; it was ducal; it was dramatically appropriate; she always spoke in character, why could not everybody else do the same? It was a perplexing business.

But then, grown-ups in real life never did behave like people in books. A quip or retort, faithfully reproduced from some witty dialogue in a story, would be received with rebuke instead of with applause. There was a little girl in some sentimental story who had stroked her mother's face sympathetically and remarked upon her "poor, thin cheeks". Katherine tried this one day upon Mrs Lammas. Mrs Lammas was not touched, like the storybook mother; she was thoroughly annoyed.

"Good gracious! It's enough to have other people telling me I look old and ill without you starting. Don't make personal remarks."

Katherine felt that Mrs Lammas had fluffed her lines. It was perhaps better to make up both sides of the dialogue for herself. In bed at night, she lulled herself to sleep with long stories, recited aloud, in which she identified herself with some hero of fiction, carrying him through endless adventures in different lands and centuries.

18 Charlotte Mary Yonge (1823–1901), author of 160 books, of which *The Heir of Redclyffe* (1853) first brought her popular success. She came under the influence of John Keble who urged her to expound his religious views in fiction. *The Little Duke*, a romance for children, was first published in 1854.

One day her Grandmother informed her:

"We heard you talking in bed the other night – you were using sacred names – you must have been preaching a sermon to yourself."

Katherine was disgusted. Grown-ups always said that eavesdropping was contemptible, yet this was what they did themselves. At a moment when you thought you were private, they listened outside your door. She passed over the ill-bred observation without comment.

Persons who knew about Katherine's story-book cloud-cuckoo-land always put her down as dreamy and imaginative. Nothing could have been further from the truth. She was purely practical and realistic. She had imagination of a sort, but it was external and creative; she never really believed in her own imaginations. She could imagine what it would be like to meet a fairy or be frightened by a lion, but she never had the slightest expectation of actually finding a fairy in a flower or encountering a lion in the laurel-bushes. It sometimes seemed wrong to her that she should be so lacking in proper feeling; the book-children did experience genuine emotions of this kind. Katherine would wander about the garden or lie awake in the dark, trying conscientiously to work herself up to shuddering-point about ghosts or angels or a man under the bed, but it was useless. The terror remained fictitious and enjoyable. The only thing she had a genuine dislike of was any sort of machinery. She was worried by the dark inside of the garden pump and the hidden intricacies of the domestic water-closet. Suppose the machinery should "go wrong" – what would happen? Curiously enough, the grown-ups had no sympathy with this particular anxiety – though if anything actually did go wrong with the water works they made a surprisingly loud outcry about it. Katherine's uneasiness troubled her but seldom and left little mark on her mind. It was probably only due to the fact that nobody had ever thought to explain to her the mechanism of pumps and water-closets, for she never had any fear of what she could understand.

Take, for example, frogs and insects. Her mother thought that, as a country child, she should be brought up in a natural intimacy with all these creatures. No living thing that crept or flew had, in consequence, any terrors for Katherine, and she prided herself on an exact knowledge of insect habits. The knowledge was derived chiefly from books, for she had no turn for patient observation of nature; as far as it went, however, it was correct, and she was always anxious to impart it to the grown-ups, whose minds, on this subject, were regrettably warped by prejudice.

"Ugh! Get away, you nasty thing!" cried Miss Martin, apostrophising a large dragon-fly, "take care, Kitty, you'll get stung."

"Dragon-flies don't sting", said Katherine, simply.

"Oh, yes they do", said Miss Martin.

"No, they can't", said Katherine, "they haven't got any stings."

At this point the inevitable relative interfered, saying, "Kitty, you mustn't contradict, it's very rude."

Katherine was amazed. Rudeness was very far from her intention. She had stated a fact – one which she had really verified by experiment. She had caught dragon-flies and handled them, and they had no stings, though they had fierce-looking jaws and could chew up flies like anything. But the jaws were harmless to human beings, and surely Miss Martin should have been grateful to be delivered from the imaginary menace of poison-bearing dragon-flies. She tried to explain, what she obscurely felt, that the establishment of a scientific truth was somehow different from the putting forward of an unsupported opinion; but her vocabulary was not equal to this, and she was left with a sense of injury. Not that she was herself readily amenable to correction. She would argue the point with obstinacy, for she had a great opinion of her own cleverness and to be proved wrong was humiliating. She did, however, understand the nature of proof, and, though she seldom admitted her mistake in words, she would not repeat the error.

It was Aunt Millicent who taught her to knit. Her first efforts on two needles were clumsy, but in time the mysterious entanglement of loops and knots sorted itself out and she produced a scarf in plain knitting, and after that, a vest for Jacko, in ribs of purl and plain. She made the fascinating discovery that the back of the purl stitch was the same as the front of the [plain] stitch, so that the ribbing pattern was formed by the knitting of purl over plain and plain over purl in consecutive rows. From this it was only a step to the manufacture of ribbed wristlets on four needles.

This led to a dispute with Aunt Millicent. The smooth ribs, said that lady, were all plain knitting; the wavy ribs, that so fascinatingly closed up and disappeared inwards as the knitting progressed, were the purl ribs. You knitted plain over plain and purl over purl – always.

Katherine denied this. "It's purl over plain and plain over purl", she insisted.

"No, it isn't", said her aunt.

Katherine remembered a phrase which she had heard some grown-up use in an argument with another grown-up. (Grown-ups, she noticed, contradicted one another with surprising freedom.)

"Oh, well", she said, magnanimously, "I expect we both mean the same thing, really."

Aunt Millicent said nothing, but Katherine was uneasy. Her aunt was a great authority on knitting; her shawls and socks were famous in the family. Katherine had a great respect for authority, but still – the purl-over-plain rule, which she had so often proved by experiment, could not, surely, fail her now. There was only one way out of the difficulty; one must experiment again. One would mark the plain-knit row with a piece of wool, and then, next time one came to it, one would know whether it was purl or plain that went on top of it.

Feb 1899

My darling Mother
How do you like being
in Oxford? Have you
visited Old Tom yet?
I went to Earith this
afternoon, and Mrs Hard
gave me an orange, I ran
all the way with my

is still naughty.
give my best love to
Margaret and ask her
when she is coming to
Bluntisham again, tell her
I want her to come.
I am sending you a few

hoop. I am going to have a
violin practice with Daddy
when I have done my letter.
I am almost sorry I have got
a holiday from dictation.
Jacko is quite well and so
is Jocko he, is good but Jacko

snowdrops with my best
love.
Now good bye darling
Mother from
your loving little
Dorothy

Dorothy's handwriting at the age of five

Dorothy with her hoop

The experiment was carried out in private, and with a sinking feeling in the pit of the stomach, Katherine realised that Aunt Millicent had been perfectly right. Plain did come over plain – but what an extraordinary thing! It seemed (and she knew the phrase) like a reversal of the law of nature. There must be a reason for it. After long and careful thought, she discovered it. When you knitted on two needles, you always began at the front end of the needle, and worked first from the outside and then from the inside of the fabric; but on four needles, you began from the back end of the needle and worked on one side only. This was most interesting and satisfactory. It was horrid to have been wrong, but on the other hand, it obviously took a very clever person to find the explanation of so odd a phenomenon. Perhaps Aunt Millicent herself had never inquired into the reason underlying her rule of thumb. If not, she would be glad to know about it. Katherine rushed off in a hurry to demonstrate the whole thing to Aunt Millicent, who was less staggered by the revelation than she might have expected. It really seemed as though she must have known about it all the time.

Up to the age of seven, Mrs Lammas herself provided Katherine's formal education. Writing was a hard subject, beginning with long rows of repellent pot-hooks,[19] a proceeding through a series of flourishing capitals and curly-tailed small letters to a series of moral maxims, all leaning at an extravagant angle across the top of the copy-book. Katherine breathed very heavily over these exercises, finding the pen surprisingly long and heavy in the hand. It came easier, she found, if one put one's tongue out, though her father thought this funny and made jokes about it. She learned the counties of England and Wales, with their capitals and rivers: five Northern Counties; Northumberland, capital Newcastle, on the Tyne; Durham, capital Durham, on the Tees; Cumberland, capital Carlisle, on the Eden; Westmorland, capital Appleby, on the Eden; Derbyshire, capital Derby, on the Trent. She could point to them with a fat finger on the map, and sometimes remembered what they were famous for in the way of manufactures. History came out of *Little Arthur's England*.[20] It was divided into good kings and bad kings and kings who were neither good nor bad, and therefore (from Katherine's point of view) unsatisfactory. William I was good, though stern; William II was bad; Henry I was good and never smiled again; Stephen was bad and everything in his reign confusing and tiresome; Henry II made laws and was good, except to Thomas à Becket, and he was very sorry about that; Richard I was good, definitely, because he was lion-hearted and popular and devoted to the Holy Sepulchre, virtues which quite outweighed the trivial facts that he levied heavy taxes and was never at home to look after anything; while John was bad with a rich and gorgeous badness. But what could you do with a king like Henry III, who was neither good nor bad, but merely weak – a word which meant nothing? Henry VIII had six wives – he divorced two and beheaded two, one died and one survived him – Mary was Bloody Mary and Elizabeth was Good Queen Bess. In the Great Rebellion, Katherine espoused the Roundhead cause, chiefly out of opposition to Grannie, who was senti-mentally Royalist. Katherine never liked sentiment. The Georges had no characters, their reigns were full of foolish politics and, by a curious coinci-dence, their dates were quite impossible to remember. History was nice when it was full of battles and stories, but tiresome when it came to laws and constitutions. The religious part was easy, because Roman Catholics were always in the wrong.

French came, together with the violin, into Miss Martin's department, but was not nearly so interesting as Latin, to which Katherine was

19   Curved strokes, formerly practised by children in learning to write. The straight strokes
      were called "hangers".
20   *Little Arthur's History of England* by Lady Callcott, first published 1835. Lady Callcott
      (1785–1842) was born Maria Dundas, the daughter of a rear-admiral. Her first husband was
      Captain Thomas Graham of the Royal Navy, who died in 1821. Her second husband was
      Sir Augustus W. Callcott. Her work was a history book for English children for over 100
      years.

introduced by Mr Lammas at the age of six. *Mensa, mensa, mensam, mensae, mensae, mensâ.*[21] It made a nice chant to sing about the house, and there were very few little girls of her age who knew Latin. *Puella mensam habet. Feminae columbas habent. Filia currit. Agricolae rosas amant. Poeta filiae rosam dat.*[22] Mr Lammas used, of course, the "old" pronunciation.[23] "Why are sailors wicked? Because they are *nautae*." Katherine chuckled at that, and did not forget the Latin for sailor. She was puzzled by the mysterious gender of husbandmen, sailors and poets,[24] but accepted without difficulty the curious phenomena of case and verb-endings, and the fact that in Latin the position of subject and object made no difference to the meaning of the sentence. It took her fifteen years and more to realise the advantage she gained from this early training in an inflected language.

The bugbear of all bugbears was arithmetic. It was a horrid lesson. The slate-pencil squeaked and errors were often washed out in tears. The only alleviation was the Twice-one-Are-Two book, which had rhymes and pictures: "Two Times – Shoe Times." "Twice one are two, here's a pretty shoe." "Twice two are four, left outside the door." Nothing that rhymed could be altogether bad. Mrs Lammas made poetry a strong feature of her programme. Verses must be recited with action and meaning. "Casabianca",[25] "The Wreck of the Hesperus",[26] "Lord Ullin's Daughter"[27] and "The Inchcape Rock".[28] Anything that rhymed could be poured wholesale into Katherine's memory and stuck there like glue. She

21   The example of Latin nouns of the first declension given in all elementary Latin grammar books.

22   Latin: The girl has a table. The women have doves. The girl runs. The husbandmen love roses. The poet gives a rose to the girl.

23   Latin was pronounced in England as though it were English until modern times. In the 1870s reformers began to restore what they took to be the authentic ancient Roman pronunciation. The old English pronunciation continued in use longest at Oxford. It is still in use amongst doctors, lawyers and botanists. The phrase "Vivat Regina" ("Long Live the Queen") is always said and sung as though the v's were English, the i's are pronounced like the word "eye" and the g is soft. If the phrase occurred in a Latin text, students would be instructed to pronounce it: weewat regeena, with a hard g.

24   The Latin nouns *agricola, nauta, poeta,* meaning respectively husbandman, sailor, poet, end in "a" and so belong grammatically to the feminine gender.

25   Louis Casabianca (1755–1798), commander of the French ship *L' Orient* at the Battle of Aboukir, blew up his ship to prevent it falling into the hands of the English. His little son was on board and died with him. The incident is the subject of the poem by Felicia Hemans (1793–1835) which begins "The boy stood on the burning deck".

26   A poem by Henry Wadsworth Longfellow (1817–1802), first published in 1841 in *Ballads and Other Poems.*

27   A poem by Thomas Campbell (1777–1844).

28   The Inchcape Rock is in the North Sea, off the Firth of Tay, dangerous to mariners, off which the abbot of Arbroath or Aberbrothock fixed a warning bell on a float. In the poem by Robert Southey (1774–1843) Sir Ralph the Rover cuts the bell from the float and is himself wrecked on the rock.

loved words. "The good old Abbot of Aberbrothock":[29] that was a grand
word. "Aberbrothock." It filled the mouth. "Roll on, thou deep and dark
blue Ocean, roll"[30] – and it did roll. "The Assyrian came down like a wolf
on the fold. And his cohorts were gleaming with silver and gold".[31] If
Katherine ever troubled to ask what a cohort was, she soon forgot it; the
sound of the word was enough.

She discovered another lovely word, almost by accident, in Church. She
sat with Nurse in the North aisle, and could only see Mr Lammas when he
came down from the mysterious chancel to read the lessons or preach a
sermon; but she followed the service carefully in her red prayer-book. Here
the "Look-and-Say" method of learning to read occasionally let her down.
At the end of "Dearly Beloved Brethren" there was a kind of stage-direc-
tion in italic. Katherine read it as: "A General Confusion" and thought it
referred to the noise made by the congregation in scrambling down on to
their knees and scraping the long wooden kneelers along the floor. She was
satisfied with this, till disabused by some grown-up or other, who laughed
unkindly at the error and heaped the confusion upon Katherine's head.
But the lovely word made its appearance only on the third Sunday in the
month, when a ritual called "the Ante-Communion" was added to
Morning Prayer. She did not perceive its beauties at first, pronouncing it
"apposso-lick", on the model of "Catholic". The true pronunciation came
one morning as a sudden and blinding revelation, and the lame cadence
resolved itself into a splendid marching rhythm: "Catholic and Apostolic
Church". Besides this rhythm, it had the merit of being incomprehensible,
like the earlier and more exciting part of the Athanasian Creed. The beauties of the Psalms, on the other hand, left Katherine cold at this period –
they were too long altogether, and there was a particularly dull section all
about statues[32] (another failure of "Look-and-Say"), which she dreaded
and hated beyond expression.

In Katherine's eighth year, Mrs Lammas decided that the educational
problem was getting beyond her, and engaged a governess.

Miss Carstairs was petite and fair and excessively refined. Her mouth
was so round that when she yawned Katherine thought it must crack at the
corners, it seemed so unequal to the strain. Katherine's own mouth was of
generous width, and she was celebrated for the extraordinary distance to
which she could extend her tongue. It came out long, stiff, pink and pointed, and she could even roll it into a tube. One day she found the governess
examining her own tongue in the glass, and discovered to her amazement

29 See preceding Note.
30 Lord Byron (1788–1824), from *Childe Harold*, Canto 179.
31 Idem, "The Destruction of Sennacherib", *Hebrew Melodies*.
32 The word misread by D. L. S. as "statues" is "statutes", which appears in several sections of
    Psalm 119, a psalm which she would certainly have found "too long altogether".

that the tongue did not come out at all. Miss Carstairs could only open her mouth and display a pale, flabby flap.

"Can't you put your tongue out any further than that?" demanded Katherine. "Look at mine!"

Miss Carstairs said that tongues should be kept inside the mouth as much as possible, but the incident added to Katherine's already powerful sense of superiority. But she could not help admiring the elegance with which Miss Carstairs dressed. She had one lovely afternoon costume of purple cloth, the front and sleeves of which were filled with a delicate pink and white floral chiffon. A hat crowned with cock's feathers and a boa and muff of silver fox made up an ensemble fully equal to any fashion-plate. Miss Carstairs further enlarged her pupil's ideas with the aphorism that a lady put on her gloves in her bedroom; only inferior persons put them on in the hall, while to postpone the matter till you were actually in the street was vulgar in the extreme.[33]

It is obvious that Miss Carstairs' thoughts took an urban turn. The long, straight, solitary Fen roads and muddy field-paths upon which she and Katherine were doomed to take their daily exercise must have made her feel like a pelican in the wilderness. She walked with little, mincing steps holding her long skirts out of the wet. Katherine scuffled beside her, kicked at loose granites, or ran loose on the wide grass verges, inventing stories about knights on horseback. Miss Carstairs' conversation generally took the form of long anecdotes about the little boy and girl to whom she had been governess before. She kept photographs of the whole family upon her dressing-table, and her heart seemed to be still very much with them. Arthur Payne had had very nice manners and his sister Betty had been so pretty and obedient. And Mrs Payne had evidently been a model employer. She knew so many distinguished people and had always treated Miss Carstairs quite as one of the family. When she called on Lady This and the Hon. Mrs That she had always taken Miss Carstairs with her. Fentisham was a horrid place, by comparison with Winchester, where the Paynes had lived. There was no society.

Katherine was very angry. Nobody had ever hinted before that her home was not perfect in every particular.

"There's lots of society", she said stoutly. "There's Mrs Welbeck."

"Mrs Welbeck!" said Miss Carstairs. "A brewer's wife!"

It was quite true, of course. Mrs Welbeck lived in St. ... ,[34] and had a daughter a year younger than Katherine, and every so often the families exchanged visits. She could take the little local train, or jog along the four miles of road. Katherine liked driving best, especially if she was put in the front seat of the dog-cart on her mother's knee, where she could watch the

<hr>

33 I received the same instruction from my grandmother, who was born in 1856. (Ed.)
34 The name is left blank in the manuscript. A pseudonym for St Ives was perhaps intended.

long bay back of Jenny the mare and the solemn jerking of her tail. Sometimes Daddy would even let one drive for a little while. The road was not featureless for Katherine. There was the humped railway bridge, which was the only break in the flatness, and where one conscientously tried to sit forward so as to throw the weight of the trap correctly on to Jenny's shoulders while she surmounted this terrible hill; there was Mrs Tebbutt's farm, where they kept a raven in the front garden; there was the field of tragic memory into which a beautiful green balloon had once floated away and burst under a hedge before Aunt Emily, energetically pursuing, could recapture it; there was the house in Heppleworth which had a window blocked up "because of the window-tax". It was a remarkable window, because the owners had painted the semblance of window-panes and a pair of Nottingham-lace curtains on the obscuring black plaster, so that you had to look quite carefully before you recognized it for the dummy that it was, and Katherine was very careful to point it out to any visitor who might be making the journey with them, understanding perfectly that visitors must be amused and interested to the best of one's ability. Further on, there was a level-crossing, where the gates marvellously opened of their own accord to let you through after the train had passed; a funnily-shaped house which marked the site of an old toll-gate, and when you got to St. ..... itself, there was the market place, with its iron pens for cattle. Monday was market-day, and then the town was full of farmers and their traps and animals, so that it seemed a most populous and bustling place. On ordinary shopping expeditions the dog-cart was left at the Golden Lion, which had an enclosed courtyard and a gallery running round it, festooned with Virginia creeper. For sixpence you "put up", which meant that Jenny was taken out and bestowed in a loose-box, but if you were only staying a short time, you had a "tie-up" for threepence, under the gallery on the left side of the yard. The ostler was a little bow-legged man in a striped waistcoat, and Katherine learned to cry out "Morning!" in a grown-up manner when he touched his cap [and to feel a friendly interest in him].[35]

Of course, if you were going to Mrs Welbeck's, you went past the Golden Lion into Broad Street, to the house with the green door, and put up there. The house seemed dark to Katherine and rather awe-inspiring. In the winter, you went upstairs to Hester's nursery, where you played "fish-pond", or sometimes, for a great treat, were allowed to look at Great-aunt Welbeck's "Bioscope or the Wheel of Life", which was like a great metal bowl, with slits in the dial. You put in a sheet of coloured pictures round the inside, and gave the bowl a twirl on its stem, and then, when the bowl revolved, you looked through the slits and saw the pictures moving. There was a boy pulling up a fish, and a clown tumbling, and a pink demon who peeped in at a blue door and out again. There was a big pile of these

---

35   The words in square brackets are deleted in the manuscript.

pictures, and it must, even at that date, have been a valuable toy. There was a piano in the nursery, much prettier than the one at home, for it had a beautiful blue panel in front, painted with white sea-gulls.

In the summer, you went down into the garden, and then Mrs Welbeck's unfortunate occupation in life could no longer be ignored, for the way to the garden ran under a flagged archway, filled with empty barrels and the sour-sweet smell of beer. Mrs Welbeck never ceased to lament the vulgarity of this approach and to apologise, with a little affected laugh, for the "horrid old brewery". Katherine found the smell and the sudden coolness and the echoing of one's footsteps beneath the arch all exquisitely mysterious and lovely. The garden itself was small, but it overhung the river, and one could fish for minnows over the railing, and sometimes one was taken out in the boat, sculled silently and efficiently by Mr Welbeck (who had no conversation) or by his sister, who was alert and practical, or by Mrs Welbeck herself, who always had to take off her rings and watch-chain first and hand them to her husband to hold. Katherine thought Mrs Welbeck wonderfully pretty, and marvelled that anybody so frail-looking and frilly could manage those enormous heavy oars. Little Hetty Welbeck was pretty, too, with big, languishing dark eyes and thick brown hair. In her presence, Katherine felt the first faint prickings of an inferiority complex – her own eyes were small and pale, her mouth so wide and her freckled nose so very snub. People were always making fun of Katherine's nose and freckles. In the early nineties it was considered right to make fun of little girls' looks, for fear they should grow up conceited.

Grown-up people and books were very confusing about this business of being pretty. It was better to be good than pretty – even being clever was better than that; on the other hand, Miss Carstairs spoke of admiring Betty Payne's pretty curls and it was quite clear that only pretty girls ever got married. In the fairy-tales, of course, it was easy, because prettiness, cleverness and goodness always went together, but in real life that did not appear to be the case. The logical inference would seem to be that it was, on the whole, more distinguished not to be married, because that only happened to the inferior pretty people, but actually, not being married was considered rather odd and disgraceful if you were a woman. (This didn't apply, naturally, to Aunt Millicent or Aunt Emily, because one's own relations were quite different from ordinary people.) Gradually it became fixed in Katherine's mind that she herself was never likely to be married, and that one must take that for granted and not mind about it, because being married was, after all, a troublesome thing to be, though, if one did succeed in getting married, all one's grown-ups would be greatly pleased with one. It is true that Katherine did not think this out very clearly – it would have been difficult to reconcile all the conflicting statements of the grown-ups on this confusing subject – but she found it quite easy to hold two irreconcilable opinions at the same time. [She did so quite firmly and quite unquestioningly – just as she implicitly believed that she was destined to be a great musician and…][36] She kept them in water-tight compartments, believing one set of doctrines on Mondays and the other on Tuesdays, exactly like the majority of grown-up people; and, like the majority of grown-up people, made little attempt to relate them.

She had, however, pretty hands; Mrs Lammas incautiously told her so. They were Warwick hands, small-boned and shapely, whereas Lammas hands were raw-boned, with ugly short top-joints and awkward knuckles, and Mrs Lammas could not help rejoicing openly that her daughter – Lammas in stature and colouring – had inherited her hands from the distaff side.[37] Katherine decided that it was more unusual and aristocratic to have pretty hands than a pretty face, and took refuge in this thought when people laughed at her snub-nose or said rudely, "Oh, what a mouth!"

In any case, one could always make up stories and games and have adventures in the garden. One was never allowed to go outside the gates alone, but inside one had perfect freedom when lessons were over and no tiresome walk had to be taken. One could sit under the weeping-ash and imagine that it was a house of one's own, or one could look for wrens' nests in the great limes on the front lawn; or one could crawl under the big blackberry bush and pretend it was a smuggler's lair; or pick forbidden (but not too strictly forbidden) fruit in the kitchen-garden, while pretending that one was Robinson Crusoe; or one could hunt for frogs behind the washhouse, or talk to Bruce[38] in his kennel outside the back door; or stare at the pig, knee-deep in straw, snuffling among the cabbage-stalks and potato-peel in the trough; or one could go into the laundry and watch Mrs Appleton the gardener's wife, as she goffered her way round interminable muslin curtains, or pashed her iron, thump, thump, over great tracts of starchy table-cloth. When Mrs Appleton took the iron from the fire, she held it close to her rosy cheek and then, if it was too hot, plunged it sizzling into a pan of cold water. It was fascinating to watch the wrinkled linen come out smooth and shiny as the iron moved over; fascinating, too, when woollens were being passed through the mangle – seeming at first far too thick to enter that tiny crack between the rollers, but being somehow miraculously squeezed in, and coming out on the other side flat as pancakes, with the water dribbling through the tray into the tub beneath. Appleton the gardener was also a grand companion. He was not the morose man with a grudge against "they peafinches", but a new one, of a kindlier disposition. He had submitted without too much grumbling when,

36 The words in square brackets are deleted in the manuscript.
37 D. L. S. was to give this vanity to Lord Peter Wimsey. See *Gaudy Night*, chapter 14.
38 Bruce was the name of a dog owned by the Sayers family.

The Parish Church of Bluntisham-cum-Earith

The nave of Bluntisham Church

The pulpit from which the Rev. Henry Sayers preached

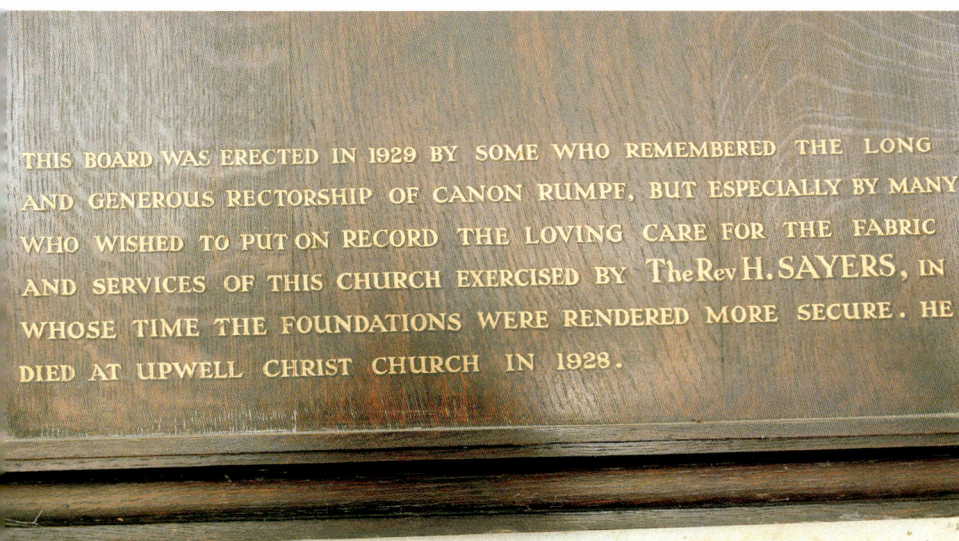

THIS BOARD WAS ERECTED IN 1929 BY SOME WHO REMEMBERED THE LONG AND GENEROUS RECTORSHIP OF CANON RUMPF, BUT ESPECIALLY BY MANY WHO WISHED TO PUT ON RECORD THE LOVING CARE FOR THE FABRIC AND SERVICES OF THIS CHURCH EXERCISED BY The Rev H. SAYERS, IN WHOSE TIME THE FOUNDATIONS WERE RENDERED MORE SECURE. HE DIED AT UPWELL CHRIST CHURCH IN 1928.

A commemoration of the Rev. Henry Sayers

The Parish Church of Bluntisham-cum-Earith

after the tomtits' nest had been three times pulled out of the pump and three times rebuilt, Mrs Lammas had said that the pump was to be left alone till the tomtits had finished with it. The birds had their entrance by the pump-handle, but they did not mind at all when the top of the pump was lifted off and Katherine held up to look at the twelve speckled eggs, and in the end they hatched a cheerful family of ten incredibly small red babies, most of whom survived to fly. This was exciting. Still more surprising was the crackbrained thrush who laid six eggs in the hollow of a cabbage-head from which Appleton had removed the heart for cooking purposes. Unhappily, some cat or other got at the fledglings. There was no official cat at the Rectory. Mrs Lammas did not like cats, so Katherine did not like them either. "I like dogs best", she said. "Dogs are faithful, but cats are cruel. Cats prefer places to people." All the books and the grown-ups were conveniently in agreement on this point, and as Katherine never knew any cat intimately, she was not tempted to oppose authority as in the distressing episode of the dragon-fly.

"But you ought to like cats", said her Uncle Robert one day, tiresomely (he was a teasing uncle and not a popular visitor), "you're a little cat your-self, aren't you?"

"No, I'm not a horrid cat", said Katherine indignantly.

"Oh, but you must be. Your name's Kitty. That's a little cat."

"It isn't", said Katherine.

"Yes, it is. Kitty, Kitty, Kitty. Come along, let's look at you. I believe you've got a tail and claws."

This, for the misguided Uncle Robert, was the cue for a display of humorous tickling. Katherine screamed loudly.

"I won't be a cat! I'm not a nasty cat. I'm not! I'm not! I'm not!" At which point she gave the lie to her assertion by severely scratching Uncle Robert.

"You *are* a little cat", said Uncle Robert, with more temper than was becoming in a grown-up. "A *very* horrid little cat. Look how you've scratched your poor uncle."

"I don't care", howled Katherine.

Miss Carstairs, arriving hastily, was shocked.

"He called me a cat", sobbed Katherine.

Miss Carstairs supported Uncle Robert in the most unfair way, and Katherine was sent to bed and told to stay there till she was sorry, and ready to apologise to her uncle.

"But I'm not sorry", said Katherine to her mother. "And I can't say I'm sorry when I'm not. It wouldn't be true."

Mrs Lammas said it was naughty to scratch Uncle Robert, but possibly she sympathised with Katherine, for when the next day came, everything went on as usual and Uncle Robert's apology was not insisted on. Nor did Uncle Robert make any further mention of cats. But in the back of her mind Katherine knew that her name was a vulnerable point, and threw up a protective shell about it.

When Miss Carstairs had reigned for about a year over the Fentisham schoolroom, it seemed good to Mr and Mrs Lammas that Katherine should be given some companions of her own age. It would teach her, they thought, to be unselfish and companionable. Only children were always spoilt children, and undeniably Katherine was becoming too self-important. In the absence of any school or companions of suitable social standing in the immediate neighbourhood, the next best thing was to board, lodge and educate the children of some stranger, following the usual practice of country parsonages. The small brother of an old Oxford pupil conveniently offered himself at this juncture, and later on, the daughter of another country parson.

Katherine was interested and excited at the idea of having Charles and Gertrude to live with her, and welcomed them politely. In the matter of developing unselfishness, however, the experiment was a failure. Intellectually, Katherine could more than hold her own with either of them; and Charles turned out to be afraid of wasps and stinging-nettles, which placed him definitely as inferior to herself. Gertrude was better-looking than Katherine, and Katherine resented this, without feeling any disposition to admire. Charles was greatly admired and petted by the grown-ups because he had curly hair and could say very amusing things at table; but in the school-room he displayed, in Katherine's own words, "his uncivilised side". Gertrude and Katherine made common cause against him when he was tiresome.

Mr and Mrs Lammas were careful to observe a strict impartiality among the children in the matter of gifts and indulgences, but this did not prevent the appearance of jealousies, spites and tale-bearing. Looking back on this period in after years, Katherine decided that she had developed more unpleasant characteristics from the companionship than compensating virtues. It did not suit her to be queen of her company. It only confirmed her in the belief that she was cleverer and more interesting than other people.

A wholesome setback to her self-satisfaction was, however, administered by Miss Weller, who succeeded to the throne of Miss Carstairs when Katherine was nine, and who was definitely a good governess. Miss Weller had only just returned from Germany, and was young, athletic and, in Katherine's eyes, beautiful. Her hair curled naturally and instead of Miss Carstairs' high-necked dresses she wore square-cut blouses which left her throat visible; she also instituted games and Swedish drill and Sandow's exercises.[39] In all these things Katherine was but a poor performer, though she did not care to admit as much. She preferred to excuse failure by a

39. Eugene Sandow (1867–1925) wrote several books on physical exercise.

Dorothy with her governess and friend

pretence of indifference. If either of the other children had happened to possess athletic genius, Katherine would probably have sulked and refused to compete. Happily, or unhappily they were little more competent than herself, so that she was able to join in games and exercises without too much damage to her self-esteem.

With Miss Weller, the question of competition did not come in, and Katherine could worship whole-heartedly. Even more than by her physical prowess, this excellent governess compelled admiration by her ready skill in painting and poker-work, and other arts and crafts of her period. She made mats and pincushions, table-centres and decorated boxes for village bazaars, and encouraged her flock to design their own Christmas cards. She could also take photographs and she had sufficient skill in botany to distinguish one field-flower from another. She was impatient of the dull, formal procession along the main road to which Miss Carstairs had confined the daily walk, and led the way into fields hitherto unexplored. Under her leadership the children went farther and fared more excitingly than before. They would picnic in "the Spinney" – a small and undistinguished clump of trees which in that flat and unwooded country took on the importance of a great forest; or they would tramp across the fields and over the weir to the village of Dykesey,[40] returning by way of the ferry at the "Roach and Carp", and feeling that they had undertaken a tremendous expedition.

One Fenland scene Katherine never forgot. In the winter of that year – the second of Miss Weller's reign – there was a great frost and the packice came down the river and jammed in great floes against the Nine-holes Bridge at Fentisham. The redness of the setting sun on the black river and the crumpled white ice was a wild and poetic marvel to Katherine.

About this time she began to write poetry. She invented a Christmas hymn, and Miss Weller copied it out in her own handwriting as an anonymous surprise for Mr Lammas on Christmas Day. He was pleased with it, and the Christmas hymn became an annual institution, for Katherine had the institutional mind that is pleased with ceremonial repetition.

Mrs Lammas was fond of poetry and delighted that her daughter should show signs of literary talent. In this, however, the child showed her usual perversity. She seldom celebrated the beauties of Nature or, if she did, they were not such beauties as the Fen displayed before her eyes. She wrote and showed her mother a poem celebrating the dawn. Mrs Lammas objected that Katherine had never seen the dawn – which was sadly true. Getting up early in the morning was not one of Katherine's virtues. Katherine's defence was to assert – quite untruly – that she *had* seen it. She had, in fact, only read about it; but what she had read was to her always just a little more real than what she had experienced. When she wrote stories, it was always about grown-up people, and about exotic or chivalrous adventures in imaginary surroundings. To the suggestion that she should confine herself to subjects she understood, she turned a deaf ear, showing herself in this of sounder literary judgment than her critics. To start with invention is the mark of the fertile mind and leads later to the interpretation of experience; to start with the exploration of experience is the infallible index of a barren invention. Katherine did not know this, and defended her correct instincts with incorrect reasoning, which naturally convinced no one.

Her mother, whose instincts were so right as to amount to educational genius, encouraged Katherine's love of reading by throwing the whole

40 D. L. S. also gives this fictitious name to a parish in *The Nine Tailors*, in which it is marked on a map.

world of books open to her. Practically no work in the house was forbidden, except *Enquire Within*[41] and *What a Woman of Forty Ought to Know*. Conventional people were surprised to find Katherine poring over *Jane Eyre* and the works of Shakespeare and other grown-up literature at an early age. But Mrs Lammas maintained that children always "passed over" what they did not understand, which was true enough. There were moments, of course, as when Katherine asked Aunt Millicent the meaning of the word "adultery", to which she had been introduced in church. Aunt Millicent said, not quite accurately, that it meant having two wives at a time, and Katherine understood that this unusual behaviour must be wrong, since she found no example of it among her friends and acquaintances. There was also a moment when Charles asked Miss Weller (while they were all driving in the governess-cart), whether there was a hole in hens for the eggs to come out of. Miss Weller sharply told him not to ask foolish questions – naturally, nothing could come out unless there was an opening for it to come out by. Katherine, who had never given the subject any consideration, laughed loudly to show her superiority and repeated Charles' question in a jeering tone. She was briskly rebuked, and carried away a new piece of knowledge from the discussion, namely that birth was not a subject for public discussion.

The person who, on the whole, gave Katherine the most thoughtful and sensible answers to her questions was her cousin Myrtle,[42] who paid her first visit to the Rectory about this time. Myrtle was only five years older than Katherine, but she had been brought up on a farm in California and had more wisdom of the rough and ready kind than any other person in Katherine's circle. She was old enough to seem like a grown-up person, and young enough to be the real companion which Charles and Gertrude were temperamentally unfitted to be. She possessed a great knack with younger children, and her extraordinary skill in such arts as the setting of butterflies' wings and creating toys out of string and cut paper induced in Katherine a profound admiration. Her great merit was that she would discuss any question seriously and thoughtfully, and that if she did not know the answer, she said so. She never gave those foolish answers which are no answer at all. Katherine was much given to asking troublesome questions and horribly pertinacious in demanding accurate and illuminating replies. She was troubled one day by the difficulty of understanding how a sharp instrument (as, for example, scissors) could divide a continuous substance (as, for example, paper). Did the narrow edge force its way somehow in between something or the other? Even if the width of the edge was reduced to infinity (a concept with which Miss Weller had made her pupils familiar in Euclid lessons), there must still be a something – a wideness – a solidity –

41 *Enquire Within Upon Everything*, a well-known domestic encyclopaedia.
42 Based on her cousin, Ivy Shrimpton, who was in fact eight years older than Dorothy..

a – Katherine found the question difficult to formulate. She asked the question, not of Myrtle, but of some grown-up who happened to be handy. It may be admitted that the problem was an awkward one. Nobody at the Rectory was familiar with atomic physics which in 1899 had not been made the subject of popular text-books. If the reply had been, "My dear, that is a very mysterious thing which nobody knows anything about", Katherine would have been excited and flattered. She would have realised that it was clever to ask so abstruse a question, and would have employed herself happily in inventing a theory for herself. But the grown-up merely replied: "Why do scissors cut paper? Why, because they are sharp, of course" – and for that, there was no excuse. Even Katherine could tell that the answer answered nothing. Myrtle's answers to questions were never of this foolish sort. She had a speculative mind, and was ready to put forward a theory as a theory, open to argument and refutation. She said, "I have often wondered about that", or "I don't know, but I should think the reason might be so-and-so." Nor did she ever grow impatient with Katherine's conversation, which was apt to be too improving for the average adult. The cousins got on famously, for their minds were cast from the same mould. Myrtle's contributions to Katherine's literary education were *The Ingoldsby Legends*,[43] *Little Women*[44] and *The Wide, Wide World*,[45] in which she displayed beauties which Katherine had hitherto not managed to see. Katherine's was a mind that required guidance, but when she had once had her attention directed to any point, she grasped it firmly and appreciatively.

Grannie, in the same way, led her to history through the gate of Scott's novels, which she read aloud of an evening, while Aunt Millicent was a great performer in the works of Dickens. Both these admirable grown-ups had the excellent habit of reading straight through an author, without skipping the parts which might be thought boring. As soon as it was possible for the children to attend to a novel as a whole, the books were read aloud from start to finish; and by this means, Katherine acquired a habit, which she never lost, of reading continuously and attentively. Miss Weller scored a tremendous success with *Westward Ho!*,[46] which for the moment eclipsed all other works of fact or fiction in Katherine's mind. She could never afterwards hear the name of Salvation Yeo,[47] without seeing the old mulberry tree in the sunlit garden, and herself with Charles and Gertrude sprawled

43   Old tales told in humorous verse by R. H. Barham (1788–1845).
44   By the American author Louisa M. Alcott (1832–1888), published in 1868.
45   A sentimental and lachrymose story by the American author Susan B. Warner.
46   A novel by Charles Kingsley (1819–1875), first published in 1855, a patriotic tale of adventure, Jesuit intrigue and naval enterprise, of the time of Elizabeth the First.
47   A character in *Westward Ho!*, who sails with the hero Amyas Leigh in pursuit of Don Guzman, who has run off with the beautiful Rose Salterne.

upon the carriage rug where they had voyaged in mind across the Spanish Main or tracked their difficult way through tropical forests to find the golden city of Manoa. How they laughed at the absurdities of John Brimblecombe and wept when Amyas Leigh was struck with blindness:[48]

"Heyday! Not past the Shutter yet! How long she hangs in the wind!…Oh, God! I am blind, blind, blind!"[49]

That disaster gave Katherine a sinking of the stomach, for blindness was one of the things she most feared. She did not gladly re-read that page, though, like most children, she revelled in sentiment and sick-room scenes. The Victorians understood children far better than their descendants do and knew well enough the lure of the death-rattle and of lachrymose piety. Katherine's Edwardian grown-ups would sometimes seek to spare her the ghoulish gloatings over last-minute repentance and the tears of bereavement which so lavishly besprinkle the pages of Charlotte M. Yonge. "This part is rather sad", they would say, "so I think we won't read it." Katherine politely waited till they had gone away and then collared the book to wallow in mournfulness herself. Grannie and Aunt Millicent were honourable exceptions, reading what was set down for them and shirking nothing. Grannie, however, sometimes showed a lack of tact, in that she would recount the illnesses and deaths of her own relations. This was not approved. Sentiment, Katherine considered, was enjoyable only when encountered in the abstract, and not made embarrassing by personal association. Similarly, it was unpleasant to hear expressions of affection which, if made, should (she thought) be conveyed under some humorous disguise.

"Auntie", said Katherine one day to Aunt Millicent, who had behaved with a pleasing generosity, "if I were a heathen I would make you my god." Her aunt was delighted with the avowal. So was Katherine; she knew that it deserved full marks for aptness, wit and originality. It bcame a most useful formula.

The departure of Miss Weller to marry a young man who collected beetles was the first severe blow that life aimed at Katherine's affections. The beetles themselves helped to add poignancy to the loss, for Katherine, knowing that her governess had a beetle-loving friend and happening to become possessed of a rather rare specimen acquired during an entomological expedition to Wicken Fen, had rather ostentatiously presented the creature to Miss Weller to hand to the "friend". She hoped to, and did, receive praise for this generous gesture, and was disgusted to learn, some months later, that she had been as it were cheated into making gifts to the enemy who was to rob her of the beloved. She conceived an intense hatred of the beetle-man, whom in her mind she imagined with extremely thin legs and a cavalry moustache, and dressed in a pepper-and-salt suit and a

48 He is struck blind by lightning, while in pursuit of Don Guzman.
49 Chapter XXXIII. The Shutter is a rock off the island of Lundy.

bowler hat. (This picture must have stepped complete from the pages of some illustrated magazine of the period.)

When Miss Weller had been driven away for the last time in the governess-cart to catch the train at the main-line station some miles off, Katherine rushed to the piano and sang with melancholy emphasis a number of sentimental songs which she had learnt from Miss Weller. "Morgen muss ich fort von hier / und muss Abschied nehmen / O du allerschönste Zier,/ Scheiden das bringt Grämen" – "Wär'ich ein Vögelein / Bald wollt'ich bei dir sein – ".[50] It was all too touching.

Gertrude – always a tactless child – would insist on intruding on this elegant grief, demanding why Katherine was so grumpy. Mrs Lammas, however, interfered and told her and Charles to leave Kitty alone, thus lending a ceremonial sanction to the emotion. The grief was genuine, but it brought with it a certain satisfaction. To be so miserable as all that had a kind of Schilleresque distinction about it. Fortunately, as the holidays were then beginning, the unsympathetic Charles and Gertrude took their departure; Myrtle arrived in their place; and Katherine found an ever-ready audience to applaud her tragic show and turn her mind to less tedious ways of exhibiting herself.

The person who suffered most from Katherine's devotion to Miss Weller was Miss Weller's successor – a quiet, conscientious and rather austere girl who had no great knack with children. She did not remain very long at the Rectory; probably the continual comparison of her methods with those of her predecessor were too much for her. Having made this poor lady's existence as burdensome as possible, Katherine thereafter displayed her usual perversity in thinking and speaking of her with a respect she never accorded to any other governess. Her successsor was a preposterous elderly person, selected by Mr Lammas at a time when his wife was incapacitated by illness. Mrs Lammas, as soon as she saw her, realised that this would never do. This person, who in appearance resembled Mrs Grundy[51] and wore voluminous flannel petticoats, became the butt, not only of the schoolroom, but of the kitchen. She even affronted the good-natured Mrs Appleton by issuing peremptory and, in the laundress's opinion, unnecessary instructions about the proper method of washing her underlinen. Lessons became occasions for unseemly riot. Nothing had so drawn the three children together as this common hatred. Mrs Grundy

---

50 "Tomorrow I must away from here/and take my leave./ O thou most beautiful jewel,/ departure that brings sorrow." "Were I but a little bird/ soon would I be with thee". The words of two German folk-songs, the first of which is included in *The Oxford Book of German Verse*, p. 48. Neither the authors nor the composers have been identified.

51 A symbol of conventional propriety, from a play by Thomas Morton (1764–1838), *Speed the Plough*, produced in 1798. Mrs Grundy is constantly referred to in the play but never appears in it.

departed at the half-term, unregretted by any, and education was carried on by Mrs Lammas with the aid of "Mademoiselle", an amiable French girl who had arrived to teach and be taught "au pair". Pleased with their victory, the children obliged by behaving, if not like angels, at least rather less like a zoo let loose, and eagerly awaited the next victim.

This was a tall sentimental young lady with blonde hair, who avenged Katherine by capturing the violent affections of Gertrude. She outraged Katherine's sense of delicacy by admitting to a love-affair – Miss Weller would have scorned the locution – and telling the two girls all about it. Katherine despised Miss Weeks for her garrulity; how dignified, by comparison, now appeared the affair of the beetle-man, which had only been divulged, by a third party, when the fact that Miss Weller was leaving to get married could no longer be concealed! Gertrude thought Miss Weeks sweet and overflowed with sympathy; it was, however, Katherine who provided the governess with a particular variety of tobacco-box, closing with a fascinating clip, in which to keep her love-letters. However foolish and trivial the matter in hand, Katherine liked to play an active and important part in it and, oddly enough, received a greater share of confidence than Gertrude. Miss Weeks was probably not a very sound judge of character, being herself but poorly supplied with the commodity; but she had her uses, for she taught the schoolroom to play bezique, and this was the best thing she did. The course of her true love was fluctuating, exhibiting itself now in tears and despair, now in the decoration of a handkerchief-box in marqueterie. After eighteen months she left, whether for the altar or elsewhere history saith not, and Gertrude suffered all the agonies she had formerly despised in Katherine.

What qualities there are in the character of children which to the adult mind appear so beautiful, and whether they have any existence, except in the eye of the observer, it is difficult to say. Faith, innocence, candour and affection, or their simulacra, are lauded in children as in dogs. But it may reasonably be argued that the faith is ignorance and the innocence confined to a narrow class of offences to which the adults have agreed to shut their eyes and ears. If egotism, envy, covetousness, greed, cruelty and sloth are sins, then children possess that original sinfulness in a high degree. Nor are they candid, except as to the requirements which they voice without reticence or regard; in the inner chambers of their soul they are secretive as cats, playing their own inner drama on an unseen stage, themselves the centre of the action; while in their affections they are catlike also, wild and capricious, leaping at one moment insistently upon your knee and the next moment yawning in your face. It is true that they are unbought, for though they will purr gratefully over a plate they will readily bite the hand that feeds them, or display a perverse fancy for some person who has never sacrificed a moment's pleasure for their sake. Everybody is flattered by the attentions of a cat or a child, knowing well enough that they are the fruit of

Two Musketeers

a cold and calculating judgment; and everybody knows the embarrassment of a cat's or a child's critical and unwinking stare. The modern fashion for abasing oneself before the child is a gesture of propitiation from the weak to the strong, from the altruistic to the egotistic, from the undirected to the determined. When Katherine in later days looked back upon the childish figure that had been herself, it was with a hatred of anything so lacking in those common human virtues which were to be attained in later years at so much cost and with such desperate difficulty. She saw herself through no rosy mist of illusion; she must, she knew, have been a disagreeable child. Strangers rightly considered her a prig. "Did you say prig or fig?" said the cat.[52] No fig, certainly, with all its soft warmth within; but something with a tooth-shattering hardness at the core.

The last governess came upon the scene when Katherine was about thirteen. Her name was Miss Dunbar and associated with her was the last and best-loved of all the mademoiselles. This period brought also the last and most flamboyant of all Katherine's impersonations. *The Three Musketeers*[53] took possession of the schoolroom and life became a flutter of flags, an incrustation of jewelled baldricks, a sheen of swords. To all the elders, Katherine allotted parts; to herself, not d'Artagnan, but Athos. Her preference for the "beau ténébreux"[54] betokened an unripe literary judgment and a necessity for sentimental expansion. The part of the Gascon

52 "Did you say pig, or fig?" said the Cat. *Alice's Adventure in Wonderland*, chapter 6.
53 *Les Trois Mousquetaires*, a romance by Alexandre Dumas the Elder (1803–1870). With its sequels, *Vingt Ans Après* and *Le Vicomte de Bragelonne*, it deals with the life of an impoverished Gascon, d'Artagnan, who comes to Paris in the reign of Louis XIII to join the king's musketeers and becomes a comrade of Athos, Porthos and Aramis.
54. "the handsome, sombre young man".

Dorothy as Athos

was handed over to Miss Dunbar, who in character bore singularly little resemblance to the hard-headed and self-confident young adventurer. Katherine did not at that time care very much for d'Artagnan; unconsciously, perhaps, she recognised and deprecated in him some of her own less amiable qualities.

A wave of dressing-up enthusiasm poured over the schoolroom. Charles had left to go to school but his place was taken by another girl, who was thrust into the part of Aramis, while Gertrude, who (to her own annoyance and the unkind amusement of her companions) was developing a regrettable amount of puppy-fat, was designated by Katherine's imperious will to impersonate the gigantic Porthos. This, however, she steadfastly refused; and the part was given to Mademoiselle. Wigs of crepe hair, ruffled shirts and boots made of buff linen were constructed by the obliging Mrs Appleton, and French oaths of the most ferocious kind resounded about the house. A small attic was seized upon by Katherine for her private use, and the servants were instructed to refer to it as her "quarters". Here she started to write cavalier poems with swaggering choruses. As soon as the day's lessons were over, she would hasten to her quarters and assume doublet and hose. If a grown-up said, as most of them tactlessly did, "Are you going to dress up?", Katherine would reply in a tone of rebuke, "I'm going to *dress*". It was impossible to make these people understand that the character of Athos was more real to her than her own.

The only grown-up for whom no part in this comedy was provided was

Grannie; for she was dying. Her life had been useful and devoted; to her Katherine owed much which she had never thought to repay and never would repay now. Mrs Lammas kept the children from the sick-room; she desired to spare them the sight of anything distressing or alarming. Mr Lammas was much distressed by the indifference shown by the school-room to the near approach of death. He interrupted a noisy musketeer episode on the lawn with the constraint:

"You children don't seem to care at all that poor Grannie is so ill."

They were abashed, yet a little hurt. In this disaster they were given no part; how could anyone expect them to bear it in mind all day?

One morning, during the holidays, Katherine came back from a walk with Mademoiselle to find the blinds drawn down. Her mother met her in the hall and told her that Grannie was dead. She felt no violent pang of bereavement, but the hush of the house was awe-inspiring. She climbed up to her quarters and sat down. Grannie was dead. It was like a scene in a book. She cried, rather luxuriously.

Presently her mother came up.

"Have you got any white stockings among your dressing-up things?"

Katherine produced a pair in which Athos had often swaggered across the green lawns. They were not of the best quality. They were, in fact, of the precise quality provided by the tradesmen of St. … for their present purpose. Katherine had purchased them herself, and Mr Brown the draper had said at the time "Cheap white stockings? Certainly. Miss Jones, show Miss Lammas some cheap white stockings" and, in a lower tone, "the quality we keep for funerals". So Grannie went to her grave, apparelled in the stockings of a musketeer.

Katherine did not see the body. Mrs Lammas said: "I would rather you remembered dear old Grannie as she was when you knew her. She has changed a good deal, dear, you know." Katherine's nervous self-consciousness was glad to be spared the ordeal. It was not that she was exactly afraid of seeing a corpse; rather that she was not sure of being able to produce the gesture and speech suitable for such an occasion. She could have found plenty of precedent for correct behaviour in books, but she knew from long experience that behaviour learnt from books was not always well received in real life. Mrs Lammas, with her uncanny insight into her offspring's mind, would infallibly have detected the underlying insincerity. Katherine was never a spontaneous child, and was exceedingly bad at aping an emotion which she did not really feel.

She did not go to the funeral. Aunt Emily and a number of Lammas relations came down for it. The house was filled with a sinister kind of excitement. Mr Lammas's voice trembled in church on the Sunday while reading the Second Lesson, which happened to be appropriate to a time of bereavement, and Aunt Emily, sitting opposite Katherine, sobbed and snuffled unrestrainedly, to her niece's scandal and embarrassment.

Aunt Emily, seeing Katherine in a white dress, said to Mrs Lammas:

"You're not going to black the child, then?"

Mrs Lammas said, No, she was not. She disliked the pageantry of woe and did not think that children ought to wear it. Aunt Emily made no further remark, and Great-aunt Agatha, who happened to be staying in the house at the time, backed up her niece.

"A lot of nonsense", said Great-aunt Agatha. "Waste of money and mostly hypocrisy. What does a child of her age know or care about death? As for you, Emily, if you had been pleasanter to your mother in her lifetime it would have done her more good than all this sniffling now. You can't help the dead. Look after the living, that's what I say, they need it a great deal more."

"Your Aunt Agatha needn't be so unkind", complained Aunt Emily. She retired into the hammock with a sunshade and a smelling-bottle, and Mr Lammas said:

"Pas devant l'enfant, ma tante."

"Fiddle-sticks!" retorted the old lady. "What do you expect, John? You've brought the child up sheltered, and you can't have it both ways. Teach her to behave decently to people while she's got them with her, that's all. I've no patience with graves and epitaphs. She'll have her troubles soon enough, and you can't prevent it with all your coddling. I'm going out for a walk. Kitty, you can come with me."

Katherine was quite pleased to accompany Great-aunt Agatha and, finding that she had now attained an advanced age without reading *The Three Musketeers* was obliging enough to tell her the whole plot of that absorbing book. She greatly enjoyed her walk.

Great-aunt Agatha was Mrs Lammas' aunt, the youngest of a very large family, and at this time was little over sixty. She was tall and upright and must have been a very handsome girl in her day. She lived alone in rooms in London and had her full share of the Warwick reticence. Nobody quite knew how she lived or what she did, except that she had an interesting collection of fossils and kept a cat. As a girl she had had a reputation as a lively wit, and her calculated indiscretions of speech made her formidable. Her hair, which had gone white early in life, was thick and piled high over a framework, and she wore a surprising number of gewgaws on her chain and châtelaine. Katherine liked her, because she never pretended to any great love for children, but conversed with them seriously and sensibly, as though they were grown-up. She treated you exactly the same, whether your age was six, twenty-six or sixty, and this suited Katherine perfectly. Great-aunt Agatha and Myrtle belonged obviously to the same breed. They never remarked in public how much you had grown, or repeated your babyish sayings to visitors in your presence or asked you how you were getting on with your lessons, or committed any vulgar familiarities of that kind.

Her remarks to Mr Lammas about bringing Katherine up sheltered were unfortunately true. Katherine's childhood belonged to a period when letting children tumble up anyhow had become discredited in favour of an anxious consideration for their bodily and mental education. Risks were not taken. Mrs Lammas, who had had to tumble up rather casually herself, as a member of a large family full of boys, had experienced a violent reaction in favour of caution. She was a born worrier, foreseeing with a dreadful vividness all the possible consequences of any unconsidered action. Katherine inherited this, and her natural timidity was enhanced by precept and example. There were moments when she rebelled against being considered soft and helpless and when she secretly envied children with more casual mothers. This made her often rude to her own mother, but had no other effect. She was herself cautious by nature and grudging of risk and inconvenience. The romantic desire for recklessness expended itself harmlessly in dramatic impersonation.

One day at Mrs Welbeck's, it was suggested that Kitty should learn to scull.

Katherine politely refused.

"I couldn't learn in one afternoon", she said, "and I should only get my hands all over blisters."

There was also an underlying certainty that she would be very bad at sculling and make a public exhibition of herself, which was a thing she did not like.

Gertrude and Hester Welbeck were exceedingly scornful.

"We asked her if she would like to row and she said she was afraid of spoiling her hands."

Katherine explained again, but her reasoning made no impression upon them and sounded unconvincing even to herself. She felt in her own heart the certainty that she was both vain and cowardly, but undertook no reckless exploit to prove the contrary to herself or the world. She hid herself behind a rampart of logic, and took up the attitude of despising all physical sports.

Within a few weeks of Grannie's death, Katherine dreamed a disquieting dream. She was in the schoolroom, and Grannie had returned from the grave, and was sitting in the basket-chair in her usual widow's cap and weeds,[55] making one of her wonderful embroidered crazy cushions, just as she had always done. But this was not a dream of the usual sort, in which the dreamer is transported back to a time before the shadow of death had fallen upon the person dreamed of. Grannie had been buried in the dream as in reality; but it had all been a mistake; she was not dead after all.

The dream-Katherine behaved to the dream-Grannie with respect and

55. See *My Edwardian Childhood*, Note 36.

politeness, but a sickening despair had fallen upon her. Grannie, it appeared, was not dead; no, but she would some time die in earnest and all the weary funeral business would be to do again. It was intolerable that this should be so – that a few years should see a repetition – the drawn blinds, the hushed house, the snuffles of Aunt Emily, the heavy feet of the under-taker's men carrying the coffin, ghastly and invisible, past Katherine's closed door. Surely the past should be past. In this world there ought to be no embarrassing resurrections. Katherine woke, and was glad that Grannie was safely dead.

She sought Myrtle out and hastened to tell her about the dream, insist-ing very much upon her own unusual feelings. If Myrtle was shocked, she did not say so; she seemed only interested.

"You see, Myrtle", said Katherine, "it was so dreadful to think it would have to be gone through again. It wasn't that I didn't like Grannie, but it was the idea of its all happening twice that seemed so awful."

Myrtle said she quite understood.

"I am afraid", pursued Katherine, "that I must be essentially callous" – this was a fine pair of words – "I expect I am one of those hard-hearted people, you know – don't you think so?"

Myrtle was inclined to take a less unfavourable view of her cousin's character. She thought that even an affectionate person might naturally feel upset at the idea of going through two unnerving periods of mourning for the same person, however nice. She felt sure that Katherine was really affectionate in spite of the curious dream. "One always behaves very oddly in dreams", she added.

Katherine was not quite pleased to be exonerated. She was proud of dreaming anything so peculiar and pleased with the new insight afforded into her own character.

"I don't think you're right, Myrtle", she declared. "I feel sure I am really heartless." And, when she thought about it she adopted a pose of ruthlessness.

"Katherine", said Aunt Millicent to Great-aunt [Agatha], "is a mass of affectations."

"Why shouldn't she be, at her age?" said the elder Miss Warwick, gruffly. "Shows her brains. She's choosing a character for herself."

"I like children to be natural", objected Aunt Millicent.

"Bosh!" said Great-aunt Agatha. "You don't know what 'natural' means. Nor do I. Nor does anybody. Man's an unnatural animal. Makes himself in his own image. The child's always acting – quite right too. She'll have to try herself out in a lot of characters before she finds the one that suits her."

Mrs Lammas, also, was a little troubled by Katherine's self-dramatising tendency.

"I want you just to be yourself", she said.

But Katherine was not sure what her self was like.

"Be herself, indeed!" was Great-aunt Agatha's comment. "I suppose you think you're asking her to do something easy. My dear Margaret, the art of appearing natural is the last word in sophistication. It's natural to children to be as artificial as possible. The more brains they have, the more they act a part. And if one acts a part long enough, one becomes it. If you pretend hard to be a Saint you may end by being a Saint. Or contrariwise. But you won't turn into a Saint by being yourself."

Poor Mrs Lammas said she would not like her daughter to be insincere.

"Then I'm sorry for you, Margaret", replied her aunt, "because she will be insincere, as sure as eggs is eggs, for another twenty years or so at any rate. You seem to think that the truth is as obvious and definite as a brass poker."

Katherine ought not to have heard this conversation, but it was carried on one evening on the lawn beneath her window, after she had gone to bed, and she had no scruples about listening to it. She knew, of course, that eavesdropping was contemptible, and that if she was found out she would be told that listeners never hear good of themselves; but she knew also that grown-up people were not above eavesdropping and spying themselves. There had been the old episode of Grannie overhearing Katherine's private story-telling at bed-time; there had been a day when Mrs Lammas herself had confessed to looking through a keyhole to see whether Katherine was really getting up as she said or merely reading a book. [Katherine] had been disgusted, and had countered this kind of supervision by hanging her skirt over the keyhole in future while she dressed.

On the present occasion she might have been pleased by Great-aunt Agatha's defence of her, but for two things. The first was that she was not perfectly clear about her Great-aunt's meaning, and the second was that she greatly resented being discussed by other people at all. She was a person, not a thing. She should be accepted as she was, and not talked over as a subject for educational experiment. If her character had to be analysed, she thought she was the right person to do it.

It seemed difficult for one's parents to realise how grown-up one was by this time. It occurred to Mrs Lammas one day that Katherine might like to possess a pet dog of her own (Bruce had died, full of fleas and years some time back) and she made the suggestion at the family table.

"It would be nice for her to learn to look after it."

Mr Lammas agreed that it was time Katherine learned to look after something and Mrs Lammas said it ought to be a well-bred dog, thus bringing up the question of expense.

"Why don't you let her buy it herself out of her birthday money?" inquired Mr Lammas.

"Oh, *no!*" said his wife. "I want Katherine to keep that for a rainy day."

"It wouldn't cost much", said Mr Lammas. "The money's there to be used. It's time she learned something about the value of money."

"She has sixpence a week pocket-money", replied Mrs Lammas, "but I don't want her to touch her savings."

"She can't realise the meaning of money if she's never allowed to spend it", argued Mr Lammas. "It's the child's own money, after all."

"Yes, but I've always told her that that was to be kept for something really important", said Mrs Lammas, sticking to her guns. "It's nice to feel that she has a little bit to fall back on."

"But what's the good of it, if she's never allowed to fall back on it?"

The argument threatened to become interminable. Katherine, who had been suffering acutely, broke in:

"Why do you talk about me as if I wasn't here? Why don't you ask *me*? I never said I wanted a dog – I don't want a dog. I should never look after it. And I'm not going to take my money out of the savings bank, anyhow, so what's the fuss about?"

"You mustn't speak like that to your father", said Mrs Lammas. And Mr Lammas said:

"That's not the way to speak to your mother."

The matter of the dog was dropped. Six months later, Katherine became madly anxious to possess a bicycle and said so, suggesting that she should pay for it out of her birthday money. In spite of her mother's reluctance, she had her way about it, the machine being purchased second-hand from the cook's sister for £5.

The bicycling craze began in the holidays; Myrtle and Kitty learnt at the same time. They made a good deal of to-do about it, and fell off a good many times. Katherine, ever interested in facts and their reasons, discovered that it was a great deal more painful to fall on top of the bicycle than to fall on the ground with the bicycle on top of her, and attributed the cause to the relative weights of the machine and herself, and the comparative contours of the earth and the bicycle. As usual, the grown-ups were blasé about these researches, and merely said, "Of course". Katherine also found that she was most liable to fall off when approaching one of her own grown-ups with a view to demonstrating the progress she had made.

"That", said Mrs Lammas, "comes of showing-off."

Katherine produced a number of arguments tending to prove that other causes were responsible. Mrs Lammas remained unconvinced and so, in her heart, did Katherine. It was the same kind of argument she had used about learning to scull – and it did not ring quite true.

It was about this time that she made another discovery – one of far-reaching importance, but difficult to describe in words. It was, first and foremost, the discovery that History, Geography and Literature were not three different things but one thing. It was first occasioned by learning that Ahasuerus (who was Bible) was the same person as [Xerxes] the Persian

The bicycling craze

(who had, up to that time, been Classics).[56] This led to other surprising identifications. The effect on Katherine was most extraordinary. It was like fitting together two pieces of a puzzle and hearing all the other pieces fall into place, one after the other, locking and clicking. She felt as Copernicus must have done when he tried placing the sun in the centre of the solar system and found that, for a complicated variety of planetary aberrations, he could now substitute a beautiful one-ness of concentric circles. She tried to explain the discovery to Miss Dunbar. "It isn't different things", she said, "it's all one thing." Miss Dunbar said placidly: "Of course it is." All grown-ups said "Of course" to one's most exciting novelties. But Katherine was too greatly delighted with her discovery of the universe to care much what Miss Dunbar had to say. Because, now, lessons ceased to be lessons – they were part of everything else. *The Three Musketeers* fitted into History and Poetry. Books had begun to make contact with life.

    In that same summer, Mr Lammas mislaid the tennis-court.

    The back lawn at the Rectory was tree-shaded and rather damp, and the grass grew fast and lush there. It was not an ideal lawn for tennis, but it was the only one that was level, and it did well enough for the children. But that Spring had been rainy and the two iron sockets that took the net-posts,

56. See "A Vote of Thanks to Cyrus", first published in *St. Martin's Review*, no. 591, May 1940, pp. 228–320. Included in *Unpopular Opinions*, Gollancz, 1946. D. L. S. has here inadvertently written "Cyrus" when she intended Xerxes.

together with the permanent metal corners of the court, had sunk out of sight beneath the close roots of the turf. After prodding about for some time, Mr Lammas found one of the sockets, and paused to wipe the perspiration from his forehead; for it was a hot day. Mrs Lammas had retrieved from some drawer the set of measurements, and Mr Lammas, measuring from the socket in what he took to be the right direction, began to prod the ground again for the missing corner.

Katherine watched the series of prods, extending in a direct line towards the mulberry tree.

"I didn't think it was so far this way", said Mr Lammas.

"You're going wrong", asserted Katherine, positively. "You want to make a circle, not a straight line."

Mr Lammas, whose natural intelligence may have been a little confused by the heat, queried this.

"It's Euclid", said Katherine, and proceeded to enunciate the properties characterising the radius of a circle.

"All right", said Mr Lammas, abandoning the string and the garden knife. "See if you can find it."

By a kind of miracle, Katherine did find it, using the Euclidean method, in a very few seconds. If the court has not been precisely laid out in the first instance, she might have had more difficulty, but the corner being accurately placed, the laws of geometry held good. In her heart of hearts, Katherine was awe-stricken. To see a prophecy made on paper fulfilled on the back lawn is a very enlarging experience, and it is unfortunate that the phrase, "There! I told you so!" should be feebly expressive of the rapturous humility which ought to accompany scientific experiment. Mrs Lammas having, in the meantime, discovered the second socket by trial and error with the point of a sunshade, Katherine went on to find the next corner, exactly where it should have been, at the point of intersection of two circles. After this, there was no holding her. She lectured the household on geometry at a length, and with a triumphant emphasis which ought to have procured her a snubbing. Rather fortunately, perhaps, she was spared this in some ways desirable rebuke. For however offensively she may have expressed her feelings, she had been brought face to face with beauty. It had risen up before her again – the lovely, satisfying unity of things: the wedding of the thing learnt with the thing done: the great intellectual fulfilment. Mathematics was to cause her infinite pains and griefs in the near future; but nothing would ever quite wipe out the memory of that magnificent moment when the intersecting circles marched out of the pages of the Euclid book and met on the green grass in the sun-flecked shadow of the mulberry tree.[57]

___

57. For explanation and diagrams, see Appendix A.

It must now have been made reasonably plain that Katherine, though much loved, was not exactly a lovable child. Her faults were of the kind that hit you in the face; her qualities were of a kind more agreeable in maturity than in the growing stage. It began to worry her a little that, on her rare occasions of social festivity, she should be somehow set apart as brainy and awkward. She would find herself standing on the edge of groups, or hauled in, with rather too-conspicuous kindness, to take part in some game at which, through sheer self-consciousness, she would acquit herself exceedingly badly. She was eager to shine, and when she could not shine she put on a pose of indifference. People said, "Kitty doesn't care for games; parties bore Kitty." It was said so often that she came to start every game and party with an inward certainty of failure that induced its own fulfilment. Cleverness is seldom popular in mixed society, and in the early 'teens assumes particularly anti-social and repellent characteristics. Relations and friends (who saw Katherine, gawky and solitary, in the midst of a crowd of people merrily fooling around with clock-golf or golf-croquet, or playing hide-and-seek or hunt-the-slipper), were wont to remove her compassionately to show her the library or a set of stereoscopic views; and never realised how much their compassion was resented. The sense of being, in some ways, a misfit, had a bad effect on Katherine's temper. Further trouble was caused by the fact that her health was rather delicate. She had had trouble with tonsils and treatings of diphtheric throat, possibly because, as Mrs Lammas dolefully asserted, the Rectory water "came through the Dissenters' graveyard". (She said it as though an Established graveyard might have had less insanitary qualities, but actually she had no sectarian prejudices. She merely felt that it was inconsiderate of the Nonconformists to bury their dead where they did, just as Mr Lammas thought it cantankerous of them to have their annual bun-fight on Good Friday.) In any case, the danger of catching cold was so impressed on Katherine, and she had so often been urged to keep her feet dry and not to sit on wet grass, that picnics and field sports were occasions of torment to her. If she refused to play in damp spots, her companions laughed at her; if she recklessly ventured where others went, somebody was sure to call out, "Kitty, Kitty! You're not getting your feet wet, are you?" and cover her with shame and confusion. Even at home in the garden, the coming-on of a slight shower was sufficient to call up the humiliating apparition of a servant laden with coat and goloshes for her. Katherine would be overcome with such uncontrollable fits of shaking rage that she scarcely knew how to speak, and there would be scenes of rudeness and temper which positively shocked her family. But if Great-aunt Agatha, who took such matters lightly, criticised this molly-coddling system, Katherine was instantly up in arms to resent the aspersion upon her mother.

Her father said one day:

"It's no good, Kitty. You've been brought up soft and it's too late trying to be hardy now."

At that moment she was angry with both parents equally.

In spite of occasional friction, however, she had a deep respect for her mother, and automatically took her side in any family dispute. Poor Mrs Lammas always regretted that, to quote her own words, "it always fell to her to say the disagreeable things". This was the price she paid for having the strongest intelligence and the most vigorous personality in the household. When Katherine was about ten years old, something happened which made an ineradicable impression on her childish mind. It happened during a rather gloomy period, when an almost unknown uncle – Mrs Lammas's favourite brother – was ill and expected to die at any moment. Katherine had innocently said or done something irritating and her mother had scolded her rather sharply. With a child's usual fatalism, Katherine accepted the idea that she was somehow or other naughty and in disgrace, and was wandering rather desolately through the hall, when Mrs Lammas called her into the dining-room. A garment was being cut out, and the sewing-machine stood on the table, surrounded by paper patterns and pieces of material.

"Oh, Kitty", said Mrs Lammas putting down the cutting-out scissors and putting her arm round the child, "I'm sorry I was so cross with you this morning. I was worried and upset about Uncle Peter and I spoke without thinking."

"It's *quite* all right, Mummy", said Katherine.

She was staggered. Never yet in her life had she known a grown-up admit to having been in the wrong, and the nobility of the gesture overcame her completely. She did not go as far as realising that she might do well to follow this excellent example herself – admitting her errors was not Katherine's strong point – but she did, from that moment, form a very high opinion of her mother's character. She also began dimly to understand that one did not become good automatically merely by growing up. Previously, it had seemed odd to her that grown people should pray so elaborately to be forgiven for their sins and wickednesses, seeing that, in her experience, they never admitted to anything of the kind. With the general clarifying of the intellect that took place about the Musketeer period, she was able to coordinate the surprising apology of Mrs Lammas with the evil conduct of historical characters. Wicked behaviour and a sense of guilt were not confined to persons in books; they existed in real life. The natural, though unfortunate result of this was that Katherine felt herself at liberty to criticise her superiors, and this in no way improved her manners.

*

"Really, Kitty", said Mrs Lammas, "you ought to have a lady's maid to tidy up after you. You'll never look nice if you hang up your clothes on the floor."

"I don't care about looking nice", said Kitty, morosely.

"And look at your hands! You had such pretty hands as a child. I remember Mrs Welbeck saying, 'Why, her hands are like velvet!' Now they're like nutmeg-graters and you've been biting your nails again. I don't think you know when you're doing it."

"Yes, I do", said Katherine.

"Well, do try not to. The first thing a man looks at is a woman's hands. Nobody would want to hold a hand like this."

"That's a good thing", retorted Katherine, "I should hate having my hand held. I think that's stupid. They won't fuss over my hands at college."

"But you might get married after you leave college."

"I shan't get married. I'm going to be a writer."

"Yes, but even great writers can look pretty and keep themselves nice."

"Oh, Mother, do leave me alone."

"Oh, dear", said Mrs Lammas.

*

"The fact is, Kitty", said Miss Dunbar, "you won't work at anything unless you find it comes easy. You can do things if you choose."

"I hate arithmetic", said Katherine.

"But you'll have to learn to keep accounts and that kind of thing."

This prospect seemed remote to Katherine. She wriggled away from the discussion as soon as possible and shut herself up in her "quarters" to write a blank verse historical play about Edward III.

*

"Oh, Doctor", said Mrs Lammas, "Kitty's got some wax in her ear, or something. She's deaf on one side. And I wanted to ask you about these spots on her forehead."

"Ah!" said Dr Bates. "Turn round to the light, would you, Kitty? Hum, ha! Yes, just a little wax, I think. I'll send you some peroxide of hydrogen to be dropped into the ear at night, and I'll come back on Friday and syringe the wax out. Now, let's look at these tiresome spots. A little acne – oh, yes. Very common about this age. Nothing to worry about. The skin is a bit irritable – look! I expect I could write your name on your arm, couldn't I, Kitty?"

He traced a capital "K" on the inner surface of Katherine's arm with the pointed end of a probe and went on talking about nerve-endings and acid conditions of the blood. In a few minutes' time he pushed back the sleeve again.

"There! You see?"

The "K" stood out, a white weal on the arm.

"I'll send a little mixture to put that right. The condition will soon pass off – temporary, merely temporary. And we'll take the spots away as well. I expect the spots worry Kitty a lot more than the deafness, eh?"

If Katherine could have spat in the doctor's face, she would willingly have done so. How *disgusting* of him to think that a trifling spottiness could be more important to her than that beastly, disabling, stupid-feeling inability to hear on one side! Grown people were revolting – men, especially. She replied so rudely that Mrs Lammas felt constrained to apologise for her.

"You mustn't speak like that to Dr Bates", she told her daughter, when this well-intentioned but tactless man had taken his departure, leaving a whiff of iodine behind him. "I think you must need a little liver pill."

How horrible people were!

*

Aunt Millicent might have sympathised with Katherine, for she, too, had a bone to pick with Dr Bates. She was a woman full of nervous apprehensions about herself – owing, as her sister remarked, to having nobody and nothing else to worry about – and she had been alarmed by a persistent pain in the lower abdomen which she decided must be due to some kind of internal growth. Dr Bates pooh-poohed this idea reassuringly.

"Nothing at all", he said – "just a little inflammation of the colon. That's the big bowel, you know. The intestine comes down like this" – he sketched an outline with his thumb-nail on the blotting-pad – "and it makes a bend just where it enters the big bowel, *here*. A trifling obstruction and irritation – that's all. Very uncomfortable, but not serious. I expect you've been taking purgatives. Well, don't. It will only increase the inflammation. I will send you something to soothe the bowel. Stick to a light diet and keep the abdomen warm. It will clear up in a few days if you don't irritate it."

"Horrid ill-mannered little man", said Miss Warwick. "I don't want to be told about my – bowel. It's not nice. When I send for a doctor I want him to make me well, not to give me lectures on my – inside. I think the less we know about these things the better."

"You always were an ostrich, Millicent", said Great-aunt Agatha, "you will stick your head in the sand. Why shouldn't you have bowels like everybody else? Good old English word, bowel. And he's quite right about those everlasting pills of yours. How do you expect Nature to do her job if you keep flogging her with medicines? All the Warwicks are constipated – except me; I've too much sense. I leave things alone. You eat too much meat and potatoes, Millicent. You always were greedy. And when things go wrong you rush off to pills and patent medicines. Your cupboard's stuffed with the things. Don't tell me – I know it."

"I think that's very unkind of you, Aunt Agatha. We're not all as strong as you are. And surely it isn't necessary to use such coarse language."

"Nonsense, Millicent. You're perfectly healthy, or you would be if you ate less and took more exercise. Why don't you go and dig in the garden or help Mary[57] a bit in the parish? Not but what Mary's just as bad as you are about pills. She's always giving them to the child, too. Kitty would be as constipated as all the rest of you by the time she grows up. No wonder she's so rude and ill-tempered."

"Kitty's growing up exrememly pert", agreed Aunt Millicent. "Mary gives way to her too much. When I was a child I wasn't allowed to answer back the way she does."

"She's getting a bit too much for all of you", said Great-aunt Agatha. "She'd be better off at school where she'll find her own level. Though she'd hate it, and they'd probably ruin her. Still it might do her good to fight her own battles for a bit. I shall speak to Mary about it."

*

"Kitty", said Mrs Lammas, as she was brushing her daughter's hair a few weeks later, "we've been having a little talk about you, and we've decided that you ought to go to school. You'll be fifteen in June, and you're rather growing out of governesses. What do you think? Shall you mind it very much? Of course, you've never been away from home before."

A curious sensation came over Katherine; she felt suddenly a little insecure. But the hint of sentiment antagonised her.

"Well", she said, "I think I should like to go to school. It would be a change. And I should like to know some other people."

Mrs Lammas felt that this might be true and natural, but she did not greatly like it. Her voice shook a little as she said:

"Your father and I have tried to do our best for you – "

"Oh, yes, – I know that, Mother", said Katherine hastily.

" – but of course, if you're going to college, you'll need a different kind of teaching. And you'll have to pass examinations and so on."

"Yes, Mother", said Katherine, determined not to feel concern.

"You'll find it very different", pursued Mrs Lammas, still hoping for some expression of regret or affection, or something. "Perhaps we've kept you at home too much. But being the only one, you see – "

"Oh, yes", said Katherine. She did not want to have anybody's feelings brought into the matter. "But I expect I shall get on all right. When do I start? Next term?"

57.   Mrs Lammas' name varies between Margaret and Mary.

BOOK TWO

I

Eager as she was that Katherine should, above all things, get "a good education", Mrs Lammas did not overlook the requirements of the body.
Great-aunt Agatha, in fact, thought she overdid the woollen underclothing
as well as the aperients. Not that Mrs Lammas was inclined to stuffiness; on
the contrary, she thought highly of fresh air (though not of draughts) and
was convinced that young people always did better in the country than in
the town. She therefore put aside her aunt's recommendation of a school in
London, though she went to look at the place.

"If you had seen it, Aunt Agatha, you would have agreed with me. All
very nice, of course, and comfortable, and I liked the headmistress. But the
dormitories seemed so dark, and they only looked out on roofs and a tiny
bit of garden."

"I daresay you are right, Margaret. I've never been there. But I know
Miss Attwood, and I like her ideas. She would understand Kitty better than
most of these educational women."

"I'm quite sure you are right. But Kitty has been brought up in the
country, and I'm afraid she'd feel very cramped at that place."

"As long as her mind isn't cramped in the country", said Great-aunt
Agatha, a little grimly. "It's a kind of mind that needs a good bit of room to
expand."

"It may need pruning", said Mr Lammas, mildly.

"Very likely, John, but that's a thing that needs doing with judgment.
Most of these schools turn 'em out pot-bound."

"It's very difficult to know", sighed Mrs Lammas. "One does so want to
do everything for the best."

"Margaret worries far too much", observed Aunt Millicent to Aunt
Emily, who was paying her usual summer visit. "Schools are all much of a
muchness, in *my* opinion."

Eventually, Mrs Lammas chose the Beaufort School at Carisbury[59] – a
group of red brick buildings perched on the edge of the downs on the outskirts of the Cathedral city. It had a large, windy garden and three raw,
new playing-fields, a small gymnasium and a large hall. The lavatory
accommodation in the School House was not very adequate nor very up-

---

59. Fictitious name for the Godolphin School at Salisbury. See Introduction, p. xvi.

to-date, but it may have been working properly on the day Mrs Lammas saw it. There were a hundred boarders in the four boarding houses and about the same number of day girls, and the headmistress, Miss Dando, was well known to be a remarkable woman. Thirty years before, she had begun with twenty pupils in little old Wellington House, now the smallest of the four; now she was getting on for seventy, and supervised every detail for the two hundred as she had done for the twenty. As she stood outside the hall to watch the school file in for prayers, she could tell in a moment if one of the two hundred was missing, and would instantly send for the house-mistress or form-mistress concerned to ask where Edith Canning was, or whether Irene Norton's cold was really bad enough to keep her away from school. It was admitted that she was not exactly a scholar; scholarship had not been expected of schoolmistresses when she began work. But there was no doubt that she was a great organiser and a great personality. The piercing glance of her blue eye was famous, and she was held to be an astonishing judge of character. Mrs Lammas, though a trifle nervous in dealing with educational details which, she frankly admitted, she did not understand, was not the sort of person to be abashed by any woman when it came to the question of her daughter's well-being. She tackled Miss Dando firmly, explaining that Katherine was an unusual girl, that she had never left home before, that she was an only child and might feel strange among other girls at first, though they had done their best to give her companionship, that her throat was not strong, that she must not be allowed to get wet or overdo herself, that she was not likely to care much for hockey, that she was to go to college if possible and would probably get a scholarship if she tried for it, that it was exceedingly important that she should have a good education and, once again, with a little thump of her sunshade on the floor, that, though Katherine was her own child, she must really impress on Miss Dando that the girl was singularly well equipped with brains.

Miss Dando gazed back piercingly at Mrs Lammas with the celebrated blue eyes and promised to bear all these points in mind. She is not to be blamed if she discounted the whole conversation. She must have heard the same thing a great many times in a longish life, and had probably very seldom found it justified by the facts.

When Katherine learned that she was to go to Beaufort, she began to take stock of herself. She knew nothing whatever about school life, except as it was depicted in *Eric*[60] and *St Winifred's*[61] and in the pages of one or two

---

60   *Eric, or Little by Little*, a story of school-life by Frederick William Farrar (1831 - 1903), published in 1858.
61   *St Winifred's or the World of School*, also by Frederick William Farrar, published in 1862.

stories by L.T. Meade[62] which belonged to Gertrude and which even Katherine felt to be lacking in verisimilitude. It was very difficult indeed to make up pictures of herself at school. She made them up as well as she could, and whether they were pleasant or unpleasant, Katherine Lammas was always in the centre of the picture.

The pleasant pictures stressed her accomplishments. Mistresses and girls were all amazed by her learning. After all, it was not every English girl of fifteen who knew so much Shakespeare, Tennyson, Browning and Malory by heart, or could speak French like a Musketeer, or was intimately acquainted with the major works of Corneille, Racine, and Molière, to say nothing of the elder Dumas and Edmond Rostand.[63]

Also, she was a poet and that was surely rather unusual. She didn't write sentimental little verses, either, about moonlight, and roses, but good, stalwart stuff; cavalier songs, ballads which really might have come straight out of Percy's *Reliques*,[64] spelling and all. And she knew that it was good verse, with metre that required no apology. Metre was one of the things she knew about, instinctively, just as she knew about English syntax. Her essays, too, were likely to be thought original and striking. She could put words together so that they marched like an army and she was seldom at a loss for an apt quotation to embellish them. And her ideas, as everybody had to admit, were extremely advanced for her age.

Her German was good, too. She had learnt to speak pretty fluently in Miss Weller's days, and though French had rather pushed German into the background of late (owing to the Musketeer craze), still it was probable that she would speak and write it a good deal better than most of the others. And she knew some of Goethe's poems and had read parts of Schiller and Lessing's *Minna von Barnhelm*[65] and *Die Ahnfrau* by Grillparzer[66] and quite a lot of other things.

Her Latin was not so good. She had gone through two books of the *Aeneid* with Mr Lammas and Ovid's *Pyramus and Thisbe* and a little Caesar and Cornelius Nepos, but it had taken a very long time. It was troublesome learning a language you couldn't make conversation in. However, she was going to be definitely on the Modern side and classics wouldn't matter so much.

---

62 Mrs L. T. Meade wrote detective stories in collaboration with several scientists. D. L. S. mentions her in the Introduction to *Great Short stories of Detection, Mystery and Horror*, volume I, Gollancz, 1928, pp. 31–32. Among her stories for young readers are *A Sweet Girl Graduate* and *The Honourable Miss*, both published in 1891.

63 For details of these authors see notes below.

64 Thomas Percy (1729–1811), *Reliques of Ancient English Poetry*, 1765.

65 A play by Gotthold Ephraim Lessing (1729–1781), published in 1767. It became and remained a set text for pupils studying German up to and beyond World War II.

66 Franz Grillparzer (1791–1872), an Austrian dramatist. *Die Ahnfrau* (The Ancestress), published in 1817, is a poetical fate-tragedy.

History? Well, at any rate she knew a great deal of history out of Walter Scott and Bulwer Lytton and even Charlotte M. Yonge. School-book history was not so easy; in fact, they sometimes seemed so different that it was a job to link them up in one's mind. But she could write a very good character of Richard Coeur de Lion (*Ivanhoe*) or Cardinal Richelieu (*Three Musketeers*[67] and *Under the Red Robe*[68]). She decided that brilliancy of treatment would probably counterbalance any haziness about facts and dates.

But lessons were not everything. There was, for example, personality. She felt herself cut out to be a leader – but she would find other leaders already established. How would she manage to dominate them? She was, as she knew, unfortunately plain. Or was she? Might she not prove, after all, to be an Ugly Duckling? On the whole it seemed quite likely that strangers would be more appreciative of one's peculiar personal appearance than one's own family. She examined herself in the glass. A commanding height (when she remembered not to stoop), blue eyes (but they might have been bigger), a snub nose (dear, dear!), and a high forehead (very unfashionable), dark hair, rather thin and soft, a long upper lip (and she had read somewhere that this was reckoned a defect), a wide, but rather well-shaped mouth, with dimples in the corner, a good skin (when it wasn't afflicted with spots – bother Dr Bates and the spots!) And, of course, pretty hands. Not a very good list of charms, but you never knew. The face must surely have character. It could not possibly help being an *interesting* face (could it?), when it belonged to such an interesting person?

And there was always the possibility of asserting one's personality in some heroic crisis, such as – ?

Unhappily, Katherine's upbringing had not fitted her to take the lead in crises. She was afraid of fire. She could not swim. She turned away hastily when anyone was ill or hurt, from helplessness, rather than cowardice, because no one had taught her about first aid. Above all, it was hardly conceivable that she could ever save the school by making a winning goal at hockey or scoring a century not out in a cricket match. And apparently those were the exploits that counted most.

The minute Katherine began to think about games, the pleasant picture receded and the unpleasant one took its place. She hated games, resented the idea of being forced to play them, and knew that she was bound to make a public fool of herself over them. And she loathed making a fool of herself – unintentionally.

Starting from hockey, Katherine saw herself hated and despised in every activity of school life. Large, powerful girls sneered at her awkwardness and made jokes about her appearance. Mistresses were coldly surprised that she should be so vague about the Constitutions of Clarendon

67   See Note 53.
68   Stanley John Weyman (1855–1928), published in 1896.

and the exports of Brazil, and told her that she would have to do mathematics in the kindergarten. And there rose up before her the wraiths of scholarly girls in spectacles, who knew the literature of five countries by heart, and clever scientific girls who laughed at her poetry as useless, sentimental rubbish, and elegant girls who had actually been abroad and learnt their French in Paris. And they all despised her for being out of things and different, and for never having been to school before.

Between dreams of glory and nightmares of humiliation there seemed to be no middle way. She could never be comfortably and ordinarily part of the general herd. She would be either the school star or the school butt. Which? She had not imagined that it was perfectly possible to be both.

The June roses fell; the geraniums and begonias flared in the formal beds in the front lawn and in the Dutch garden behind the shrubbery. Katherine had a curious feeling as though she were about to die and were seeing these things for the last time. Mrs Lammas, assisted by Mrs Appleton, struggled with the school list of requirements. Six flannel blouses, of which two must be white. One black and red games blouse, material obtainable from the school. One long dark coat (school regulation supplied if required). One dozen stiff white collars. Two sailor hats. Blue serge coat and skirt. White party dress with high neck. Strong boots for hockey. Flat-heeled shoes. Underwear, sheets, towels, handkerchiefs. Hairbrush and comb in bag. Everything to be marked with initials of Christian names and surname in full. Mrs Lammas made the blouses herself. She cut them a little too short on the shoulder, so that the neck-band continually escaped, shamefully, from under the stiff collar, and the love and devotion put into the stitching was no compensation for that.

Lessons became more and more of a picnic. One was only marking time. Katherine wrote the words of a Cantata on the Death of Athos, a Ballad on the Death of d'Artagnan, a Farewell Ode to Porthos. The brave company of the Musketeers was to be broken up, and in this mood of rich melancholy it seemed at times that there was nothing left remarkable under the visiting moon. But there was consolation in words:

> Shadowy, shadowy, thin and pale,
Far in the west
The light slides and the sunbeams fail,
> Sinking to rest…

Tears of pure intoxication came into Katherine's eyes as she wrote:

> What say the wailing trumpets
As they return from war?
They say that he is fallen,
D'Artagnan fights no more.

Sung to the tune of *Malbrouck*,[69] the lament resounded about the house and haunted the shrubberies of an evening.

> What spoke the mighty captain,
> What said he as he fell?
> "Athos and Porthos, greeting,
> "And Aramis, farewell!"

It was beautiful to be so sad.

> "Porthos, mon vieux, nous n'oublierons jamais les beaux
>   jours de la jeunesse."
> "Mais non, mais non, mon bon camarade. Tu m'écriras?"
> "Bien sûr, je t'écrirai. Dire que nous ne nous reverrons
>   jamais – c'est triste, hein?"
> "C'est triste, oui. Mais il nous reste toujours le souvenir."
> "Ah, parbleu, oui. Et peut-être tu reviendras nous visiter."
> "Ce serait charmant. Merci, cher Athos. Voyons, ne t'attriste pas
>   trop. Tu trouveras de nouveaux amis."
> "Ce n'est pas la même chose. Ce ne sera jamais les mousquetaires.
>   N'oublions jamais notre serment. Tous pour un, un pour tous!"
> "Parbleu!"
> "Fidèles jusqu'à la mort."
> "Fidèles jusqu'au tombeau."[70]

Nothing could be more satisfying than that. C'était beau, mais c'était triste. Tout le monde pleurait, jusqu'au capitaine des pompiers, qui pleurait dans sa casque.[71] …It was, indeed, so beautiful that Katherine almost believed it must be true, and that she would not forget to write to Porthos, as she had – so strangely soon – forgotten to write to the beloved Miss Weller. She had been a child then, but at fifteen one's affections were more important and established. And besides, here there was a whole life-time of memories – the siege of La Rochelle, the diamonds of the Queen, the execution of Charles I – to look back upon – all real, all far more real than French lessons and the rambles across the fields and long summer days beneath the mulberry tree.

The last day came. D'Artagnan departed. Aramis and Constance Bonacieux went their way. Porthos set his face toward France, in a shower of ecstatic French. Athos was left to brood solemnly alone in the deserted

---

69   "Malbrouck s'en va-t-en guerre…" an old song, commonly associated with the Duke of
     Marlborough and the Battle of Malplaquet (1709) but said to date from the time of the
     Crusades. The traditional tune resembles that of "For he's a jolly good fellow".
70   For translation, see Appendix B.
71   It was beautiful but sad. Everyone was crying, even the captain of the firemen, who was cry-
     ing inside his helmet.

garden, which was never again to ring with the cries of what an irritated neighbour had been heard to call "the Rectory parrots". The previous October, Porthos had planted a white rose-bush in the Dutch garden. A lingering blossom still hung upon the stem. Athos went to water it with a tear and remained to remove some green-fly.

The arrival of Myrtle afforded fresh opportunities for the parade of grief. Also, for speculation upon the future. The prospectus of the Beaufort was discussed from end to end, and the names of the mistresses suggested an entertaining series of prophecies about their appearance and character. It was distinguished and noble to mourn over the past, but a bold Musketeer must, after all, march breast forward. There was no doubt that an era had come to an end – *Ah! Les beaux jours que ce siècle de fer!*[72] – but the future held infinite possibilities. School, however strange and alarming, could only endure for a few years. Behind it, dim in a haze of gold, rose up the familiar spires of Oxford.

II

There are no lands unhabitable, nor seas innavigable.[73]

Katherine Lammas started her school career unfortunately. She contrived [to] get an attack of chicken-pox at the end of the summer holidays, and was not passed for general release until three days after term had started. This put her at once in a position over which even new girls could look down on her.

She lunched in Carisbury with her parents, and then they all drove to the school in a curious open fly with an ancient horse that could only plod up the hill at a snail's pace. Girls were coming in from the garden and playing-fields for afternoon school. They all wore blue pinafores and they all seemed to know one another. The machine had started, and already every smallest wheel of it knew its own place and turned relentlessly.

Miss Dando received the party cordially, but was astonished to find Katherine so big. Could it be that the famous memory had slipped a cog? Or that she had not listened to a single word of Mrs Lammas' detailed account of her daughter's past history and achievements? Surely that was impossible – yet the fact remains that she had expected to receive a child

72. The correct quotation is "O le bon temps que ce siècle de fer!" (O the fine days of that age of combat!), Voltaire, *Le Mondain* (1736), line 21.
73. Quoted from Robert Thorne by Richard Hakluyt in *The Principal Navigations, Voyages, and Discoveries of the English Nation*.

of eight years old. She hoped that Kitty would be happy at Beaufort, supposed that she would like to go and see the school while parents and headmistress had a little chat together, and rang the bell for the matron, who was also surprised to find Katherine so big. Matron was a depressed-looking woman, probably chosen by Miss Dando for her powers of self-effacement. Her duties were to see to the servants, deal out medicines and games excuses when required and remember that Miss Dando, and not herself, was house-mistress at School House. She showed Katherine her cubicle in the Short Dormitory, her locker in the School House dining-room and her book-shelf in the sitting-room, and informed her that no girl was allowed in the dormitories except at the regular hours for dressing, changing and sleeping, unless by special permission. She then showed her her hook in the cloak-room, with its pigeon-hole for boots below, and explained that all these places had to be kept tidy. Katherine, who never kept anything tidy, said "Yes", and was corrected and told to say, "Yes, Matron". In the Hall, a class was doing drill, and this reminded Matron that Kitty would have to be measured for her gym-tunic in the morning. At the upper end of the Hall was a platform, with a grand piano and a row of aspidistras in pots, and over it a stained glass window, with the arms of Lady Margaret Beaufort, founder of the school. Katherine noted the royal arms with their border compony, and they told her that this famous lady's line had sprung illegitimately from Plantagenet blood; but she had the wit to keep this deduction to herself.

Round the Hall and the gallery which ran above it were class-rooms, from which the voices of teacher and taught came dimly through closed doors. One could not go in there, but Matron opened the door of IV, which happened to be unoccupied, and disclosed several rows of desks, a black-board, a window-sill full of flower-pots, and a gloomy little book-case caged across with wire, containing only a few abandoned-looking volumes, and a notice-board covered with form-lists, time-tables and grim lists of homework. Beyond the Hall were the Mistresses' Room, two dismal cells known respectively as the Big and Little Division-Rooms, and a staircase leading up to IV-a and the Studio. The thing that struck Katherine most about all these rooms was their peculiar smell. She grew used to it later, but it always surprised her afresh at the beginning of every term. It was the smell of human beings, and she had never met it before.

As they returned from their excursion, past a row of music-rooms, each labelled with the name of an eminent composer, and all competing in a horrid and simultaneous cacophony, they encountered Miss Dando and the Lammases, preparing to go over the grounds together. Katherine was restored to her parents, and said it was all very nice. They went through the garden, by way of a herbaceous border, still full of bloom. "We are very proud of this border", said Miss Dando. There were three games of hockey proceeding on the playing-fields, and while Miss Dando explained that

The Godolphin School, Salisbury

Lacrosse at the Godolphin

The Hall at the Godolphin

The VIth form room where Dorothy studied Molièr

Miss Douglas ("Miss Dando")

Fräulein Fehmer ("Heyser")

they were also very proud of these playing-fields – recently acquired to accommodate the growing numbers of Beaufortians – Katherine thought what a horrible and difficult business hockey looked and felt that the unhappiest hours of the next three years would be spent on those wind-swept plâteaux.

When they had finished seeing all that there was to be seen, Miss Dando gave them tea, and then graciously permitted Katherine to have dinner with her father and mother in the town. First, however, she had better go and unpack her things, under Matron's eye. Matron checked all the mark-ing-tapes with an approving eye, but looked a little surprised at Katherine's winter coat which was her old dark-brown tweed.

"You aren't having a regulation coat?"

"No", said Katherine. "The list said any dark coat would be all right."

"It's quite all right, but most of the girls have navy blue. Give me those boots; I'll send them down to have bars put on for hockey. Haven't you any gym shoes? Well, never mind, I'll have some sent up tomorrow for you. And you must go to Miss Clark for your school tie and hat-band and your school hymn-book. Your sponge-bag isn't marked. Have you brought some spare tapes? That's right. And your work-basket. Yes. No – don't sew it on now. You can do it tomorrow after supper. That's the proper time for sewing."

A proper time for everything. Of course. That was how things were done. But it was depressing. And Katherine had never mended anything yet.

"Now, take all these books down and put them on your shelf in the sit-ting-room. And these other things in your locker. And if you come along with me now, I'll measure you for your gym-tunic and pinafore."

Dinner in the Minster Hotel was rather melancholy. Mrs Lammas was full of questions which Katherine did not know how to answer. How could she tell whether she would like the school when she had seen so little of it? Mrs Lammas was full of reminders about looking after herself and writing home every Sunday. Both were obviously *trying* to appear cheerful and at ease. Katherine knew that the time was coming when she would be expect-ed to show some appropriate emotion. The thought made her self-con-scious and drove all the emotion away. When she did say good-bye at the school gates, she was more off-hand than she meant to be. She entered the front door with a guilty feeling that she had been unkind and ungrateful.

She stood in the vestibule, wondering where to go and what to do. Presently, a door opened and Matron popped out.

"Oh, here you are. That's right. Tomorrow, of course, you must come in by the girls' door. Hang up your hat and coat on the cloak-room peg. Have you forgotten where it is? I'll show you. That's right. Now come along to the sitting-room, and I'll introduce you."

She smiled amiably as she opened the door.

The room seemed very full of girls of all ages in navy-blue skirts, white blouses and pale-blue pinafores. Matron picked out a tall, fair girl of about sixteen.

"Oh, Rose – this is the new girl, Kitty Lammas. She's next you in the dormitory. Will you look after her and see she's all right. And tomorrow morning, will you take her to Miss Clark for her exam papers. You missed the entrance, exam, of course", she added, turning to Katherine, "but Miss Clark will see to it all for you."

She nodded and went briskly out.

Rose looked at Katherine. Everybody looked at Katherine.

"Why", said Rose, "how old are you? They told me I'd got to look after a very little girl and see that she didn't fall out of the window."

Everybody laughed.

"Fifteen", said Katherine.

"Are those your books on the shelf there?" inquired another girl – dark, with a flat, sallow face that looked as if it were made of india-rubber.

Katherine glanced at the familiar backs of *The Three Musketeers*, *Cyrano de Bergerac*,[74] Shakespeare and the *Morte d'Arthur*,[75] looking unhappy and iso-lated in these surroundings.

"Yes", she said, as though owning to some not-too-reputable acquaintance.

"Somebody's too learned for the likes of me", said the dark girl, pulling a face.

"Shut up, Bungie-face", said Rose. "I'm Rose Mason. That's Dorothy Hendon. And that – "she indicated an older girl with red curly hair, "is Marjorie Kerr. She's head of the house. You'd better come and be shown to her."

Marjorie Kerr received Katherine with an aloof kindness, heard with resignation that she knew nothing about organised games, and explained that the "examination" that Matron had talked about was for the purpose of determining which form Katherine would be in.

"I expect it'll be V-b", said Rose. "You'll be with Miss Bellows."

"What's she like?"

"Bellows? Oh, History. She's not a bad old sort. Why did you come late?"

Katherine explained about the chicken-pox.

"Oh, bad luck! It makes it awkward for you, starting after everybody else. But you'll soon settle down. Ever been to school before?"

"No."

"Oh, bad luck! But you'll soon get used to it. I suppose that's why you've

74 Cyrano de Bergerac (1619–1655) was a French soldier and the author of comedies. He is the subject of a play by Edmond Rostand (1868–1918).
75 By Sir Thomas Malory (fl. 1470).

never played games."

"Yes, And I don't think I shall like games much."

"Oh! Well, I shouldn't shout about that too much, if I were you. You'll soon get to like them."

"What's that?" said somebody.

"The new girl says she doesn't like games."

"Well, she'll have to."

"She only likes French and Shakespeare."

"Shut up, Bungie-face. *You* weren't much good when you came. If you like French, you'll appeal to Eglantine."

"Who's Eglantine?"

"Miss Lamotte. She teaches French in V-b. She's only half French, but she pretends she's Parisian. Dresses with lace on them. Elegant Eglantine we call her."

"She's very nice", said a brown-haired girl.

"Oh, of course, Millie. We know you've got a pash for the Egg. She's all right, really. Hullo! There's the bell for prayers. We have them in the dining-room. You'd better stick to me, Kitty – I suppose you haven't got your hymn-book yet."

"Clear up all these things", called Marjorie Kerr.

Books and writing-materials were put away. The bell rang again. A procession of blue pinafores passed out into the corridor.

Matron took prayers. She read a few verses of the Bible in what Katherine, judging the performance professionally, considered a dreary, unimaginative way. A hymn was sung, accompanied by a girl at the piano, who struck several false notes. Everybody said good-night to Matron and shook hands with her.

"Lights out in a quarter of an hour", said Rose, as they entered their cubicles. "Except people having baths – they're allowed a bit longer. Put your light out when the bell rings. We can talk through the curtain till it goes."

*

"Well", thought Katherine, "here I am at school. I wonder what the exam will be like. I wonder what all these girls will be like. I wonder what the mistresses will be like. I wonder if I shall be miserable. But anyhow, a term isn't really a long time."

She had pinned up a calendar on the wall by the looking-glass. With a sense of doing the correct thing, she took out a pencil and crosssed off her first day at school.

*

The next three days passed for Katherine in a haze of confusion. She went down to prayers with V-b, under the grimmish guidance of Miss Bellows, who was immensely lean and tall, with a gruff voice, and had pink fingers. Then, while bells rang for other people's classes, she was pushed into any form that happened to be engaged in preparation or something quiet, and set to do examination papers. Some of these were childishly easy; others were hopeless – such as geography and mathematics. She had no idea how to tackle an examination question or to keep her papers neat. She made a dash at one thing after another, putting down what she knew in a formless, amateur way. When the bell rang and she had not finished, she could explain anxiously to the mistress in charge that she had only done four questions, and the mistress would say that it didn't matter, and gather the papers up, leaving Katherine feeling as though she was all unravelled at the edges. Working to time was a new thing to her. At break, she considered vaguely about looking for Rose, or for some other School House girl who might take notice of her, or else stood forlornly in a corner of the play-ground, eating squashed-fly biscuits[76] and drinking milk, which she detested.

On the second afternoon, while she was struggling with a geometry paper in a large, remote form-room, a girl came in and said that Miss Dando wanted her. She looked up, alarmed, and began to gather her pen and paper together. She had already learnt that nothing must ever be left about. But the mistress said, rather sharply, "You can leave those, Kitty. Don't keep Miss Dando waiting."

Miss Dando had a number of questions to ask and instructions to give about the subjects Katherine was supposed to take. Violin. Piano. Drawing. This and that. Katherine said, "Yes, Miss Dando", without taking in very much. Bells rang, but Miss Dando talked on unmoved. When at last she dismised Katherine, the cloak-room and corridor were full of girls. They all looked large and busy. Katherine had no idea what the time was, or what she ought to be doing. She was haunted by the recollection of the geometry paper and her pencil-box. Somebody caught and questioned her, as she was scurrying madly along a passage.

"Where are you going? You aren't supposed to go up there now."

"I've been with Miss Dando. I was in the middle of a geometry paper. I don't know where it was, the room, I mean", panted Katherine. "I've left my things there."

---

76   Garibaldi biscuits.

"You'd better come along down to tea", said a voice. It sounded rough and scornful.

"But my paper – I want to get back to the room where I was –"

"Poor little thing! She wants to do her exam paper."

"Ha, ha!"

"You can't do that now – we've just come out of prayers."

"You'll catch it if you're late – you won't get any tea."

"Well, what room were you in?"

"I don't know", said Katherine. New places bewildered her. "It was a big room – a long way off –"

"Now then," said a voice with authority. "What are you girls hanging about here for?"

"Oh, Miss Clark – it's this new girl – Kitty Lammas. She's left her papers and things in some form-room, but she doesn't know where."

"Miss Dando sent for her."

"She's doing her exam papers."

"If I can't find them", explained Katherine, feeling more and more hopelessly at sea, "I shall get an Untidy Mark."

"Well, where were you?"

Katherine tried again to describe the large room a long way off.

"Up in IV-a, I expect", said Miss Clark. "I shouldn't trouble, now, Kitty. Somebody will have put them away for you. We'll look for them later on. Run along down to tea now." She paused, and, catching Katherine's scared eye, said:

"Forgotten where the dining-room is? I'll show you. Try not to be so absent-minded."

"No, Miss Clark."

In the dining-room, among the group about the tea-urns, Katherine discovered Rose Mason and poured out her troubles.

"All right", said Rose. "I'll go up presently and get the things for you."

The pencil-box and papers were discovered, neatly put away in an empty desk in IV-a. Katherine never had to finish the geometry question. Everything was confusion in her mind.

As Rose had predicted, Katherine found herself in V-b, along with Dorothy Hendon, three other School House girls and a number of unknowns from other houses. She now learned the true nature of a time-table. Everybody in form at 10 minutes to 9. Each one in her desk and silent when the bell began to ring for prayers. At 5 to 9, Miss Bellows stood up and the form monitor stood by the open door. Wait till Form V-a passed on its way to the Hall. Then fall in behind in single file. The monitor came last and shut the door. Form up in the Hall behind Form V-a. No talking. At 9 o'clock, the bell stopped ringing and Miss Dando came up from the bottom of the Hall and mounted the platform.

"Good morning, girls."

"Good morning, Miss Dando". (The instructions were that the greeting was to be said heartily.)

Hymn. Bible. Psalm. Prayers. Lists of marks. Notices. Dismissal. March out. Bell. Geography. Bell. History. Bell. Arithmetic. Break. Biscuits and milk. Bell. English. Bell. Divinity. Bell. Wash. Bell. Dinner. Half an hour's recreation. Bell. Crocodile, two and two, for those not playing games. Back and change. Bell. German. Bell. Preparation. Bell. Tea. Bell. Preparation. Bell. Wash. Bell. Supper. Then mending, or doing what one liked in the sitting-room. Bell. Bed. Bell. Lights out and stop talking.

Six and a half hours work for each girl each day, except Saturday half-holiday. No more. No less. No over-work. Only so much time for games – no over-exertion. But no privacy.

Difficult – answering questions in class. Writing neatly. Keeping a Rough-Note-Book tidy. Remembering to take down the prep. Remembering to include *all* rough working in the margin of the arithmetic book. No excuses. No putting off a piece of work that one did not like. No chance of getting out of anything.

Humiliating – to answer a question in an unexpected manner – not out of the book. To know so little. To be so mixed-up in one's mind.

But one day there would be French. Then one would find out whether what one knew was any good.

V-b. Stuffy. The smell of people. A fine morning outside, but V-b looked out westward and was dark and gloomy of a morning.

Dorothy Hendon at the door.

"Shut up, you! Eglantine's coming."

Elegant Eglantine, with her hair piled up in stiff little curls over the back of her head. A small, thin face, with a long nose and dark eyes. A blouse with a lace collar. Small feet in high-heeled shoes. Small, plump hands with rings on them. Age perhaps twenty-eight.

"Bonjour."

"Bonjour, Mademoiselle."

"Nous allons parler aujourd'hui de Molière."

That was all right. A really good accent. Spoken slowly for dull ears, but the real thing. And Molière, too – what luck!

"Pouvez-vous me dire qui était Molière?"

Silence. Should one put up one's hand? Or would that look too pushing? Better wait.

"Voyons. Vous avez entendu parler de Molière. Qui était-il?... Dorothy Hendon? Non? Marjorie Baker? Non? Personne ne sait rien de Molière?"

The dark eyes scanned the rows with a pretence of surprise. It was not really likely that anybody had heard of Molière or, having heard, would volunteer information in French. But schoolmistresses always have that air of hoping eagerly for the impossible.

Katherine raised a modest hand.

"Ah!...C'est Kitty Lammas, n'est-ce pas? Eh, bien, Kitty. Pouvez-vous nous dire quelque chose au sujet de Molière?"

"Molière, c'est le plus grand écrivain comique de la France; un des plus grands, peut-être, qui aient[77] jamais vécu."

This time Katherine had made her impression all right. There was no doubt of that. The high, clear voice, with the r's rolled in the throat and the intonation singing up and down like the note of a foreign bird, brought every head round with a jerk to stare at the strange phenomenon in the back row. Miss Lamotte, who had never before in her life heard the subjunctive accurately and readily placed[78] within the walls of the Lower Fifth, reeled slightly under the shock, but recovered herself sufficiently to reply:

"Ah! très bien. Et qu'est-ce qu'il a écrit?"

"Des pièces de théâtre, dont les plus importantes sont: *Le Tartuffe*, *Le Festin de Pierre*, *L'Avare*, *L'Ecole des Femmes*, *Les Femmes Savantes* et surtout *Le Misanthrope*, qui est son chef d'oeuvre."

("That will show her", thought Katherine. "There aren't many people who would mention *Le Festin de Pierre*." She was a little flushed and breathless.)

"Et dans quel siècle a-t-il vécu?"

"Au dix-septième siècle, à la cour de Louis XIV, pour qui il a écrit la plupart de ses comédies."

"Bien".

Mademoiselle paused. That was enough attention to bestow on a new girl. She took some books from the desk. "Nous allons lire *L'Avare*. *L'A-var-e*. Qu'est-ce que cela veut dire, *l'Avare*? Winifred? Edith? 'The Miser'. Bien. ..."[79]

"Here, you new girl", said Margaret Watkins of Wellington House, when the forty minutes' lesson was over. "Where did you learn all that stuff? You'll have to help me with these beastly exercises. Eglantine must be hopping for joy."

Katherine mumbled something. It looked as though one part of her dream was fulfilling itself to some extent. In this curious new confusion, she found something in common between herself and Miss Lamotte – they were fellow-competents in a crowd of incompetents. But there was a snag about this. She did not see where or when Eglantine Lamotte and herself could meet to enjoy rational conversation about Molière. The school time-table did not provide for that sort of thing. The only thing one got out of being ahead of one's companions was the privilege of yawning through

---

77 This verb is correctly in the subjunctive, following a superlative.
78 See preceding Note.
79 For translation see Appendix C, p. 163.

four periods a week while they stumbled and fumbled along a path of which one knew every step by heart. This was but a poor set-off to the weary humiliation of being behind-hand with most other subjects. There did not seem to be much entertainment to be got from the prolonged contemplation of one's own superiority.

*

"Hullo, K. Lammas!" said somebody from the crowd milling round the games notices. "You're down to play right half on Number Three."

"Oh, lord! am I?"

"Mean to say you didn't look?"

Katherine had not looked. For a week she had scanned the notices at break with a terrified feeling in her stomach. She had not seen herself there, and she had begun to have a faint, unreasonable hope that her existence had been forgotten altogether.

"Slack kid!" This was Minnie Rogers, the School House girl with a pash for Miss Lamotte. She was in V-a, and therefore not in direct competition with Kitty, but she had heard tales of the sensation in V-b, and had no notion of allowing the Lammas nuisance to show off.

"The first thing you've got to do every break is to look at the games lists. You'll catch it if you don't."

"Who's taking Number Three?" Rose thrust her fair head over Minnie's shoulder. "Oh, the Paragon. What luck for you!"

Miss Paradine was a former Beaufortian who had returned as a mistress. She taught various subjects to the Lower Forms and assisted Miss Waterhouse, the Games Mistress. It was the fashion, for some reason, to find her "sweet". She was – or so Kitty was informed – much nicer at taking games than Miss Clarke, who was apt to be "sniffy". The best luck of all, of course, was to be in the game taken personally by Miss Waterhouse, but she was seldom to be found on Number Three, which was the least good of the playing-fields and usually given up to scratch games, composed of the untried, the hopelessly feeble and the unenthusiastic.

In a cold wind, after afternoon school, Katherine found herself clumsily thumping in her barred boots down the wood steps which led to Number Three. Her limp, soft hands grasped a hockey-stick. The other three people from her own house – a fat, short-sighted person of imperturbably good temper, a coltish youngster from IV-a with a loud voice and slangy manner and a new girl who had the enviable knack of appearing to be perfectly well established the minute she was put anywhere, like a pot-grown plant – had been absorbed into a large group that was familiarly discussing the probable make-up of the First XI. Katherine, dawdling forlornly on the outskirts, wondered how in the world the other new girl had managed to pick up so much about the form of all these people in the time. But Vera Temple had been to school before and knew all about everything. It was popularly supposed that she would not long remain playing in scratch games on Number Three. The wind blew Katherine's dark blue skirt about her knees. Her legs, in their awkward pads, felt stiff, and as though they did not belong to her.

Miss Paradine came briskly down the steps with a devoted attendant carrying her hockey-stick for her, in case she decided to give a personal demonstration of how it should be done.

The game sorted itself out. Katherine mournfully approached Miss Paradine.

"Please, Miss Paradine, what have I got to do?"

Miss Paradine looked her up and down. She was a very plain woman with a curiously flat face and unbecomingly dressed hair. She was thin, and wore a costume of grey cloth with the coat cut very long, a workmanlike flannel blouse and a leather belt with a whistle stuck into it at the end of a chain.

"Oh, you? You're new, aren't you? Kitty Lammas, isn't it?"

"Yes, Miss Paradine."

"You've never played hockey before, have you?"

"No, Miss Paradine."

"Well, where are you supposed to be playing?"

"Right half, Miss Paradine."

"Oh, I see! Well, you come over here. You stand here. You've got to mark the opposite forwards and stop them from getting past. You have to try to pass the ball to one of your own forwards." Miss Paradine indicated those stalwarts. "You must only play with the face of your stick, and you mustn't raise the stick above your elbow. Do you see? Like this."

"Yes, Miss Paradine."

"You'll soon find out all about it."

With this optimistic prophecy, Miss Paradine withdrew. Katherine, ready to howl with resentment and gloom, grasped the hateful stick firmly. She could run pretty fast, anyway. Perhaps a miracle would be worked in her favour and she would find in herself an inborn genius for hockey. But she did not feel confident about it.

A whistle blew. There was a scrimmage in the middle of the field and the ball flew away towards the opposite goal. Everybody surged after it. Katherine surged too. Something seemed to be happening just ahead of her. There was a further scrimmage and the whistle blew again. Miss Paradine, superintending some operation on the edge of the field, caught sight of Katherine. The ball came in again and was pounced on by one of the forwards. Miss Paradine made a gesture which Katherine did not understand. The ball came back a little, and was sent forward again and shot away behind the goal line. Whistle. Miss Paradine ran down to Katherine.

"You're much too far up the field. Get back to your place. Look! Watch Molly Dwight over there. Don't come further up than she does. You're supposed to be down near your own goal in case the ball comes back."

Katherine looked vaguely across at Molly Dwight (whoever she might be), and saw her standing well down on the opposite side of the field, legs well apart, stick balanced across idle hands. She appeared to be grinning. Everybody was grinning. The game was held up. Katherine said, "Oh, I see. Thank you, Miss Paradine", and walked back till she was in a line with her left half. The whistle blew, and the game proceeded.

After a little time, Katherine found it possible to get on by watching Molly Dwight. She could copy the careless stance when the game was at the other end, the alert crouch as the ball came back towards goal, the rush half-way up the field, the casual slouch back to one's allotted position when the whistle was blown for a bully – even the headlong rush to meet a galloping forward, and, after a time, she found out how to stop the ball and hook it away without turning on it or giving occasion for a cry of "Sticks!" But having got the ball, she never could do anything with it. While she was making up her mind, somebody would snatch it and drive it past her. Or if, seeing an opponent thundering up alongside, she contrived to smite it out, it always went with diabolical directness to the stick of the opposing centre. "You must *look* where you're passing", said Miss Paradine. But Katherine couldn't look. The field was always a blur. If she stopped long enough to locate anybody, then the time for striking had gone past.

She gained no clear idea of the game as a game; and it may as well be said at once that in three years she never did. She sometimes thought that if she could read a book about it, or see it all clearly explained on a blackboard she might understand about corners and bullies and offside and all the rest of it; but it never entered anybody's head to teach a game that way, nor was she sufficiently interested to ask. In any case, she could never have become more than a theorist, because she had no games eye and no games sense. She saw people who began to play in the same term that she did rise into the First XI, and could not imagine how they did it. Not that she felt any particular envy of them; she was quite sincere in her dislike and scorn of the pastime. But it was uncomfortable to know one's self such a fool. Also, it was annoying to waste so much time on anything so unprofitable. If the physical exercise had made her feel hearty and happy, that would have been something to the good, but it merely made her feel limp. She hated the acute pain of breathlessness, and standing about in the freezing wind, and getting her ankles hacked; most of all, she hated the unaccustomed roughness of her hands after an hour and a half in a north-easterly blast; it set her teeth on edge.

Rose asked Kitty how she had got on with her first game of hockey.

"Oh, all right", said Katherine.

"Think you'll like it?"

"No – I think it's a beastly game. But then I don't like games."

"It's not elegant enough for our Kitty", said Minnie Rogers. "She doesn't like nasty, rough games."

That was, unfortunately, true; and as the weather grew colder, Katherine liked rough games less and less. She was eccentric enough to rejoice when games were scratched, even though the alternative was a school crocodile. The only unhappy part about a crocodile was the difficulty of securing a partner. Kitty Lammas was not a popular companion. She was frequently the odd girl out, who had to walk with the mistress. Actually, the mistress was often a better companion than a girl, but to say so branded one as an oddity of the first water. Unless, of course, you happened to be keen on the mistress. But you never knew which mistress was going to take the crocodile till she appeared, and then there would be either an unedifying rush to walk with her or a still more unedifying rush to avoid her. A dull mistress would suffer the mortification of seeing her crocodile suddenly start away with surprising animation and, scanning its ranks with an eagle eye, would perceive an unlicensed "three" concealing itself in the ranks.

"Stop! What are you doing, walking together? You know that's not allowed. One of you must come and walk with me."

"Oh, so sorry, Miss Jenkins. We didn't notice…"

"Well – ?"

Then the hasty and insincere request:

"Oh, *may* I walk with you, Miss Jenkins?"

"Certainly" (with a grim expression).

After which, the luckless partner might have some difficulty in making conversation for Miss Jenkins. After all, if anybody had had the wit to see it, it was galling for Miss Jenkins when this kind of thing happened, especially as she had seen Miss Waterhouse (who was extremely handsome) greeted, as she rounded the corner of the cloakroom, by an eager, lurking couple, with cries of "May we walk with you, Miss Waterhouse?" Katherine did, sometimes, dimly guess that the Miss Jenkinses and the Kitty Lammases of the school world might have something in common. But her frequent position at the tail of the "croc" was more often due either to making a virtue of necessity or to that thirst to win notice and approval from authority which was called (by Minnie Rogers and others) "sucking up".

Katherine's letters home always said that she was well and happy, and contained details of her daily life. She would never have acknowledged that she was not a success. That was not the kind of thing one admitted. Her parents knew, naturally, that she disliked games, but that, she explained, was because she despised such activities. Though she felt that an expression of her mental and spiritual state was called for, her pen refused the task. She filled in the blanks with descriptions of her lessons, of the mistresses, of the form-room, of the curriculum. From time to time she was

haunted by the idea that she ought to say that she was homesick. It would
be only polite. But actually she was not homesick at all – not at any rate, in
her first term. Her mind conceived the thirteen weeks of the autumn term
as a definite period, reasonably short. She could see to the end of it.
Though not altogether at ease, she was interested, and while she was interested and in sound health, it was impossible for her to feel any sense of
hopeless and endless desolation. It worried her a little. It seemed wrong to
be so impervious to natural sentiment. But she could not admit any defect
in herself and therefore decided that homesickness was foolishness. As a
sop to parental feeling, she mentioned in every letter that she was looking
forward to the holidays.

She was confirmed in her attitude by a letter she received from Mrs
Lammas about the middle of term. It appeared that the daughter of a
neighbour, who had gone to boarding-school at the same time as herself,
had pined herself sick and had to be sent home.[80] Katherine was elated by
the news. "How feeble", she thought, "and how inferior to me." She wrote
as much to Mrs Lammas, though expressing herself with a modest
hypocrisy. She kept her mother's letter by her for some time; it was a com-
forting salve to her self-esteem, which was receiving a number of severe
blows.

There was the matter of the overcoat. Hers was the only coat in the
school that was not of the regulation pattern, and her house prefect and
house-mates continually made comments about it. And there was the matter of the gym-knickers. "Three pairs of dark-blue knickers" had been
specified in the school list, and these had been duly supplied. At her first
gym-class, Katherine found herself mysteriously an object of attention,
and presently Miss Waterhouse, examining her tunic to see that it came to
the regulation inch above the floor when she knelt, cleared up the mystery
by saying with a smile:

"You must get some proper knickers, Kitty; these don't look nice at
all."

Katherine looked round. The other girls were all grinning. They had
knitted knickers, ending above the knee in a neat band of ribbing.
Katherine's knickers were woven and buttoned beneath the knee. A hot
flush of resentment surged into her face. It was monstrous that the school
should deliberately subject her to humiliation of this kind. Mrs Lammas
would be worried by the expense of providing a new coat and knickers.
How could she know that what she had bought would not be correct, when
the list did not make itself clear on these points? The other new girls in the
class had managed to get the right kind of knickers, and were grinning as

80   This is based on the experience of her cousin Margaret Leigh. See letter to her mother,
      dated 7 February 1909, Volume I, p. 17.

widely as all the rest. How did they know these things? They could not possibly have wiser mothers, for Katherine Lammas' mother was as perfect as all Katherine Lammas' other belongings. They had been lucky, that was all. Katherine mumbled, "Yes, Miss Waterhouse", and cherished fury in her soul. That same evening, the School-House prefect also mentioned knickers, and Katherine was rude and off-hand about it. For the rest of the term gym-classes were occasions of horror and shame. She tucked the offending knickers as high above the knee as she could, but the wrongness of their shape was still apparent.

Then there was hat-elastic. The hard and ugly straw boater sat uncomfortably on Katherine's large head and thin hair. It was secured in the traditional way with an elastic under the chin. "Only third-form kids wear their hats like that", said the prefect. "Can't you put yours under your pig tail?" Katherine's pig tail caused her acute mental distress as it was. It was a poor little thing, short and thin. She could not believe that it would hold the hat in place, and said so. She was too angry to try. She did not like to submit to correction. Later in the term, however, she did, very quietly – almost surreptitiously – transfer the elastic to the back of her head. The change remained unnoticed for some time. Then somebody exclaimed:

"Oh, good! Well done, K. Lammas! Look! She's got her elastic at the back."

They were quite kind about it. They expressed genuine pleasure. Katherine sulked. The heartiness of the approval was the measure of their former criticism.

"Well, I suppose you're satisfied now", she said, sulkily. "The beastly thing will always be blowing off, now, but if it makes you happy, I don't mind."

It did blow off, but no more than other people's hats. Hats were made to be blown off. Secretly, Katherine was glad to be no longer criticised. In time she even began to feel strongly herself about the proper position of hat elastic. Leaven, if left long enough and kept warm enough, will move the stickiest dough.

Another shock was administered personally by Miss Dando. She taught Divinity, with a Low Church dullness which turned the study of the Bible into a dreary collocation of texts. Owing to the presence of the Headmistress and the unattractiveness of the subject, the Divinity Class was a model of well-behaved torpor. While the girls laboriously wrote out Miss Dando's laborious notes, Miss Dando herself would prowl up and down between the desks and peer over their shoulders.

"You're doing it quite nicely", she said to Katherine, "but your writing is rather terrible, isn't it?"

Katherine gaped with surprise. The class, delighted to be momentarily relieved from the teachings of St Paul, sat up and took notice.

"Is it, Miss Dando?"

"The letters are quite well formed, but they're much too tall. They stretch nearly from one line to the other."

Miss Dando drew a light pencil line through the tops of the offending letters.

"Try to improve that. Take somebody who writes nicely and model your hand on hers."

Tears came into Katherine's eyes. Anger always made her cry easily, and this time she felt rather more than anger. Neither her mother nor any of her governesses had ever said that her writing was bad, and this easy dismissal of it as "terrible" was a reflection upon them. It was all very unkind. It was as though she were being asked to admit that everything they had done for her was done in vain.

"Yes, Miss Dando."

"Now, go on with your work", said Miss Dando, addressing the class generally. "You need not pay attention to what I'm saying to Kitty." Heads bent industriously over the Epistles of St Paul. Miss Dando continued to engage in the matter of handwriting, setting a copy in her own hand for imitation.

Of course, if the Headmistress had spoken about it, the writing *must* be changed. Katherine set herself to alter the hand she had written ever since she could write at all. She evolved a slow, square, extremely affected writing, as unlike as possible to Miss Dando's old-fashioned Italian hand. When Miss Dando said she was glad to notice a great improvement, Katherine ground her teeth.

In the matter of the patched pinafore, Katherine did not really deserve the pain she underwent. In her very first week at school, she tore one of the blue pinafores on the sharp edge of a nail in the cloakroom. This was a matter for mending-day. Once a week the School House mending was done, under Matron's superintendence, while some other mistress read a literary classic aloud. Matron supplied Katherine with a piece of blue material to make a patch, and instructed her to stitch it closely and finely along the edge.

Katherine's heart sank; she felt bemused. She had never been made to do her own sewing. Mrs Lammas had seen to all that as she saw to all the dull domestic duties at the Rectory. Sometimes she told Katherine "You really ought to learn to look after your own things." But she had never insisted, or taken any definite steps to make her do so. Katherine loathed sewing, and the only effect her mother's remarks had had upon her was to induce a sense of guilt and what would have been called in later days an inferiority complex about it. Now she threaded her needle with fine thread and began her task with a premonition of defeat. She knew what "stitching" was, and began, very slowly and clumsily, to execute it as instructed, using very small stitches of perfect evenness, and advancing at the pace of a very rheumatic snail. It didn't look right, but she was sufficiently ignorant of the art of putting in patches to believe that it must be right if Matron had said so. Miss Clark's voice droned on through *Peveril of the Peak*.[81] Katherine, huddled in a far corner of the sitting-room, toiled on till the first bell rang for house-prayers. Then she caught Matron and exhibited the work.

"Is that right?"

"Oh, no", said Matron, "that's not right at all." She looked at the work which was certainly very neat and careful in spite of being so wrong and so small in quantity. Was this just stupidity? No. Kitty Lammas wasn't a stupid girl. With a little thought she found the right explanation.

"I'm afraid it was my fault", she said. "I expect you call it over 'over-sewing' or 'whipping'. A great many people do. Never mind. I'll show you next time."

"Oh, I see", said Katherine. "Thank you, Matron. I didn't understand. I know what you mean by 'oversewing'."

"What did you do, Kitty?", asked ……. curiously. "Let me see."

"No", said Kitty, bundling the pinafore together and pushing it into her work basket.

Matron had gone; possibly she told the other mistresses about the peculiar girl – so ignorant that she did not know how to put a patch upon a garment, or so blindingly exact in following a verbal instruction. Or perhaps she neither said nor thought another word about it. She was not a very speculative woman.

*

About the middle of the term, Katherine was sent for by Miss Dando, and told that it had been decided to transfer her to the Upper Fifth.

"On the strength of your Languages and your English", explained Miss Dando. "You are bound to find some of the other work rather hard for you, but I think it will be good for you to make the effort. And you will find the Languages and Literature more interesting. That, you know, is the Higher Certificate form. They are half a term ahead of you, but you will be able to catch up on them if you give your attention to it and work hard. I have told Miss Greene to expect you and Miss Bellows knows all about it, so you can take your things upstairs at once."

Katherine was delighted. Authority had been obliged to acknowledge her capabilities in one direction at any rate. She entered V-b and walked up to the Mistress' desk with a slightly self-conscious smirk.

"Oh, Kitty?" said Miss Bellows, smiling her usual grimmish smile.

81   A novel by Sir Walter Scott (1771–1832), published in 1822, containing portraits of Charles II
      and **Buck**ingham and glimpses of Titus Oates and Colonel Blood, romantic characters dear
      to the imagination of D. L. S.

"You are promoted, I understand. Yes, you can take your things up to Miss Greene. Do it quickly and as quietly as you can. Leave your desk tidy."

Kitty gathered her books together and carried them to the Upper Fifth, at the end of the gallery above the Hall. The room was lighter and pleasanter than the Lower Fifth. Miss Greene had grey hair and blue eyes as unusual in their way as Miss Dando's, but instead of being hard and piercing they were liquid and tending in colour to violet; and the whites were blue-tinted like a delicate egg-shell china.

"Ah, Kitty", said Miss Greene, in a deep, soft voice, "so we are to have the pleasure of your company? That will be very nice. Put your things on that empty desk for the moment. It's too small for you, but after prayers we will try to find something more suitable. Marjorie Rush, will you see that Kitty Lammas has her fresh book-labels and the form time-table?"

The form-prefect said, "Yes, Miss Greene" and grinned faintly as Katherine squeezed her lanky legs under a desk some three sizes too small. The bell began to ring; a hush settled over the form; Miss Greene, turning her violet eyes compellingly from one composed face to the other, appeared to summon her flock to participation in some solemn and sacrificial rite.

One fly in the ointment of Katherine's promotion to the Upper Fifth was the severance of her connection with Miss Lamotte. Miss Greene took the Higher Certificate French herself, and while her accent was good, it was synthetic, nor had she in dress or person anything suggestive of Parisian chic. It soon turned out, however, that she was an inspired teacher of literature, and this suited Katherine very well. The set books for that year's examination were chiefly selected from the classical period of French literature, and here Katherine felt at home. *Le Misanthrope*[82] she already knew by heart and *Le Cid*[83] was familiar ground, and so were the works of Racine,[84] that poet of passion in hooped petticoats, here harmlessly presented to the adolescent in the alexandrine severity of *Britannicus*.[85] Ground in the slow mill of textual criticism,[86] these works surprisingly acquired a new and more luscious savour. Either you enjoy this kind of thing or you do not. It is a mistake to suppose that a work of art is damaged by being shredded word from neighbour word to make a grammarian's holiday. This happens only in nine hundred and ninety-nine cases out of a thousand. When the work itself will stand the strain and when the mind to which it is presented for trituration happens to delight in that

82   A comedy by Molière.
83   A drama by Pierre Corneille (1606–1684).
84   Jean Racine (1639–1699), dramatist, younger rival of Pierre Corneille.
85   A drama by Racine.
86   D .L. S. is referring to the French exercise in literary analysis, "l'explication de texte".

particular exercise (two factors not always found in combination) the result is satisfaction of a peculiarly rich kind. If once you have seen the wood as a whole, it will afford only an added delight to number and admire the infinite variety of the trees. When Katherine sat down to prepare a passage of Molière she experienced the actual physical satisfaction of plaiting and weaving together innumerable threads to make a pattern, a tapestry, a created beauty. Into the picture, silken and stately, came le Roi Soleil,[87] small, bewigged, superb, and with him all the people from *Le Vicomte de Bragelonne*,[88] rustling through the sun-drenched parterres to view the latest triumph of the court poet, that wandering player with his melancholy eyes, worn lungs and broken heart. Candles to light the stage! Marquises with their tall canes, delicately absurd in their petticoat-breeches, displaying their lace ruffles, peacocking amid ribbons. The literary quarrels of an *Impromptu de Versailles*,[89] fought out in a show of disputatious adjectives. Clamour over a broken hemistich. Whispers in the *ruelles*.[90] Literary abbés taking snuff and sneering at a caesura. Corneille, old and obstinate, with his heroic fires eclipsed in the rising of the sun of passion and fashion. The balance of a hexameter. The enriching of a rhyme. The schismatic licence of a tentative *enjambement*.[91] The dying actor acting the *Malade Imaginaire*.[92]

"N'y-a-t-il pas de danger à contrefaire la mort?"[93]

The darkened room, and two nuns only to help him as he coughs out his soul. Black night, and glimmering torches, and the corpse huddled with maimed rites into the wrong earth. Picture after picture and all one tapestry, every least stitch a marvel.

Rose was in the Upper Fifth, too, and it was agreeable to have an ally. Rose, from being merely protective, had become friendly. She could speak French and read Shakespeare with relish. Together they strove with the footnotes of *Twelfth Night* and *Coriolanus*, under the painstaking, though not brilliant guidance of Miss Goodman. Rose did not think it screamingly funny that one should be carried away into a dream of fine melancholy by the rapture of words:

---

87 The Sun King, Louis XIV.
88 A novel by Alexandre Dumas, the Elder (1802–1870), published in 1847. D. L. S. mentions it in her Introduction to *Great Short Stories of Detection, Mystery and Horror*, Gollancz, 1928, p. 21. See also Note 53.
89 A comedy by Molière.
90 Rooms used in 17th-century France as literary salons.
91 A term meaning the carrying over of the sense from one line of verse to another.
92 *The Imaginary Invalid*. Molière acted the title role when he was gravely ill himself. During the fourth performance he collapsed and later died. Not having received the last sacraments, he was buried without ceremony in an unmarked grave.
93 "Is it not dangerous to imitate death?"

O, it came o'er my ear like the sweet south
That breathes upon a bank of violets.94

"Some commentators", said the footnote, "have suggested the emendation 'Sweet sound' ". Rose and Katherine agreed that some commentators displayed their folly. How could a sound steal and give odour? "The sweet south", yes indeed. "That strain again… It gives a very echo to the seat where love is throned."95 "What is the opinion of Pythagoras concerning wild fowl?"96 One knew that. "Did you ever read Marlowe?97 No? Quick! Send home for the book. "Ha! Pythagoras' metympsychosis!" One can get quite giddy on Marlowe. "Was this the face that launched a thousand ships and burnt the topless towers of Ilium?" Words, words, words.

["Your majesty will shortly have your wish]
And ride in triumph through Persepolis."

"Is it not brave to be a king, Techelles,
Usumcasane and Theridamus,
 Is it not [passing] brave to be a King,
And ride in triumph through Persepolis?"97

Words to be chanted, shouted, bawled aloud to the winds! "Shut up, you ass! Everybody'll think you're crazy." Well, let them. "Why this is hell, nor am I out of it." …Come and stay with us one holidays, and we will act it together. … "O lente, lente currite, noctis equi!"99

*

"Miss Paradine is coming over tonight to take the house-marching."
"How sweet of her."
"We've got to get the cup this year."
"Yes, rather."
"Well, it's simply ripping of the Paragon."
"She *is* so ripping."

94   *Twelfth Night*, Act I, scene i, lines 5–6. The reading "sound" for "south" has now been accepted by editors of Shakespeare.
95   "That strain again, it had a dying fall" is the fourth line of Duke Orsino's opening speech in *Twelfth Night*. "It gives a very echo to the seat/Where love is thron'd" is Viola's reply to Duke Orsino's "How dost thou like this tune?" in Act II, scene iv, lines 20–23.
96   Ibid. Act IV, scene ii: Clown to Malvolio: "What is the opinion of Pythagoras concerning wild fowl?" Malvolio: "That the soul of our grandam might haply inhabit a bird."
97   Christopher Marlowe (1564–1593). All except one of the quotations are from his drama *The Tragedy of Dr Faustus*. See note following.
98   Dialogue from Marlowe's *Tamburlaine the Great*, Part I, Act 2, scene v, lines 48–54.
99   Latin: "Run slowly, slowly, horses of the night!" Also a quotation from Marlowe's *Dr Faustus*.

*

"Left, left, left, right, left, right, left…left…Hold your head up Marjorie.
Right about *turn*. Heads *back*. Left…left…left…"
    The solemn circling of the hall smote Katherine's sense of humour
under the fifth rib. She began to cackle helplessly.
    "Come on, Kitty, you mustn't laugh."
    Miss Paradine was smiling, though. For one moment that shaft of
uncontrollable mirth from the hand of innocence must have found its way
between the joints of her conventional armour. The House looked
shocked.
    "I'm sorry, Miss Paradine. We all looked so funny."
    "Well", said Miss Paradine, "you must get over that feeling."
    "Left…left…left…"

*

"Oh, yes", Katherine said, when she returned home for Christmas, she
was getting on quite well at school. The mistresses were very nice. Some of
the girls were very nice. Rose Mason was a great friend of hers. The School
House was a very good house, the best in the school. She didn't care much
for hockey, of course, but she got on all right. Next term it was lacrosse, and
she would have to buy a stick. It sounded as though it was a nicer game
than hockey. Not so rough? Well, very fast, she was told, but you were not
so likely to get your teeth knocked out.
    It was ripping to be home again. How do you do, Mrs Appleton? How
do you do, Ethel? How do you do, Cook? Yes, it was quite jolly being at
school. Hullo, Appleton, how are you? Yes, school is very jolly, but it's ripping to be back.
    Christmas visits in the village. Mrs Lammas putting up holly in the
church. Everything as usual. The world has not stopped, but it already
seems to be turning a little more slowly than usual.
    "It'll be a help to have you back in the Choir", said Mr Lammas. "We're
doing *While Shepherds Watched*. Coming to Choir-practice?"
    "Oh, yes, rather."

*

A moonless night with stars, and fumbling down the narrow path to the
wicket gate. A touch of frost in the air. The church-door open, a smell of
tortoise stoves and paraffin. The sexton on a step-ladder, lighting the choir
lamps with a blazing taper thrust upward through an opening at the base of
the bowl. "Good-evening, Simpson". "Good-evening, miss. Back from

school?" "Yes." "Liking it where you are, miss?" "Yes, thank-you,
Simpson – but it's nice to be back." "I'll be bound it is, miss." "Good-
evening, Maud. Fanny. Good-evening, Tom, how's Toby? What, Toby
dead? Poor little Toby, I'm so sorry. Yes, I'm back from school. Oh, yes,
thank-you – it's quite jolly."

Toby dead. Toby who used to sit in the cobbler's window and bark at
people coming down the street. Katherine and the others used to play
"Outdoor Grab" in Miss Carstairs' time. One for a bird, two for a dog,
three for a cow, four for a horse, and anybody seeing a dog or cat looking
out of the window won the game at once. Katherine used to cheat. She
always chose Toby's side of the street, in the hope of winning the game at
once. She knew about Toby; the others didn't. But Toby had never been
there when they were playing. And now he was dead.

Mr Lammas tapped the side of his desk with his baton. The organist
blew her nose and pulled out some stops. The *Te Deum* first. Stanford in
C.[100] That was ambitious. The trebles were out of tune. Old Jim Tabbitt,
clutching the music in his gnarled hands was dragging the basses back as
usual. Such a dear old man, Mr Lammas always said, but you couldn't
make him keep up with the others.

"Now, the altos do that bit by themselves. *The glorious company of the
Apostles.* Now, all together again from there." Well, it might be rough, but it
was hearty. School prayers were thin stuff by comparison.

"And now we will go through the anthem."

Easy music this; carol music.

"While she-heperds watched their flocks by night, All slee-heeping on
the ground…" Home was pretty good, after all. It was jolly to get up late,
and jolly not to have every second of your time filled in for you.

Among Katherine's Christmas presents were the books she had asked
for: Malory's *Morte d'Arthur*[101] and Percy's *Reliques*[102] Words to dream over;
words that painted the world scarlet and cobalt and vivid green, like a pre-
Raphaelite picture; gold on belt and bridle; a spray of eglantine over a
corselet of steel.

So it befell in the month of May, Queen Guenever called unto her
knights of the Table Round; and she gave them warning that early
upon the morrow she would ride a-Maying into woods and fields
beside Westminster. And I warn you that there be none of you but

100 Charles Villiers Stanford (1852–1924) set a number of Anglican services. His service in C is
      the easiest. D. L. S. says that she sang it many times in her father's village choir. See her let-
      ter to Herbert Byard, 1 October 1945, Volume 3, p. 165.
101 D.L.S. has forgotten that Katherine already possessed this and had brought it with her to
      school.
102 See Note 64.

that he be well horsed, and that ye all be clothed in green, outher in silk outher in cloth.[103]

That was real, somehow: more real than the hall at the Beaufort, with its aspidistras and the hot-water pipes which one sat on when one was cold (though sitting on the pipes was forbidden).

> I heard the water lapping on the crag
> And the long ripple washing in the reeds.[104]

That was beautiful; but Malory's prose was simpler:

> "Sir", he said, "I saw nothing but the waters wappe and the waves wanne."[105]

More beautiful still, perhaps? Difficult to tell. One could at any rate mouth them both aloud, and not be called crazy.

> And lang, lang may the ladies sit
> Wi' their fans into their hand…[106]

One could not say that often enough. Say it, sing it, fifty times, five hundred times, and it was as new as the day it was written.

> Wi' their fans into their hand…
> Wi' their gowd kaims in their hair…[107]

They burned against the darkness, row upon row of ladies, stiff, silent, like images, more real than flesh and blood.

Katherine spent much time and made hideous noises upon the piano, till she had made a tune for herself that fitted *Sir Patrick Spens*.[108]

> Half ower, half ower from Aberdour
> 'Tis fifty fallen deep;
> And there lies gude Sir Patrick Spens
> Wi' the Scots lairds at his feet.

Mr Lammas, who had himself just given birth to a new and rather fine

103 Malory, *Le Morte d'Arthur*, Book XIX, chapter 1.
104 Tennyson, *Morte d'Arthur*, lines 116–117. D.L.S. has misquoted from memory. The original lines are: "I heard the ripple washing in the reeds,/And the wild water lapping on the crag".
105 Malory, *Le Morte d'Arthur*, Book XXI, chapter 5. wappe (arch.), to splash; wanne (arch.) to wane, to ebb.
106 From the ballad "Sir Patrick Spens". See also Note 108.
107 Ibid.
108 An old Scottish ballad in Percy's *Reliques*, on the subject of Sir Patrick Spens who set out on a sea voyage for the king in winter and perished.

setting of "Bright the vision that delighted",[109] listened critically and thought Katherine's tune a good one; but Mrs Lammas enjoyed hearing the words of the ballad. Or perhaps she chiefly enjoyed hearing Katherine sing them, in her loud, hoarse, untrained contralto.

Malory and Percy went back to school with Katherine at the beginning of the Easter term. So did her own beloved set of Racine, in the eight tall eighteenth-century volumes, with the lovely Bodoni type and the classical engravings.

"They are too good for school", said Mrs Lammas. "You must take care of them."

*

The term opened a little more brightly for Katherine. She had a regulation coat and three new pairs of proper gym knickers, and Rose seemed really glad to see her back.

Better still, there was a new girl in the house – a timid and awkward creature, whose parents lived somewhere abroad and whose wits seemed to be still abroad with them. Coming in the middle of the school year, she was at a far worse disadvantage than Katherine had ever been. Katherine was able to patronise her and show her where to put her things, explain what the bells meant, and warn her about untidy marks and not using coloured hair-ribbons.

The strange and hostile faces of V-a had turned into those of familiar friends. People said, "Hullo, K. Lammas!" as if she belonged there.

As the year went on, she began to feel, herself, as if she did belong there. Ignominies were forgotten. Threatened terrors smoothed themselves away to nothing. She began to find a measure of self-assurance, and, where she could not find it, the courage of defiance. When she was cornered, she could sulk and snarl like a trapped rat, or dig out an underground way of escape with argument and excuse.

Before very long, the question of her music became critical. She had arrived at the Beaufort hugging her violin case and repeating her childhood's creed: "I believe in my musical ability"; though her faith had already been a little staggered by her failure to pass the L.R.A.M. and L.R.C.M., Intermediate.[110] Now for the first time she faced a specialised teacher of music who had no temptation to please her family by smooth words. Miss Playfair heard her attempt one of her late examination pieces,

---

109   The words of this hymn, based on the account of Isaiah's vision, are by Bishop R. Mant. The usual setting is by R. Redhead. The manuscript of the setting by Henry Sayers has not been found.

110   Licentiate of the Royal Academy of Music, Licentiate of the Royal College of Music.

and said briefly, "Yes, I think I know why they failed you." Miss Playfair was energetic, enthusiastic, sharp-tongued, an excellent musician, but tactless. In informing Katherine that her intonation was faulty, her execution careless, her tone thin and her bowing rough, she let it be seen that she thought her badly taught; and Katherine was instantly up in arms, though she had herself had her suspicions and though Mrs Lammas, ignorant as she was of musical technique, had had her suspicions also. But it was one thing to harbour these ideas one's self, and quite another thing to hear them expressed by other people. "Je me les sers moi-même avec assez de verve,/ Mais je ne permets pas qu'un autre me les serve."[111]

The preliminary antagonism might have been overcome if Miss Playfair had not been, by nature or training, chary of expressing praise. There is a superstition current among educators that young people should be nipped, like young chrysanthemums, to prevent them from growing above themselves. This treatment is, naturally, applied most vigorously to those who exhibit a strong growth of self-esteem; by a malignant arrangement of Providence, it is more damaging to them than to any other kind, producing the oddest and spikiest offshoots in unexpected places.

Katherine sulked. She entered upon a violin lesson with the expectation of failure, and left it in depression and sometimes in tears. Her practising grew worse and more scratchy and mechanical. The more critically she listened to her own intonation, the more she found herself unable to distinguish false from true; though when she sang, she sang by nature dead on the note. She conceived the notion that Miss Playfair disliked her. Miss Dando, not altogether aware that the trouble was due to a fatal clash of temperament, intervened with considerable sympathy and kindness. She spoke warmly in praise of Miss Playfair's ability and character.

"I know", she said, "that she thinks really well of you; but she is apt to speak very plainly when she has to find fault. She is a very good musician and a splendid person. You must really try to get on with her."

After this, Katherine did try hard; but she seemed to make no progress. In the end she asked her parents to release her from the study of the violin. "I don't think I really care enough about it", she wrote to her mother. "Dad always thought I did, but I don't feel that it's my line. I *really* prefer Languages and Literature, and I expect I shall be a writer some day."

Mr Lammas was bitterly disappointed. He always hoped gaily and was proportionately surprised when things did not turn out as he expected. But his affection overcame his personal desires.

"Your mother and I don't want you to feel worried", he wrote himself, "and we have written to tell Miss Dando that you are to give up the violin.

111 "I present myself with thoughts like these with ample vigour/ But cannot tolerate from others equal rigour." Edmond Rostand, *Cyrano de Bergerac*, Act I, scene iv, lines 363–364. The words are spoken by Cyrano.

I expect you have quite enough work to do with the Higher Certificate syllabus."

Miss Playfair said she was sorry about it.

"I hoped you would play the solo at a school concert before long", she said. Katherine was astonished to hear this.

"At any rate", added Miss Playfair, "you are still going to keep on with the orchestra."

Katherine said "Yes", and explained that she had a very full time-table.

"I have to do extra Maths for the Higher Certificate, you see, because I'm very bad at that. But I do enjoy the orchestra."

"That's good", said Miss Playfair briskly, and nodded her away.

The piano, though Katherine played it worse than the violin, could under no circumstances be given up.

"You will want to be able to play accompaniments", said Mrs Lammas. "A good accompanist is always welcome everywhere."

Katherine agreed, though she pointed out that her fingers were double-jointed and that, for that reason, she could never be a pianist. She had actually read a magazine article by Pachmann,[112] which said that hands like that were hopeless. Mrs Lammas took this to be an excuse.

"There's nothing the matter with your hands", she said, indignantly. "They're very nice hands."

So that there was no escape from Fräulein Heyser, who sat all day in "Chopin",[113] saying "Na!" and writing in fingering on one's "pieces" in a thin, Teutonic handwriting. She found fault a good deal, but for some reason Katherine liked her.

"Na", she said, "zo you have given up the violin. Good. You will have the more attention to devote to the piano."

Katherine explained again about the extra Maths.

"You do not like to take trouble, no?" said Fräulein Heyser.

But she understood rather better than Mrs Lammas about double-jointed fingers.

"Let me see. Zo. That is true, They have no strength. They turn up. Na! It is more difficult for you zo, but you must practise hard and then they will become strong, like mine."

No excuse was ever valid with Fräulein Heyser; it broke itself helplessly against the strong flat-featured leonine mask of her face. But when she played Chopin, she could magic the soul out of your body. Katherine dared not neglect practising for Fräulein Heyser and cherished her rare words of praise.

It was perfectly true about the extra Maths. The Upper Fifth standard

112   Vladimir de Pachmann (1848–1933), Ukrainian pianist.
113   One of the music rooms, all of which were named after composers.

was far above Katherine, and she joined a melancholy little band of inca-
pables who strove with Miss Peacock in the Little Division Room. Miss
Peacock was very small and very plain; she was like a conventional carica-
ture of a Maths mistress. Her short-sighted agate eyes gleamed stonily
behind thick spectacles; her scant hair was scraped back into a hard bun.
Having a sallow skin and a shining red nose, she chose to wear coats and
skirts patterned in strong brown checks, or striped zebra-wise in black
upon sage green. Her cold little red fingers were always blooming with
chalk-dust. She taught her subject like an angel. Even to Katherine's confused mind, she could make a long and complicated equation seem clear,
relevant and almost beautiful. If you did not understand the working, she
would explain it patiently until you did. If she discovered, in the middle of
working an advanced bunch of quadratics, that your mind had suddenly
become a blank about the factors of X squared minus Y squared, she
would cheerfully rub the whole thing out and refresh your memory from
the beginning, observing that a little revision would do everybody good.
She was never tired, never exasperated, never in a hurry. At the end of a
lesson with Miss Peacock, Katherine would feel sure that she had the whole
theory of quadratic equations firmly in her head, and that nothing could
ever muddle her up again. This exaltation lasted only till her next period of
preparation.

Then she would stare hopelessly at some repugnant expression bristling
with brackets, and find no chink into which she could insert a factor. The
margins of her algebra book were grimy with erasures, the pages hideous
with problems that had no answers, or that petered out into sinister and
impossible combinations of fractions, such as, X = 259 over 8 times Y, or X
squared = 5YX over .19 over 4, X =? Miss Peacock marked these mon-
strosities with the severity they deserved.

"Now, *here* is where you went wrong", she would say brightly. "Look!"
And capering like an elf in a cloud of chalk she would cover the blackboard
with her neat figures.

"Multiply both sides by 7 – take the factors – *quite* right – there, you see –
X squared = 81, X = 9. Now, are you *quite sure* you understand?"

And one could not help understanding. But it was like the revelation one
has in dreams, and did not survive into the waking hours. Katherine felt
sure that Miss Peacock had the poorest opinion of her, and she could do
nothing about it. A problem was either right or wrong. You could not
obscure ignorance by turning it into English verse, as you could with a
French Unseen, nor could you ever lure Miss Peacock from the stern path
of duty as you could Miss Naylor, the Classics mistress, who could easily be
distracted from close enquiry into an ill-prepared passage of Cicero by a
judiciously-placed question about Roman monetary systems or domestic
arrangements in Athens. Miss Peacock was formidable, in spite, or possibly
in consequence, of being a member of some obscure Puritanical sect,

which forbade her to countenance inebriety even to the extent of passing the sherry in the mistresses' Residence. Her pupils nicknamed her "Sister Dinah", and made fun of her hats, but even the most impertinent – even Mary Hocking, with her loud voice and long face like a horse, and Judith Hearn, with her coarse black hair and vulgar manners – wilted under the sharp glance of those agate eyes.

What with Miss Playfair and Fräulein Heyser and Miss Peacock and the games mistresses, there grew up a settled understanding in the Staff Room that Kitty Lammas was a shirker and needed to have her Character Developed. Miss Dando, who was a great believer in Character, took notice of this state of affairs and read Katherine a lecture.

"You work hard at the subjects you like, but you don't want to grapple with Difficulties. You don't like being found fault with. You make too many excuses. Now, that won't do, you know. You have got plenty of brains, but you are one-sided, one-sided. We want you to be a fine, all-round person, with Character. Then we shall be proud of you. Character is shown in overcoming obstacles. I'm sure you don't want to be a feeble person without Character, do you?"

Since, even for argument's sake, Katherine could hardly say that she didn't want to have Character, she said gloomily, "No, Miss Dando", and fiddled with her pinafore.

Well, she was going to be a failure at school, she supposed. The accusation had enough truth in it to take the stuffing out of her. All these people must be right. They were right, she admitted it. It hardly seemed worth while to try very hard, with all these hopeless defects in her character. Though it was true she was double-jointed; true that she had never really loved the violin; true that she was minus the mathematical faculty. She would never be any good.

Every so often, she was visited with a curious sensation of power. "Let them say what they like: I have something that none of them has got – not one. One day I will show them. I will set my feet on their heads. Put the world in my hand like clay, build, build – something enormous – something they never even dreamed of. It is in me; it is not in them, and I know it."

Those of Katherine's fellows who tolerated her found her rather a scream. Sometimes she was ready enough to play the buffoon for them. *Mon panache.*[114] One could disarm ridicule by out-clowning Grimaldi.

But there is nothing more humiliating than to be despised by one's inferiors.

---

114 "My bravado". Edmond Rostand, *Cyrano de Bergerac*, Act V, scene 6.

*

The period of puberty is notorious for the rapid and ungainly development of the emotional and religious instincts. All educational systems recognise this truth, and make such provision for dealing with it as seems good to them. In Katherine's young days, this provision consisted, first and foremost, in leaving the subject of the experiment as little time as possible for private meditation. Psychological theory was in its infancy; but a rule of thumb empiricism had satisfactorily demonstrated that fewer immediate disasters occurred at this unfortunate period when every minute of the time-table was accurately accounted for, from first bell in the morning to last bell at night. The self-assertion of the body was humbled by a determined hideousness of costume and exhausted by the energetic performance of physical exercises. This was, perhaps, bad luck on the body, which had quite enough to do to look after its own internal economy; but it was found to give less trouble that way, while any ill effects usually remained hidden until after the subject had left school, and so demanded no particular consideration. The emotions were more difficult to canalize, though something was attempted along the lines of religious observance; while manifestations of extravagant feeling were snubbed and discouraged – so far as authority could effect this – in the name of common sense and good form. The intellect, forging ahead as fast as it could to keep pace with the rest of the development, was kept busy with the performance of scholastic tasks. Whether this was the most useful task it could perform at the moment might be doubtful; but here, the school authorities had no choice. An authority higher than theirs – an ineluctable social necessity – had ordained that these years of physical and psychological instability should be appropriated to the passing of difficult examinations. Perhaps it was as well. To think about one's self is always dangerous. It may lead to an unhealthy curiosity, and is probably best avoided.

In the matter of religion, however, the Establishment takes a slightly different view. Disregarding the plain directions of the Prayer-book, ecclesiastical tradition has determined that a thorough shaking-up and settling-down of the religious feelings shall be undertaken, not as soon as the young Christian is able to say the creed, the Lord's Prayer and the Ten Commandments and to receive instruction in the Church Catechism, but at that later period when intellect and emotion (both of which have a word to say in the matter) are most violently and indecorously at strife. The intention is, no doubt, to sublimate the emotions by offering them an object exterior to the self: but in view of the fact that the Kingdom of God is within one, the externality of the object is not so well preserved as it ought to be. And in the meanwhile, what is to be done with the intractable intellect? A strict course of exact and dogmatic theology might well provide the intellect with a good, strong bone to cut its teeth on; but theology is a science which has fallen upon difficult days. To worship with the understanding had already, in Katherine's school-days, become unfashionable. Moreover, in a school, it is impossible to teach a coherent theology without offending some parent or other. All circumstances combine to foster the delusion that right living is easier without clear thinking. "Be good, sweet maid", said Charles Kingsley, "and let who can be clever".[115] His followers – feeling that cleverness was a kind of legerdemain that anybody could bring off with a little misdirected application – altered the words to "let who will be clever"; thus creating an opposition where the worthy cleric intended, at most, a distinction. Theologically, the result of all this was a divorce between the human Jesus and the everlasting Wisdom which was certainly undesirable, probably heretical and from every point of view unattractive.

The Christianity cultivated at the Beaufort was of this Established kind. It was not in any way calculated to produce a rich crop of faith upon a soil rocky with critical judgment.

For a daughter of the parsonage, Katherine was oddly uninstructed in Christian dogma. Mrs Lammas, while unostentatiously practising in her daily life the nobler Christian virtues of charity, self-sacrifice and sincerity, shrank instinctively from doctrinal argument. Much of it appeared to her to be difficult, probably if the truth were known, repulsive. She had always eagerly begged that Katherine should not be "bothered" with these questions. Mr Lammas, actuated by God knows what sense of personal inadequacy or nervous dread of intimate personal contacts, had sedulously refrained from giving any religious instruction to his daughter beyond what she might pick up from regular weekly attendance at Morning and Evening Prayer. Miss Warwick, while occupying her seat in the Rectory pew once every Sunday, as a proper example to the parishioners, declared bluntly in private that she was really a heathen and that church-going "meant nothing to her".

The governesses were told that they were not expected or desired to teach Divinity, and were doubtless thankful enough to be spared the task. Old Mrs Lammas had experienced some qualms of conscience on the matter, but had too much good sense to run counter to the express wishes of her son and daughter-in-law. She was, however, always ready to explain knotty points of dogma when requested to do so, and in casual conversation often took the opportunity of pointing out the beauty of Christ's life and character. But Katherine, when she emerged from an early period of hero-worship, experienced a kind of revulsion against gentle-Jesuism with which her grandmother was constitutionally unfitted to deal. Even as a

115   Charles Kingsley (1819–1875), "A Farewell", 1858.

small child, Katherine had shocked her parents by innocently inquiring: "Why does Grannie always pronounce God 'Gawd' ?" Mr Lammas had rather hastily told her not to talk like that; but the impression of senti-mental absurdity remained. In Miss Dando, Katherine again encountered the familiar hesitation, the reverential dropping of the voice, the pious deformation of the vowel. Indeed, the whole spiritual atmosphere of the Beaufort was permeated with "Gawdliness".

The Beaufortians prayed a great deal. They prayed every morning and every afternoon in the School Hall; they prayed in their houses every night; they prayed at the beginning of each Divinity lesson ("Lawd, open thou our eyes that we may see wo-ondrous things out of this Thy Wo-ord"); they were marshalled to Church and Cathedral every Sunday; and on every Wednesday afternoon in Lent they had a Special Service in place of games, which involved, among other inconveniences, the seating and subsequent unseating of the Hall. The general tone of these religious exercises was Low Church, unctuous and unintellectual; they produced in Katherine a powerful agnostic reaction.

Two factors combined in Katherine's second term to make religion stink in her nostrils. One was the business of Confirmation. Miss Dando, having communicated with her parents, called her in for "a little talk". The lowered voice, the solemn and loving expression, warned Katherine at the start that something more than usually disconcerting was to be expected. Miss Dando had informed Mrs Lammas that the Bishop was holding a Confirmation at the end of the term; a number of Beaufortians were to be confirmed. Katherine's parents agreed that it would be nice if she were to be confirmed with her schoolfellows; it was time, really, that Katherine undertook the solemn vows made for her by her godparents in her bap-tism. Miss Dando, fixing the famous eyes piercingly on her pupil's reluc-tant face, felt sure that Katherine was willing and eager to be initiated into the full privileges of a Christian.

Katherine, with the sensation of one drowning in a flood of treacle, said desperately that she would rather wait – she was not sure – she did not think she believed in anything very much.

Miss Dando replied that some doubts were only natural. The Sacrament of Holy Communion would, she thought, strengthen one to encounter any such doubts and difficulties. "Lawd, I believe, help Thou mine unbelief". There would be special Confirmation classes held by Canon Tusher[116] – "he is such a good, sincere man" – which would help to clear up any points which were not plain at the moment. Katherine's parents wished her to be confirmed. "You will think about it, dear, will you not?"

116 A pseudonym of Canon Charles Myers of St Martin's, Salisbury.

Katherine submitted to the affectionate pat on her shoulder and escaped just as she felt that she must burst into tears of helpless anger. After all, she was not helpless. She could always write home and explain that she didn't want to be confirmed and then she wouldn't be. Miss Dando would look upon her as an outcast, no doubt, but that wouldn't matter. She wrote home confidently.

Mrs Lammas' reply took her like a blow between the eyes.

"Dad and I feel it would be so much better if you were confirmed at school."

And this and that. Katherine, to use her mother's favourite expression, could "read between the lines". Mr Lammas did not care for the job of preparing her. Mrs Lammas did not like the idea of her attending classes with the village girls. The whole thing was a little embarrassing and would be far better got over at school, among strangers and at a convenient distance. The suggestion that one did not really want to be "done" at all, fell upon deaf ears, or ears conveniently closed.

If one had to be "done", then far better (Katherine readily agreed), to have the thing tackled by Canon Tusher. It would be ghastly to sit in Dad's study (connected in one's mind with *ut* and the subjunctive, Balbus building a wall and the second book of the *Aeneid*) to attend to one's own father's exposition of Church Catechism. And it was quite evident that to get out of being confirmed altogether would mean telling the truth a great deal more brutally than one was prepared to do. Dad would be hurt; Mother would be worried. One would have to make a strong stand in defence of one's disbeliefs and one would labour under a sense of guilt for years. Even Katherine's disbeliefs were not very robust – they were more in the nature of distastes. There would, indubitably, be a fuss. And her moral courage, never very strong, had been rudely shaken by the explosion of this bomb under its foundations. For the first time in her life, her parents had failed her. She had thought that a hint of distress would have brought them hastening to the rescue. Instead, they had gently pushed her back into the trap and clicked its jaws together.

It was quite useless to struggle. Rose, who had been confirmed the previous year, was of no assistance in this predicament. She did not seem to sympathise with Katherine's grumblings, which were both uttered and heard with embarrassment. It was all very unpleasant. In any case, that was not the kind of thing one talked about. The awkward stutter and hush that accompanied the word God was even more indissolubly attached to the words communion and sacrament. As "the Almighty" or "the Creator" was to be preferred to the first, so "Early Service" was to be preferred to either of the other two. To these rites that were held in secret a strong flavour of the indecent seemed to cling. Like the central act of marriage, concerning which Katherine had by now gathered a good deal of more or less inaccurate information from her miscellaneous reading, the central mysteries of religion were by common consent exceedingly sacred and beautiful but, on the other hand, indelicate and only to be mentioned in a periphrastic whisper.

Gloomy and rebellious, Katherine informed Miss Dando that she was ready to submit to the Laying on of Hands.

Through the benign intervention of those early Fathers of the Church who tied up the festival of Easter with the vagaries of an imaginary Paschal moon, Katherine's first year at school was rendered peculiarly suitable for her confirmation and first communion. Easter fell in the first week of April. It was therefore convenient that the term should run on until after Easter. This would prevent the Spring term from being too short and the summer term from being (in consequence) too long; it would also incidentally allow the Confirmation candidates to make their First Communion in the Cathedral on Easter Sunday in the parish where they had been prepared for this ordeal, and enable Canon Tusher to see his flock through to the finish. This suited Katherine well enough, so far as it went. To make her first appearance at the Altar under her father's eye would have been too much for her altogether. But there were drawbacks.

The Spring term is a dismal term at best – a season of coughs and colds and epidemics, of chilly winds and lowered vitality. There was to have been one thing to look forward to – a small form-play, in which Katherine had been given a minor part. This should have been performed in Easter week, immediately before breaking-up. Though dramatic performances must not be given in Lent, rehearsals were allowed, seeing that the acting was to consist of one or two scenes from the Shakespeare set book, and that the undertaking might be held to be in the nature of work.

But to Katherine, studying her few "lines" with absorption, came a summons to Miss Dando's room.

"I feel, dear", said the headmistress, "that, as you are being confirmed this term, it would be better that you should not take part in the play. Not, of course, that there is anything wrong about acting. But at this very special time it would not be suitable that your mind should be filled with those particular interests. I hope you won't be too much disappointed."

Katherine muttered some incoherent protest.

"There will be plenty of other opportunities for acting", said Miss Dando, "and I know you enjoy it very much. Miss Goodman tells me you act quite well. Don't think for a moment that we want to prevent you from enjoying your life and all your school activities. But confirmation is such a very solemn thing, is it not? You will want to keep all your thoughts free to look forward to the Great Occasion." She paused. "Miss Goodman quite understands, and I am sure you do, too, don't you?"

"Yes, Miss Dando", said Katherine, fury pricking her eyeballs.

"That's a good girl", said Miss Dando.

Dorothy in costume for *Coriolanus*

Katherine went out, raging. To Rose, and to anybody who would listen to her, she said:

"If they *wanted* to put people off religion for good and all, they couldn't do it better. It's absolutely sickening."

Rose was non-committal. One or two other girls said carelessly and a little contemptuously: "Poor old K. Lammas!" Rehearsals took place without Katherine; another girl had the reversion of her part; for the rest of the term she went about feeling that Christianity had marked her out as a leper, unfit to associate with her kind.

Canon Tusher's classes were held at his home, in a small, melancholy room whose walls were adorned with theological works and photographs of churches and college groups. The class learned the catechism and fidgeted while the good Canon explained what was meant by a Sacrament and how the Sacraments, as understood by the Reformers, differed from the sacrifices of Masses, as understood by the rest of the Catholic world. Katherine knew most of the catechism already, and was little interested in the distinction between Transubstantiation and the Real Presence. Her duty towards her neighbour, picked phrase from phrase and subjected to comment and expansion, increased in her the already painful sense of guilt and spiritual leprosy from which she was suffering. The Canon was a stout man, and rather short-winded; he wheezed a good deal as he talked. Katherine received the impression that he had gone over all this ground a great many times, and found little difference between one year's set of candidates and another. The sense of butting against something soft and stuffy became over-powering as Holy Week approached. It did not occur to her to make a clean breast of her repugnance to Canon Tusher; she felt that it would have upset his routine and produced nothing but some concerned wheezings and another interview with Miss Dando. Nor could she summon up any powers of dissimulation so as to present an appearance of stubborn and unconquerable imbecility. It would have been ridiculous to pretend that she could not learn the catechism or remember what she had been told about Sacraments. The trap was well padded, but inexorably shut. The dreariness of submitting was easier than the effort to escape. One could not always be making efforts. There was Maths, there was Lacrosse, there was the Piano, there was Gym, there was trying to keep things tidy and to get up in time for breakfast – those things took all one's energy. After all, everything must come to an end; the classes would be finished, the hypocritical horrors of being confirmed could only last for a day; the musty sanctities of Early Service need only happen once a month at most; and surely when once one had obliged the authorities by professing the faith of Christ crucified, they would leave one alone. In the prayers which she said, hurriedly and formally, night and morning, she had the decency not to allude to the privileges in store for her. If there was a God – and there were passages in G.K.Chesterton[117] that made her think there might be – He was probably no party to this kind of thing.

"And now", said Canon Tusher, wheezing a little more than usual, for he was suffering from a cold, "I am sending in your names to the Bishop. Can you tell me your full names and where you were baptised?" He sniffed, blew his nose, and dipped his pen in an inkpot which had suffered from periodic overfilling and bore a thick crust of ancient ink all round its rim.

The list droned on. "Agnes Brown – no other Christian name? Born 1888. St Etheldreda's, West Puddleton." Sniff. "Marion Phoebe Butler –

117 G.K.Chesterton (1874–1936), whom D.L.S. later knew personally, had an important influence on her religious belief. She read his work *Orthodoxy* while still at school. See her letter to Mrs Chesterton, 15 June 1936, Volume 1, p. 394.

1887 – St Dunstan's, Boggleton." Sniff. Dip. Scratch. ..."Katherine Lammas? Is that your full name?"

"Katherine Warwick Lammas."

"Born?"

"February 15th, 1889."

·"Baptised?"

"Christ Church Cathedral, Oxford."

Canon Tusher broke off in the middle of a sniff. His pen hung poised over the list. Everybody in the class turned round and stared.

"Are you sure?"

"Quite sure. My father was connected with the Cathedral." Katherine added convincing particulars.

"Oh, yes, I see." The sniff had become dangerous. Canon Tusher blew his nose, dipped his pen again and set down the towering name of Christ Church Cathedral among the parish churches, like a triton among the minnows.[118] Then he said kindly, for he was a most excellent and amiable man:

"You will have the unusual distinction of being both baptised and con-firmed in a Cathedral."

"I shall have to aim", said Katherine, "at being buried in Westminster Abbey."

The canon laughed pleasantly, and the rest of the class realised that K. Lammas was drawing attention to herself, as usual. The moment passed. It was the only bright spot in Katherine's progress towards the Central Mystery, and she sucked from it what comfort she could.

The veils provided for the candidates were of an excessive ugliness.

"Everything plain and simple", said Miss Dando. "This is not an occa-sion for looking dressed-up. I like my girls to be neat. Not so much hair showing, Dahlia Perkins; that looks rather common. Let me show you how to arrange it."

The dead white made Katherine's pale eyes and high forehead look plainer than even she could have believed possible. Beneath the white frock, with its high boned collar, stiff tucks and gauffred embroidery, one wore black woollen stockings and heavy black shoes. One felt all feet, till one put on one's white cotton, three-button gloves, and then one felt all hands. The day was wet, and the candidates went down to the Cathedral in three moth-eaten fourwheelers, smelling like damp and ill-ventilated loose-boxes.

There were a great many candidates. In front of the Beaufortians sat a row of girls from a secondary school in the town. Their veils looked cheap and many of them showed too much frizzed-out hair. One wore a white

---

118 D. L. S. is echoing "Triton of the minnows", *Coriolanus*, Act IV, scene i, line 90.

cotton blouse and cream flannel skirt. Perhaps there was something to be said after all for Miss Dando's point of view. Phoebe Mortimer nudged Katherine and said: "Doesn't Evelyn look sweet?" Katherine said "Sh!" Less, perhaps, because whispering was unseemly than because it seemed unfair that Evelyn Bond should have such a good profile, when Katherine Lammas had no profile at all. Katherine fixed her eyes on the hymn-sheet and thought how awful it was and what a hypocrite she was. Suppose that when everybody else audibly answered "I do", Katherine Lammas said nothing. Nobody would ever know. Would it invalidate the whole thing? Could it invalidate it any more than saying "I do" without meaning it? Canon Tusher's instruction had not laid down any very clear doctrine about the necessity of a right intention in the matter of sacraments. Indeed, he had not made it at all plain whether Confirmation was a sacrament or not, but had rather left it to be inferred that before the Reformation it had been one, and was now so no longer, except for Roman Catholics. The Prayer-Book called it an "order" – and an "order", in the most hortatory sense of the word, Katherine did indeed feel it to be.

Her eyes roamed about the Cathedral. Its architecture was beautiful, but predominantly Early English. "The most perfect period of all", said Mr Lammas. At that time, Early English was the correct period to admire, and Katherine duly admired it. If anybody had said to her that thirty years later she would openly express a preference for Perpendicular and Tudor fan-vaulting, she would have been shocked. Perpendicular was the most "debased" of all the great periods. Norman, now – it was possible to admit that one liked the Norman solidity best, so long as one made it clear that one knew Early English was really the best. So when, gazing up at the clus-tered shafting and the groined roof with its crossing ribs, Katherine felt a chill strike to her heart, she put it down, not to the Early Englishness, still less to the uniform greyness of the stone, but to the paucity of stained glass – a decoration in which Carisbury is indeed not rich. Stained glass, as Katherine knew, is a proper adornment for churches – though the same cannot be said for painted stonework which is Romish and vulgar. In fact, Katherine was ashamed of the sensation of warmth which sneaked about her heart when she looked at the screen, which was wooden and coloured and gilded, and – what was worse, "late". It was, in fact, modern imitation Gothic and really and truly rather "debased"; nobody with any proper feeling for the right thing would have admired it for a moment. Katherine knew this well enough, and always said loudly to anybody she wanted to impress what a pity it was that the original stone screen should have been destroyed. But some instinct, buried under a load of acquired information, was struggling to tell her that windows and screen and ribbed vault and sanctuary and service and congregation should all have been glowing with colour together, and that everything then gathered together in Carisbury Cathedral, from the bare communion-table to the respectably drab company of parents and guardians who sat meekly bowed over the service-papers, was as wrong and unsuitable as anything well could be.

The Bishop[119] was droning through the preface. The awkward moment was close at hand. He had already requested the candidates to speak up audibly. Katherine set her teeth.

"Do ye here, in the presence of God and of this congregation, renew the solemn promise and vow that was made in your names at your Baptism...?"

Katherine said "I do", in a loud, savage tone, which plainly asserted: "I've got to, but I'd much rather not."

Responses.

The Bishop's voice, in that peculiar clerical sing-song which is imposed upon speakers in large buildings with poor acoustic properties.

Then the prolonged and tedious shuffling forward of people in sensible shoes over cocoa-nut matting.

Katherine's turn at last. She took her place in a long row of candidates, and was suddenly overcome by the horrid certainty that Miss Dando, somewhere far behind her in the nave, was earnestly praying for her.

The Bishop sat in a high-backed chair. He was an elderly man with strong, stubby hands, which looked very thick and clumsy, emerging from the mutton frills at his wrists. [120] The amethyst in his pastoral ring winked a light.

The candidate in front of Katherine rose from her knees and was shepherded into the retiring queue. Katherine took her place. The Bishop's hand pressed on her bent head with surprising heaviness. She jerked up, startled at the rough touch, but his wide palm held her fettered.

"Defend, O Lawd..."

It was over.

Katherine staggered up ungracefully from her knees and was instantly collared by a verger, or clerk, or some such official – she saw nothing but the lower part of his black cassock – and directed into the right path. She found her way back to her own row. It was all very well organised – out one way, in the other – no feet to stumble over. She seized the book of devotions[121] presented by Canon Tusher to each of his candidates, and read some prayers with concentrated inattention.

The newly-confirmed Beaufortians were given a special tea when they got back to school. The prevailing note was one of quiet cheerfulness. A

119 The Rt. Rev. John Wordsworth.
120 A leg of mutton used to be served with a paper frill round the end of the bone. See John Tenniel's illustration in Lewis Carroll's *Through the Looking Glass*, reproduced on p. 117.
121 *Before the Throne: A Manual of Private Devotion* by William Bellars, 1907. D.L.S. kept and used this book, as its condition shows. See photograph, p. 118.

A mutton frill

peaceful evening, with suitable reading was arranged for them. It would have relieved Katherine's feelings if she might have joined the rest of the School House and played knucklebones on the sitting-room table. But that would not have done. She was still a leper.

She wrote, as in duty bound, to her people, giving a detailed account of the ceremony. But that would not do by itself. She chewed her pen. To write a direct lie was impossible. How to get over the difficulty?

"I won't say anything about *feelings*", she wrote at length. "I can't express those very well."

Dorothy Leigh Sayers
with the best wishes of
Charles Myers
St. Martin's
Salisbury   Easter 1910

Before the Throne.

By the same Author.

Confirmation Papers.

The first five of these papers are meant to present in a concise form an *outline* of the instruction to be given to Confirmation Classes. It is suggested that (as a general rule) *after* the candidates have been fully taught the subjects treated of in the several papers, a copy shall be given to each, in order that they may be helped to understand, and to remember, what they have learned. But if preferred, the papers may be given out *before* the instruction, so that it may be more readily followed by the candidates. This may be specially suggested in case of the fourth paper. The subject of a single paper may, of course, form the subject of instruction at more than one class, if desired. The last two papers are meant to help the candidates practically, as the time draws near, to prepare to receive the Ordinance worthily.

SUBJECTS OF THE PAPERS.

1. WHAT is CONFIRMATION?
2. The PERSON and WORK of the HOLY SPIRIT.
3. The GIFTS and FRUITS of the SPIRIT.
4. The DUTY of those who are BAPTIZED and CON-FIRMED.
5. HOLY COMMUNION.
6. THOUGHTS before CONFIRMATION.
7. The DAY of CONFIRMATION.

Each paper is sold in packets of 25, at 1s. per packet. The complete set of seven packets, 5s.
A specimen book, containing one copy of each paper, 6d.

SWAN SONNENSCHEIN & CO., LIM.,
25, HIGH STREET, BLOOMSBURY.

iv

Before the Throne.

A MANUAL OF PRIVATE DEVOTION.

WRITTEN AND COMPILED BY

WILLIAM BELLARS, M.A.,
Vicar of Margate.

WITH A PREFACE BY

ARTHUR JAMES MASON, D.D.,
Canon of Truro, Vicar of All Hallows Barking, London.

"Let us therefore come boldly unto the Throne of Grace, that we may obtain mercy, and find grace to help in time of need."—HEB. iv. 16.

London:
SWAN SONNENSCHEIN & CO., LIM.,
25, HIGH STREET, BLOOMSBURY.
1907.

Book of Devotions presented by Canon Myers

Indeed, she could not.

Among the protracted horrors of Holy Week, only two episodes made any permanent impression on Katherine, whose mind seemed by that time to have been battered into almost complete insensibility.

Good Friday was observed as a day of religious service and school preparation: a kind of ghastly parody of a holiday. Running rather hastily upstairs to fetch some work from V-a, Katherine almost cannoned into Miss Dando who, for some inscrutable reason, was coming down them. She stood aside, panting.

"My dear", said Miss Dando, "do remember what day it is, and don't run about so noisily."

"I'm sorry, Miss Dando."

"I always remember", pursued Miss Dando, "something that was said to me by a *very* old and dear friend who has now passed away. She was a *real* saint – always cheerful and happy – and her religion meant a great deal to her. And I remember that one Good Friday I was laughing at something – because, you know, I was thoughtless then as young people always are – and she said to me: 'I don't think I *could* laugh and run about on Good Friday as if it was an ordinary day. I always feel as if there was somebody lying dead in the house.' It made a very deep impression on me."

Having recounted this nauseating anecdote in a suitably hushed voice, Miss Dando added:

"So you will try to be very quiet today, won't you?"

Katherine said, "Yes, Miss Dando"; and when the grey-clad figure had vanished downstairs, mounted rebelliously to her form-room, while fury uncoiled in her soul like a released spring. It made her feel quite sick; she did her geometry more incapably than usual, and was only relieved by her knowledge that, as it was so nearly the end of term, a bad mark would not matter very much.

Morning prayers that week took longer than usual, and were of a penitential nature. Katherine knew, from early upbringing, all about penitential forms of service, and was perfectly well acquainted with the traps which they lay for the thoughtless.

"Our Father", said Miss Dando.

"Our Father", repeated the school loudly and earnestly, "which art in Heaven. Hallowed be Thy Name. Thy Kingdom come. Thy will be done in earth, as it is in Heaven. Give us this day our daily bread. And forgive us our trespasses, as we forgive them that trespass against us. And lead us not into temptation, but deliver us from evil."

"Amen!" said Katherine, briskly, hoping that the fun would come.

"For thine is the Kingdom, the power and…"

Miss James's voice soared out into the hush in a powerful solo – faltered, and died away in confusion. Two or three people sniggered faintly.

"My dear!" said Katherine, when the ceremony was over. "Did you hear Jimmy? Wasn't it gorgeous? I *knew* she'd do it."

"She was simply *crimson*", said Minnie Rogers, exultingly.

"Miss Dando simply *glared*."

"So *loud*."

"Serve her right, always trying to sound more 'pi' than anybody else."

"It just shows she wasn't *really* attending."

"I thought I should have *died* laughing."

"It was absolutely *gorgeous*."

"*All* by her little self."

"She *must* have felt an ass."

"*Everybody* in the Sixth was looking at her."

"Shut up!" said the form prefect, hurriedly. "Here's the Greenery!"

The melancholy business of Early Service was made a little more tolerable to Katherine by the recollection of Miss James's lapse. However distasteful the rite, one could at least mug up one's part in it and not make one's self a spectacle for gods and girls.

*

Towards the beginning of the Summer Term, it occurred to Katherine that something was lacking to completeness. Life was less of a strain in the summer. Hockey and lacrosse could be forgotten – and were forgotten, in more senses than one. (Indeed, the effort to memorise the rules of lacrosse and the placing of the team had driven out everything that she had painfully memorised about hockey, and established a mental confusion that was never cleared up.) Cricket she had resolutely determined not to play (the excuse being that it was too *good* a game to be messed about by girls). Tennis, since it was not a team-game, she could better endure to play; she exhibited a bored incompetence three days a week without active protest. Swimming, again, she contrived to get out of (excuse: that it made her blue and shivery). The corridors and class-rooms were less bitterly cold than in the winter terms. There were fewer crocodiles and more permissions to watch cricket-matches in lieu thereof. There was time to indulge one's emotions. But what emotions? Religion had been tried and found worse than wanting. Clearly the correct thing was to have a pash on some mistress or other. Everybody else had one; and it did not pay to appear singular. Katherine looked about for someone on whom she might reasonably fix her affections. Miss Waterhouse had many admirers; but it was impossible to compete for the favours of a gym-and-games mistress against hockey and tennis champions. To adore Miss Peacock would be original, but, admirable as Miss Peacock was, considered mathematically, it was doubtful whether she would respond comfortingly to adoration. Nor could she get up much ecstasy about Miss Goodman or Miss Bellows, or Matron, or the swift-striding Miss Clark ("incessu patuit dea"),[122] whom some brave spirits professed to worship. With Miss Lamotte Katherine had now no contact; Fräulein Heyser scarcely invited adoration, though she could be pleased and propitiated with the gift of a flower sent from home. Examining the staff-list carefully, Katherine decided tentatively that one might feel passionate affection for Miss Naylor, who was young and rather handsome, and at the moment had no special follower except Marjorie Kerr. The competition was formidable, since Marjorie was not only Head of School House, but also an apt classical scholar. Still, one could try. For a fortnight or so, Katherine succeeded in getting a factitious thrill whenever Miss Naylor entered the room and strove hard to express her emotions in terms of Latin prose.

It was in this mood of love-hunger that, in the middle of a lesson about *Polyeucte*,[123] she became aware that Miss Greene possessed a voice of exceptional charm and richness. "O, it came o'er my ear like the sweet south!"

From that moment the half-sketched image of Miss Naylor was erased from Katherine's heart, as though by the sweep of a wet duster. She adored, she doted on Miss Greene. It was an exceedingly fortunate choice, because no extra scholastic effort was necessary in order to win smiles from the goddess. She was already accustomed to see her French books marked in Miss Greene's angular hand with the coveted α of perfection. A good foundation was laid. All that was required for the full expression of one's devotion was to gaze upon the beloved with dog-like eyes of submission, to keep one's desk neat and immaculate, so as to avoid the horrors of a form untidy-mark, to rush to carry Miss Greene's books down to the mistresses' room after class, to enter in one's diary (in cipher) brief records of rapturous moments and to hang about the staircase, hoping for the opportunity to present some trifling gift or to ask an intelligent question.

Miss Greene showed no reluctance to be adored. She was quite used to it. Besides, an adorer or two was a help in the maintenance of discipline and came in very handy when any special job required a willing assistant.

Katherine's "pash" thus ran its course with no more deviation from traditional lines than an L.C.C.[124] tram. She suffered exquisite pangs and enjoyed herself enormously. Here she could dramatise life to her heart's content. The ridicule that she inevitably encountered she did not resent; for she was playing her chosen part, and the laughter of the audience was the world's tribute to the accomplished comedian.

High summer. Preparation in the Upper V. The sun shining hotly on the red bricks outside. The hum of the mower coming up from the tennis-courts, and the gardener's voice crying "hup!" to the school pony. A bee

122 Latin: "in her step she was revealed a goddess" (Virgil, *Aeneid* I 405).
123 A drama by Pierre Corneille, 1641.
124 London County Council.

that buzzed in from the climbing rose beneath the window-sill and, finding the form-room dull enough, buzzed out again. The Higher Certificate Examination drawing very near now. Act [II] of *Le Misanthrope* to be revised for tomorrow. Katherine read on, steadily, competently, certain of herself.

"La pâle est au jasmin en blancheur comparable."[125]

She sat up. It was as though the whole scent of summer had poured suddenly through the open window and intoxicated her. For the first time she heard the mower, smelt the roses, noticed the rich buzz of the satisfied bees, became aware that the sky was blue and drenched in sunlight. One line, in a string of peevish complaints against social hypocrisies. One line with the mysterious power to unlock the heart. Why? The old recurrent surging-up of some inner well-spring of strength and splendour flushed Katherine's cheeks, mounted to her head, made her instantaneously and unbearably happy. She held the world between her hands and turned it over and over, like some curious jewel.

"La pâle est au jasmin en blancheur comparable."

A symphony on the vowel "a" – there was the simple and practical explanation. That, and the fortuitous associations of the word *jasmin*. (The bee was back again, and though there was no jasmine on the School House walls, the scent of jasmine came with him into the room.) Katherine made a note of the line for that week's essay, which happened to be on "Molière as a Poet". A rapture of summer, still fragrant after two-and-a-half centuries. Compare Tennyson's vowel-music in *Sir Galahad*[126] – these proofs of wide reading always went down well. Corneille: "Cette obscure clarté qui tombe des étoiles" – another strange, isolated, exquisite hexameter.[127] Then there was that line of La Fontaine which was always held up for admiration: "Il choisit une nuit libérale en pavots".[128] Not to be compared with the others – *libérale* was a word without charm – but there was the same evasive beauty of association: the poppies, with the heat of August in

125 From an ironic speech by Eliante in Molière's comedy (misquoted here: *au jasmin* is *aux jasmins* in the original), of which the meaning is that a lover will exaggeratedly compare the pallor of his lady to the whiteness of jasmine.
126 The poem beginning "My good blade carves the casques of men...", in *English Idylls and Other Poems*.
127 From *Le Cid*, IV 3. Rodrigue is describing how his army waited during the night for the advance of the enemy. The complete sentence is: "Cette obscure clarté qui tombe des étoiles/Enfin avec le flux nous fait voir trente voiles" ("This dark clarity which falls from the stars/ at length with the tide reveals to us thirty sails").
128 *Fables* XI iii 20: "He chose a night liberally scented with poppies". La Fontaine's line refers to the resolve of a fox to attack a hen-run while every creature is asleep, drugged by the scent of poppies.

their drooping, opium-scented heads, their scarlet dusky with the nightfall, drowsing in sheaves in the dim arms of Morpheus, lurking in the corn, the tender bowed heads of the corn – image after image overlapping, mingling, slipping in and out of consciousness. Once again, the lovely linking of things together, and the many becoming the one. If one could somehow catch and possess them – if life were not so full of tiresome irrelevancies – examinations, games, mathematics, prayers, pinafores, bells, remembering to order one's stationery on Tuesdays, stupid intrusions, claiming time and attention, when there was, after all, something enormous, enormous, something –

"La pâle est au jasmin en blancheur comparable."

The Higher Certificate Examination was hedged about with a quite remarkable number of formalities, the chief of which was that every desk must be separated from its neighbour by not less than four feet of space in all directions. An inch or two short, even by accident, and the entire examination would be invalidated. So, at least, the legend ran, though whether the Examining Board would or could ever have discovered such an irregularity, had it existed, or whether any such dramatic consequence had in fact ever followed upon such discovery, could only be surmised. The fun of the thing lay in the complete upheaval of the ordinary school arrangements which this regulation involved. For the subjects which were taken by a large number of candidates, only two or three form-rooms were big enough – IV-a, for example, and the big room which could be created by pushing back the sliding doors between V Special and the Lower Fourth. This meant that mistresses ran about frantically for a couple of days before the exam began, armed with lists and yard-sticks, while the passages and galleries resounded with the rumbling of desks being moved. Since Miss Greene took an energetic part in these arrangements, Katherine made herself conspicuous as an ever-ready desk-pusher. She had no great dread of the examination, since this year she was not taking the dreaded Mathematics – only French, German, English and History. If she could scrape through the History, she had a pretty good chance of distinction in all the other subjects. Her mind was therefore free to concentrate on the worship and service of Miss Greene and a general enjoyment of the uproar. Moreover, as a candidate of whom great things were expected, she achieved a certain importance, even in the eyes of the other girls. She had refused to play cricket, and her tennis was not good; but for once, games seemed to drop into the background.

Sometimes, when she thought about that matter of the swimming-baths, she began to doubt whether she was as admirable a character as she liked to suppose. She had hated her first day at the baths. In fact, ever since her childish experience of Broadstairs she had always loathed and feared water, and her first efforts at swimming had been ludicrously feeble. She

loathed, too, the hasty rub-down in a dank cubicle, the rough, uncomfortable feeling of clothes on her damp skin, the chill discomfort which the
crocodile-tramp back through the streets did nothing to dispel. If the
Beaufort had had its own swimming-bath, it might have been bearable, but
the ugly squalor of the town Baths combined with her genuine dread and
loathing of cold water to bring on a fury of hatred and depression whenever swimming was mentioned.

In the end, she had funked it altogether. She wrote home that swimming
gave her a chill, and Mrs Lammas – always ready to take alarm, since
Katherine was very subject to colds and chills – had interfered. The School
despised Katherine, and she knew it. She thought she ought to despise herself. It was the affair of the rowing-boat all over again.

However, this trouble was now forgotten. Higher Certificate people
received the same kind of consideration that a condemned criminal enjoys
between sentence and gallows. And there was another advantage – during
the days of the examination they were excused all ordinary preparation,
and on the afternoons when they had no papers, were given special leave to
lounge about the grounds and talk – the one occupation for which
Katherine felt herself peculiarly fitted.

The best incident in the Examination period was the pigeon in IV-a.
Katherine, riding lightly and easily through a paper on Shakespeare Set
Books, was roused by a flutter of wings. Everybody stopped writing and
looked round. The bird flapped noisily about the room and perched on a
high beam in the roof. Miss Pratt, a very prim, though pleasant mistress,
who was invigilating, put aside the books she was correcting, walked down
the room and looked up at the pigeon. The pigeon dopped a card,
splashily, just avoiding Miss Pratt's shoulder, and a subdued giggle went
round. The charm of the situation lay in the fact that the invigilator could
not leave the room – otherwise, of course, the exam would be invalidated
just as hopelessly as though the desks had been disarranged. Miss Pratt
looked up at the pigeon from a safer distance. The pigeon put its head on
one side and said Kooroo! Kooroo!

"Pay no attention to it", said Miss Pratt, rather helplessly, and went back
to her desk.

The pigeon sat the examination out, and provided a good deal of conversation afterwards. "Poor old Prattie", said the candidates. "She didn't
know what to do! Wasn't it simply killing? I say, K. Lammas, what is all
that stuff about 'Taurus, that's legs and thighs'?[129] I got all that question
wrong."

Four-a was a class-room fertile in events. The very next day, Rose had a

---

129 From the dialogue between Sir Andrew Aguecheek and Sir Toby Belch, *Twelfth Night* I iii,
     133–139. Taurus, the Bull in the Zodiac, was supposed to govern certain parts of the body.

nose-bleed in the middle of a History paper. This was all very complicated, for the invigilator, Miss Goodman, not daring to leave the room, nor to allow any candidate to leave it alone, was forced to stand at the door and cry for assistance to Miss Chapperly in the studio. Miss Chapperly came bustling along, talking, as was her wont, nineteen to the dozen, and Rose was conducted away, to be laid flat on her back in the book-cupboard, under strict supervision, while helpful people put keys and cold sponges down her neck. She returned presently to finish her paper, looking damp and sheepish, and snuffling gently into a discoloured handkerchief. Katherine was duly sympathetic when the papers had been collected, but her chief emotion was one of gratitude for so entertaining an interlude.

"Poor old Goodman", said everybody, "she didn't know *what* to do. She was as pink as anything. Right up to her ears. And *did* you hear the Chapperly chappering away? I nearly *died*."

Rose went home with Katherine to spend part of the holidays at Fentisham. Here they learned in due course that both had passed the Higher Certificate, both with distinction in French and English and Katherine with distinction in German as well. School was not so bad after all. They walked round the Rectory garden arm-in-arm, and ate a good many peaches, and discussed Miss Greene and read poetry together, and Katherine showed Rose her Musketeer poems and Rose showed Katherine some little things of her own.

"Of course", said Katherine to her mother, "there's one thing they do teach you at school which you can't learn at home, and that's how to pass exams."

Mrs Lammas was pleased to hear this, since exams were necessary evils. She was sorry, however, to find Katherine's manners more abrupt and offhand than before. Nor was her dogmatism in any way decreased. Though rebelling against all institutions while at school, she adopted an aggressively Beaufortian attitude at home, and was able to patronise her elders from several new standpoints. And as, at school, she bitterly resented any criticism of her home so, at home, she resented any criticism of the school. But it was true that, between continual criticism on the one hand and continual solicitude on the other, she began to feel continually badgered. In between moments when the strong sense of power visited her, she was always searching for alleys of escape.

"Another of Kitty's crazes", her elders would say indulgently, when the house was swamped with stencil-paints, dressing-up garments, photographic materials, needle-work and other paraphernalia; "they always get crazes at that age." And when Katherine suddenly decided to spend hours at the piano, composing tunes to ballads and singing them in a very loud voice, they shuddered, but were indulgent.

During her next year at school, Katherine wrote a good deal of poetry –

much of it openly or secretly dedicated to Miss Greene, who now was firmly enthroned as her presiding genius. But here, a disconcerting element
intruded itself. The verse, all things considered, was rather good. It showed
clearly the influence of the Pre-Raphaelites and Percy's *Reliques*, but there
were also many attempts at sonnets, Shakespearian and Petrarchan, exercises in mediaeval fixed forms, determined wrestling with the difficult balance of blank verse, and, in fact, a preoccupation with metre and stanza
that appeared to argue almost greater interest in the poems than in their
ostensible subject. Having completed a volume of ballads and songs,
Katherine one day summoned up courage to submit it to the Rev. Mr
Stark, a kindly cleric of literary tastes who occasionally gave lectures and
took English classes at the Beaufort.

"I don't know if they're any good", said Katherine, hypocritically (who
should know better than she that they were works of genius?) "but anyway,
I've never written anything that I'd be ashamed to show people."

"No, no", said Mr Stark. "You mean you've always put your best work
into what you've done."

Katherine had not meant that, and the remark took her aback. That
sounded better and worthier than what she actually had meant. She
explained:

"Not that, exactly. I meant they weren't the sloppy sort of poetry, you
know."

"Oh, I see. Quite so", said Mr Stark. He took the manuscript in a large,
genial hand and put it away in a bag. No doubt he eventually produced
some kind of criticism of it, but his words did not dwell in Katherine's
memory. What did remain to trouble her for many years was the trivial
fragment of dialogue and the clergyman's puzzled face. How was it that
she had somehow failed to say the expected thing? Why had she been so
quick to forestall and repudiate any suggestion that her emotions were concerned in her writings? Surely it was deep emotion that gave value to all
great literature – or so all the authorities agreed. She had spoken as if her
emotions could not be genuine – but surely they were agonising and genuine enough. Or weren't they? Did her instinctive certainty that they
would somehow contaminate the verse mean that there was something
wrong about them? It was all very disquieting. And again, why had she not
instantly put forward the claim to having "put her best work" into her
verse? That would have been the right and proper claim to make. But she
simply had not thought of it.

Twenty years later, with a more analytical and better-trained mind, she
wrote in a critical essay:

> A man's fundamental beliefs are to be found, not in his expressed opin-
> ions – for to express an opinion is to admit that a contrary opinion may
> exist – but in his unexpressed assumptions. A thing really believed has

passed beyond possibility of discussion, and to say I *believe* is to say I *doubt*.[130]

When she had written that, she knew suddenly that the old, teasing riddle was answered at last. At the time she consoled herself with the verbal distinction between sentiment and sentimentality.

"But you *are* sentimental, K. Lammas", said a schoolfellow, who had suffered many things from Katherine's continual ravings over Miss Greene. "It's no good pretending you're not. Very sentimental."

"*Distinguo*",[131] said Katherine, who had learnt the schoolman's phrase and was proud of it. And she proceeded to distinguish the two emotions at great length; for at this period she exulted in dialectic.

But there were times when her ego worried her. "Brilliant but superficial" was the verdict of the Mistresses' Room upon her work; and "insincere" was the reproach levelled against her character. She felt obliged to accept these pronouncements, which were made so unanimously by those who should know.

It was to Myrtle, one day during the holidays, that she made a statement which alarmed herself. She had been talking about Miss Greene.

"You must be very fond of her", said Myrtle.

"Oh, yes, I am", said Katherine. "but you know, right inside me, I shouldn't care a bit if she died tomorrow."

"You don't really mean that."

"Oh, yes, I do. Right inside, you know."

"I don't think you do yourself justice", said Myrtle, kindly.

That was the worst of it, thought Katherine. When you really did tell the truth about yourself, it looked too bad for belief. People persuaded you that you were something quite different from what you were. No wonder you ended by being insincere. Because you *were* insincere – everybody said so. Katherine even prayed earnestly for the gift of sincerity, and in so praying, felt that she was being more insincere than ever.

"Just be yourself", as Mrs Lammas said. But what was "self"? You could take off layer after layer, like peeling an onion, and there was always another self down below, watching and mocking. If anybody had offered Katherine the doctrine of "serial consciousness" at that time, she would have embraced it eagerly and found it most illuminating; but nobody at the Beaufort dreamed of offering "the girls" any such complicated system of metaphysics. You had your "real self" (a smooth, round self-contained

---

130 D. L. S. retained a sense of this paradox throughout her life. In a letter to C. S. Lewis dated 8 August 1946 she said: "...you say that a doctrine never seems dimmer to you than when you have been defending it. Well, naturally — but I doubt if that has anything much to do with, or against your faith. It is a nemesis that attends *all* art, and *all* argument".

131 Latin: "I distinguish".

entity as hard and clear as a crystal ball) and anything superimposed on that was insincerity or showing-off.

*

Katherine was now in the Sixth Form, where you sat at a table instead of a desk and enjoyed certain prefectorial responsibilities. What you did not get was privacy or leisure. Katherine liked responsibilities, which added to her self-importance. But she was beginning to feel the strain of a life lived perpetually in public. She would wake in the morning with a heavy certainty that she *could not* get through the day. Something must happen – some catastrophe, some intervention of hell or heaven – to relieve her of the burden of living. Nothing ever did happen; but she came to the end of the term almost too exhausted to speak or move.

It had been a wrench to leave V-a – though the parting from Miss Greene had been made more bearable by an incident which took place at the end of the Summer Term.

The Upper Fifth were at preparation one afternoon, supervised only by a prefect. Outside the window arose the sound of music. It was the Lower School, rehearsing an open-air dance for an end-of-term function. Heads were thrust out of the window. The form prefect herself succumbed to the general atmosphere of frivolity. The whole form leaned out, staring and giggling. Miss Greene, entering the room quietly on silent-slippered feet, was confronted by a panorama of navy-blue backsides and black-ribboned pig tails. She rapped the desk.

Nothing very much was said, beyond a mournful intimation that, if the Upper Fifth could not behave properly when put upon their honour, they would have to be invigilated like the lower forms, by a mistress.

After prayers, Miss Greene cornered Katherine in the passage.

"I was very much grieved", said Miss Greene, "to find you misbehaving yourself, Kitty. Some of the others – yes – but I did not expect that kind of conduct from you. I am very much disappointed."

"I'm sorry, Miss Greene."

One always said one was sorry. But to one or two friends Katherine expressed a sullen indignation.

"Of course she knows I'm keen on her. But she's no business to trade on it. It's not fair to pick me out specially from the other people in the form. I've as much right to break rules as anybody else."

The friends were not very well able to disentangle this problem of personal and public obligations. The incident passed over; Miss Greene still taught Katherine French after her elevation to the Sixth Form; the worship was resumed with no apparent diminution. But the idol had displayed too open an appetite for the sacrificial meats, and Katherine had mingled her incense with the sharp odours of criticism.

In the meantime, Katherine had found other friends besides Rose. There was Elizabeth Cornish – at first a deadly rival in Miss Greene's affections, but later an ally; there was Marjorie Rawlings, who was potty about the theatre, and with whom Katherine's natural passion for acting could display itself without fear and without reproach; there was Barbara Haines, who, of all Katherine's contemporaries, was the best able to hold her own with her intellectually. There were also quite a number of people whom Katherine liked and whom she rather expected to dislike her, but who, on occasion and surprisingly, were known to express the opinion that K. Lammas was quite mad, of course, but had her good points. With these last, however, Katherine always felt herself to be at a disadvantage; she believed herself hated and despised, and this caused her to anticipate criticism by a calculated buffoonery and a prickly assumption of independence. Except with Rose, Elizabeth, Marjorie and Barbara, she was never at her ease. A still more difficult situation arose when she became aware that Rose was showing a genuine affection for her. This embarrassed her dreadfully. She was eager to admire and be admired; but she did not like the obligations imposed by either loving or being beloved. They made her impatient and angry. They were unseemly.

This sensation was so directly opposed to everything she had read and learnt about the emotion of love, that she became more convinced than ever that she really was a rather worthless and wicked person. Insincere, shallow, unfeeling, self-centred – it must be that she was all that. She certainly did not want to sacrifice herself for others; and it nauseated her to think that other people should sacrifice themselves for her. Yet she passionately wanted friends. And still more passionately, she wanted approval. Most passionately of all, she wanted to attract attention. In this last object she succeeded only too well, and probably lost thereby both approval and friends.

Katherine's second winter at school was enlivened for her by conflict with London Matriculation. There was no sense whatever in sending her in for this examination, for she was entered only in a small group of subjects which were insufficient to qualify her for entrance at Oxford. The theory advanced was that it would be "good for her" to tackle the thing; and it is likely that the appearance of her name in an Honours List was thought desirable from the Beaufort's point of view. She gained one great pleasure from doing the set books; namely, a close acquaintance with Goethe's *Faust*. This work was considered rather dangerous and improper, and Miss Greene had to employ a certain amount of persuasion to induce Miss Dando to pass it for Katherine's perusal. Katherine, to whom the subject of betrayed maidenhood had been long familiar in ballad and story, was rather amused. She took little interest in Margaret, but a great deal in Mephistopheles. This was a far more interesting view of the devil than the one presented by traditional theology. "Der Geist der stets verneint"[132] – that was a new idea, intelligible and provocative. It chimed in well with her own tendencies of the moment, which were anything but negative. Long and delightful coachings, alone with the beloved Miss Greene, on the philosophy of *Faust* offered the very acme of emotional and intellectual bliss; and for their sake she grappled, in a determined way, with the other, less exciting, set books – such, for example, as a wearisome correspondence between Goethe and Schiller, in which poor Schiller seemed always to come off second-best. The examination itself depressed her horribly. She was sent to stay with some strangers in London, and voyaged out each day, terrified, through unfamiliar streets to a gloomy examination room, to struggle with her papers among a horde of strangers. To keep up her spirits, she wrote an account of her odyssey to Miss Greene, couching her letter in a rather exalted vein of seventeenth-century *galanterie*, and concluding: "I kiss your hands and your feet."

On her return to school, she found that this effort had been an error of judgment. Fräulein Münster, who had coached her in German prose, had been deeply offended: why had Katherine written to Miss Greene and not to her? Miss Greene was offended also: "I did not like the tone of your letter; it was *schwärmerisch*."[133] Katherine dismissed Fräulein Münster from her mind as a jealous fool: it was unseemly that a mistress should appear eager for the favours of a pupil, and having lost her dignity, the poor lady was merely contemptible. As for the letter – why, this was Duke Richard of Normandy all over again. Katherine had presented an impersonation, and it had been taken seriously. She mumbled that she was sorry, suffered a good deal of private humiliation, and avenged herself on the world by a buffoonery more marked and irritating than usual. Some years later, she suddenly realised with satisfaction that there had probably been a good deal of heartburning in the staff-room over this episode, and laughed heartily. But at the time it seemed preposterous that two grown people could seriously desire attention or consideration from herself. The entire mechanism of school life was directed to proving the social unimportance of pupils, and this, she supposed, was another manifestation of the itch to snub.

But the whole episode of the London Matriculation was a kind of sideline. The really important thing now was to pass a qualifying examination for Oxford. Miss Dando sent for papers and syllabuses, and emerged from her study of them with the following conclusions.

Since Katherine had small Latin and less Greek, it was hopeless to try to get her through Responsions.[134]

---

132 Goethe, *Faust* Part I, Mephistopheles is speaking: "Ich bin der Geist der stets verneint" ("I am the spirit that always denies"). D.L.S. quotes this in the Preface to her play *The Devil to Pay*.
133 German: "sentimentally devoted".
134 The first of the three examinations which candidates for the B.A. degree at Oxford were required to pass.

The Higher Certificate would be accepted for entrance in place of Responsions if Katherine could be crammed through in Maths.

Therefore, she must do the Higher Certificate again; and Miss Peacock must somehow contrive to haul her neck and crop to the logarithm point. This must have been the most wrongheaded decision ever arrived at by any educational muddlers. With an ounce of good will, Katherine could have furbished her Latin to the Responsions standard (which is not high) and crammed the Greek in a couple of terms; for languages came easily to her. But mathematics demanded the exercise of a faculty that she simply did not possess. And there was a further disadvantage about the Higher Certificate scheme, which she did not discover till later, but which Miss Dando, had she read the papers forwarded to her with any attention, ought to have known. But the Beaufort had a great record for scholarship and small experience in dealing with college authorities. It was determined that Katherine should struggle with the Higher Certificate that summer and go on next year to try for a scholarship, either at Shrewsbury College[135] or Queen Anne's.[136] And since Miss Dando said so, and the Lammases knew no better, and Katherine was helpless to object, it was so.

Katherine sometimes thought afterwards that the question must really have been decided by the characters of Miss Peacock and Miss Naylor. For one or the other of them a hopeless-looking task had to be set. Both of them knew Katherine Lammas as a girl who persistently shirked her work for them. Neither could have expected anything but disaster from a prolonged and uphill struggle with this immovable mass of wilful ignorance. Miss Naylor, younger and more temperamental, may have thought and said that the task was beyond the wit of mortal woman. Miss Peacock, valiant little pack-mule, supported by an indomitable will and an inflexible Non-Conformist conscience, would never permit herself to refuse anything. She accepted Katherine grimly and yet cheerfully, as she would, if necessary, have accepted fire and faggot. She took on extra hours of work. She sacrificed precious leisure to the explaining of mathematical puzzles before prayers in the Little Division Room. With fingers that grew pinker and chalkier with every desperate moment, she worked the long rows of equations upon the board and patiently disentangled the knots into which Katherine contrived to tie any problem, however simple.

It was not really Katherine's fault that the difficulties were so great. She was, mathematically speaking, on a level very little higher than that of Sally the almost-human chimpanzee. She could not do an addition sum without counting on her fingers. Oddly enough, it was not the mathematical principle of a problem that was her greatest stumbling-block; it was simply that

---

135 D.L.S. had already invented this name for a fictional Oxford College which she was later to use in *Gaudy Night*.
136 This is another fictitious name.

she could not do the working. She felt like the princess of fairy-tale who was required in one night to sift the millet from the wheat: the mass of detail paralysed her. It haunted her dreams and oppressed her waking hours. Yet from this wretchedness she made no attempt to deliver herself. Behind the barren playing-fields, the stuffy class-rooms, the uncompromising red brick houses of the Beaufort, stood thin and clear on the horizon the pale spires of Oxford, her spiritual home, the Holy City

> ...like one pearl
> No larger, though the goal of all the saints....[137]

It was unthinkable that Oxford should be lost. She was perfectly convinced that there, somehow, miraculously, she would find the freedom and the balance that she could not win at Carisbury. If Oxford could only be won over the bodies of dead logarithms, then the logarithms must be hacked down; even though heaven had provided her with nothing but a tin sword. Happily, the maths was the one lion in the way. The history that she had done the previous year would serve again; and the Modern Languages and English she could do on her head.

*

The puzzling thing about life when one is young is its refusal to show its significant pattern. Over the surface of things at the Beaufort there played a thousand lights and shadows which acquired a fleeting importance and then were forgotten. A good English essay written for Miss Chepstow in the VIth. A walk with a house-mate, made memorable by discussion of Goethe. A week out of a holiday spent with Marjorie Rawlings, and a resolution to go on the stage in consequence. Going home for the holidays and being filled with refreshment by the mere sight of a table beautifully laid with glass and silver. A performance of *The Three Musketeers*[138] seen in Town and reviving old loyalties. An expedition with others from the school to see a world-famous ruin. The discovery of Edgar Allan Poe's *Tales of Mystery and Imagination*[139] and of Morris' [*Defence*] *of Guenevere*. A curious recollection of being found by another girl reading the latter work and of being asked, "And does he say anything to justify her behaviour?", and of knowing instantly that a person who asked such a question could never understand the answer. The colour of the beech-leaves on the downs. These seemed good – but had they any bearing on reality?

137 From Tennyson's "The Holy Grail", lines 526–528: "I saw the spiritual city and all her spires/And gateways in a glory like one pearl/No larger, though the goal of all the saints..."
138 See Note 53.
139 Edgar Allan Poe (1809 –1849), born in Boston, Massachusetts. His *Tales of Mystery, Imagination and Horror* were published in 1852.

Then there were queer humiliations and angers. Once, Miss Dando was late for dinner, and Katherine, as the only VI form prefect at her table, had to begin carving the round of beef. She performed the task delicately, pleased to find that she could cut the slices paper-fine and even from edge to edge. Then came Miss Dando; she took the knife and fork, saying "You're doing it very nicely, but you're taking far too long". Then, while the table sniggered at Katherine, she attacked the joint in the manner of one who will have no trifling, hewing it down into a hideous saddle-back, carving it in thick gobbets. Twenty years, thirty years later Katherine could see the mangled and insulted joint and feel the old, angry sense of injury at work ill-done, at the placid indifference to clean performance.

Another scene: she was shifting desks in Form V, to assist Miss Greene in some activity or other. She said, "Shall you want me again after dinner, Miss Greene?" And Miss Greene replied, "Do you come from up North? What makes you say 'shall' instead of 'will'?" There was no English grammar-book available to expound for Katherine the intricate rule of "shall" and "will" that she observed by training and instinct. She brooded darkly over this rebuke for many years, till the admirable Mr Fowler[140] came somehow into her hands, and justified her of her natural Englishry.[141] Rebuke that was deserved she could forgive but not forget; undeserved rebuke was neither forgiven nor forgotten.

This unamiable trait had its good side. It made her cautious in condemnation. She would never rebuke a sin that she had shared. "I don't object to so-and-so", she would say, "I often do it myself." This condescending indulgence annoyed people. "I suppose", said an angry prefect, "you think you're such an important person that anything *you* do is justified." It did sound like that. "I only mean", said Katherine, "that *I'm* not justified in condemning it." The prefect snorted; and Katherine, deeply humiliated, made a mental note that she must find some more tactful way of expressing herself. Tact was, however, a subject not taught in school and is a difficult virtue to exercise when one is conscious of a continual angry sense of inferiority.

About this period, the game of knucklebones became a craze in School House. After lunch, the red serge coverings would be hastily snatched off the tables, and for half an hour the ear would be deafened by the furious clatter of the bones. Katherine tried her hand: this game attracted her, for

---

140 H. W. Fowler, author of *A Dictionary of Modern English Usage*, 1926. D. L. S. discussed the matter in an article entitled "The King's English", first published in Nash's *Pall Mall*, May 1935, later included in *Unpopular Opinions*, Gollancz, 1946, pp. 89–97, where it is entitled "The English Language"; for the point in question, see pp. 92–93.

141 It is said that Oscar Wilde (who was an Irishman) asked his editor to correct his use of the "wills" and "shalls", about which he never felt certain, in the manuscript of *The Portrait of Dorian Gray*. The classic Irish misuse is quoted in the cry of a drowning man: "I will drown and nobody shall save me!"

it did not call for team-spirit or for violent running, being a matter of individual sleight of hand. In the holidays, she searched the garden for the relics of by-gone legs of mutton and practised assiduously, returning to school an accomplished performer and the owner of one of the finest sets of bones in the house. She liked the names of the movements: creep-mouse, crawl-rat, horses in, piggies out, through'ems, pot'ems, everlastings; they held the smack of tradition. And those soft, loose-jointed hands with their great span, setting thumb and little finger in a line and straddling ten white keys at a stretch – those hands that were useless for hockey, incapable at tennis, feebly double-jointed at the key-board – they could gather and hold the widely scattered bones, even in "squares", and do it with some pretensions to a pretty style of play. Unhappily, knucklebones is not officially recognised in schools and places where they play games.

The year wore on once more to summer. Again the rumbling of desks resounded along the corridors. Katherine sat for the Higher Certificate in a grimmer spirit than she had done the year before. No pigeon came to play "coo-my-doo" in the rafters and wake memories of Earl Mar's Daughter.[142] Nobody's nose bled. There were grisly days when one went in, sick at the pit of the stomach and clutching a logarithm book.

Katherine attained the usual distinctions in the language subjects and scraped through the Maths with a mark or two to spare. Miss Peacock, in her neat, round hand, wrote her a letter of congratulation when the results were known.

"I am very pleased", she said, "with the way you put your back into the Mathematics. I did not think you had it in you."

Indomitable Miss Peacock; rigorously honest in her dealings, unshrinkingly candid with herself and with her fellows! "Sister Dinah" was never called "simply sweet"; nobody was ever known to have a "pash" for her; she was seldom given flowers, and there was no mad competitive rush to walk with her or carry her books. But for her was reserved the greatest tribute that the ruled can pay to the ruler. "You couldn't help liking and respecting Miss Peacock", said Katherine, "she was just."

So the gates of Oxford were taken by siege. It remained to storm the citadel of the college, and for that, an assault by scholarship was necessary, if Mr Lammas, harassed by the care of a church and rectory perpetually tumbling into disrepair, was not to be unduly pinched in the matter of fees.

Miss Dando, arming herself with a fresh array of forms and syllabuses, summoned Katherine to an interview. The Higher Certificate would serve as a passport to either university: did Katherine feel strongly in favour of Oxford, or would Cambridge do as well?

In face of this shock, Katherine showed a vigorous determination that the religious question had failed to arouse in her. She showed no signs of

142 Alexander Pope (1688–1744), *The Art of Sinking in Poetry*, chapter 2.

referring the decision to her parents or of being ready to submit to any-body's judgment. "Oh, no", she said, "it must be Oxford. All my people are Oxford." Miss Dando looked as though she found the reason inade-quate, but Katherine was firm. "I've never thought of going anywhere but to Oxford. I couldn't bear to go to Cambridge." "You would be nearer your home at Cambridge", suggested Miss Dando. This seemed to Katherine to be a ridiculous reason for choosing a university, but what could she reply that would be cogent? One could not say that it would be impossible to wear light blue on boat-race day, though the thought of one's self and one's father in opposite camps on such an occasion was quite dreadful. One might say that Cambridge was sacred to science and math-ematics; but there was a Modern Language Tripos there, undoubtedly, and for all one could prove, it might be a good one. Miss Dando waited. Katherine fell back upon the categorical imperative. "I don't want to go to Cambridge", she said, "I want to go to Oxford."

"Very well", said Miss Dando.

The next question was, "Which college?" Here again, Katherine knew what she wanted. "Somerville", she said promptly.

"Why?"

Katherine gave as her reason the fact that Somerville also was "in the family", though only (as it were) by marriage, for her late Uncle Peter had married a Somerville girl.[143] Her own most heartfelt reason was that Somerville was undenominational.

She was unhappy at this time about religion. There seemed to be two different Christian religions, which had nothing in common except that both were connected with the same set of historical facts. The Christianity which surrounded her at school gave her that curious sense of physical repulsion which afflicts healthy people at the sight of the village idiot: it was ugly; it shambled in its walk; it fawned upon one with an odious and leering familiarity; when it uttered the lovely speech of the Scriptures, the words came out distorted – thick and unlike themselves. She could not believe that it was the same Christianity that had built the great churches and sur-rounded the name of God with scarlet and blue and gold and strange birds and flowers in the painted missals, and set the story of Calvary to lilting dance-music "all under the leaves of life".[144] In the book called *Orthodoxy*[145] there were glimpses of this other Christianity, which was beautiful and adventurous and queerly full of humour; but if that was orthodoxy, what

143 D. L S.'s uncle, Henry Devenish Leigh (d. 1903) married Alice Maud Bayliss who was at Somerville Hall (as it was then called) from 1881 to 1884.

144 In the first chapter of her novel *Busman's Honeymoon*, published in June 1937, D. L. S. quotes the following lines: "My lady gave me a tiger,/ A sleek and splendid tiger,/ A striped and shining tiger,/ All under the leaves of life". In a reply to a reader who asked her who the author was, she said, "I wrote it myself".

145 See Note 117.

doxy did the Establishment embrace? If only, thought Katherine, one could get to a place where religion was not bound up with the constitution, one might clear this difficulty up. An undenominational college sounded like the right sort of place. In the meantime, one kept a firm grasp on the solid bulk of Mr Chesterton, while one sought to withdraw one's feet from the sticky slough of gawdliness that threatened to suck one down.

Miss Dando accepted the choice of Somerville in so far as she wrote that college down as "first choice" upon the entrance forms. She was not unaware of Katherine's spiritual instability; rash words and unseemly paradoxes had been reported to her. The method she used in dealing with such cases was to select the waverer to walk with her to early service. Thus, one approached the Altar with the pleasant certainty in one's mind that one was at the very least a lost sheep, if not an accomplished goat. One was, unhappily, not past praying for; in the deep, fervent bleating of Miss Dando at one's side – "the reme -e -mbrance of them is Grie-ievous to us, the Burhden of them is Intohlerable" – one recognised the vicarious expression of what ought to have been one's own abasement. At Somerville, surely, no don would have the presumption to pray loudly for one's sins into one's own ear. In the meantime, one must put up with it as best one could, and attend early service only just so often as was necessary if one wished to avoid enquiry and explanation.

*

In her third Spring term at school, Katherine had the interesting experience of nearly dying. Measles broke out in Wellington House, at a moment when Miss Dando was away at a Headmistress' Conference. In her absence, Miss James the House-mistress sensibly shut up the Wellingtonians and forbade all intercourse. This naturally interfered very much with the school work.

It was commonly said at the Beaufort that Miss Dando recognised only two kinds of illness: one was asthma, from which she suffered herself; the other was broken bones, which she could scarcely ignore; though she made a point of cheering the sufferer by telling her that it was all her own fault for running about so clumsily and carelessly as to break her arms and legs. Common report may have been too sweeping in its assertions; the fact, however, remains that Miss Dando, on her return, called the school together and issued a speech from the throne about measles.

"In my absence", said she, "Miss James very rightly and properly segregated Wellington House. That was *quite* the correct action for her to take under the circumstances. I do not think, however, we need go quite so far as that. I have let the *well* people at Wellington come back. I have put the *house* out of bounds for the rest of you. Now, you must all be sensible and not sit about closely together *indoors* or run into infection. I have arranged that everybody shall have extra opportunities for *fresh air* and *exercise*. The great thing is not to *think* you are going to catch measles and you won't get it."

Whether the fresh air and exercises were insufficient or the psychological defences inadequate, or for some other reason, the result did not justify this bold course. Out of two hundred girls, every girl who had not had measles before succumbed. The small sanatorium was packed to suffocation. Two trained nurses arrived, and spoke loudly and bitterly of the lack of sanitary convenience. Katherine and one other girl got the disease in a severe form and developed pneumonia. She was soon too ill even to be excited by the visits of the doctor – a very handsome man of whom it was the fashion to be enamoured.

Mrs Lammas came down and established herself firmly at Katherine's bedside. What she said to Miss Dando is not on record; the worst had happened, and no words now could mend it. Mrs Lammas was a skilful and devoted nurse and contrived to secure the good-will of the professionals, who, overworked and harassed to death, were probably glad enough of her help. In the end, Katherine attained the alarming dignity of a day-nurse and night-nurse of her own.

She had never been really homesick till she fell ill. Now, through days and nights of misery and delirium, she pleaded weakly and repeatedly to be allowed to go home. She felt that she must be well again, if she could only get back to the cool green garden with its ancient ivy-hung trees, to the seemly beauty of crystal and silver and fine starched linen, away from the ugly school surroundings and the harsh clamour of bells. She was a good patient, taking what she was told to take and submitting herself readily to sick-room discipline. After the first day of terror, when she knew she had pneumonia, she never consciously thought of death; but there was something unconscious within her that knew the menace and resisted it with the ferocity of a trapped rat.

A night came when they called up Mrs Lammas hastily. A specialist had been sent for, but he had not arrived, and the school doctor said: "I think I must act now, if at all." Mrs Lammas replied, "Do as you think best." In a dim dream, Katherine was aware of the doctor doing something with her arm, sitting beside her, handling an apparatus of rubber and glass. She learned afterwards, with interest, that it had been a matter of a saline injection. It was a pity that all these things were done when she was too ill to sit up and take notice.

The miracle was worked. The disease withdrew, snarling and baffled. Convalescence began. Reluctant, not mollified even by the unexpected relish of weak tea administered through a spout, Katherine came back to the realisation that she was still there, that the burden of living must be taken up again, with exams to be faced and the wearisome routine of school life to be coped with. She was annoyed that she should not have been allowed to die peacefully. Mrs Lammas and the doctor, having seen well enough how the school preyed on her mind, had her removed, as soon as possible, to a nursing home. The transit was amusing; one was taken down the town, swathed in blankets, in an open fly, and was carried head-first up an outside staircase to a balcony and so through a window. Everything was fresh, clean and attractive. School receded into the distance. The home was full of entertaining gossip about the doctor and about other patients. The appendicitis next door got on too fast, over-ate himself and was sick in the night. An unexplained trampling of feet went past one's door one evening – heavy, mysterious. "It sounded", said Katherine, mischievously quoting "like a coffin a-walking upstairs",[146] and was delighted to note, in the nurse's embarrassed face, that her shot had hit the mark.

One piece of knowledge that Katherine gained from this experience was that the act of dying was probably not formidable. If only one was ill enough, one did not care.

She was also touched and surprised to find that, in spite of everything, many Beaufortians liked her. They sent anxious messages and gifts of flowers. One pair of girls, who she had supposed despised her, came in person, carrying a freesia in a pot.

She also discovered that brilliance in one subject did not prevent a person from being oddly limited in his ideas on other unrelated topics. When she was well enough to need the consolation of words, she asked Mrs Lammas to read to her. "I want", she said, "to hear 'The Lady of Shalott'." Mrs Lammas, knowing her offspring, found nothing odd in this request. She departed forthwith to the school, secured the loan of a Tennyson, and read as desired:

> Willows whiten, aspens quiver,
> Little breezes dusk and shiver
> Through the wave that runs for ever
> Flowing down to Camelot....[147]
> The gemmy bridle glittered free
> Like to some branch of stars we see
> Hung in the golden Galaxy....[148]

The doctor was uneasy. Would not a nice detective story be better for his patient than wearying her brain with this hard stuff? Poetry and all that? Katherine said, No, she couldn't fix her mind on detective stories. How could any sort of story be more soothing that those rich, lovely, familiar words flowing so easily into their smooth and satisfying pattern? Was it

146 R.H.Barham, *The Ingoldsby Legends*, "Patty Morgan the Milkmaid's Story", Fytte 1, stanza 16, line 10.
147 Part I, lines 10–14.
148. Part III, lines 10–12.

possible that anyone so clever about pneumonia could be so stupid about poetry? Mrs Lammas, between the doctor and her daughter, stood by her daughter. Here, her instinct was infallible. When they had had all the favourite bits out of Tennyson, she produced "Up at a Villa, Down in the City". Katherine had somehow missed reading this poem before, but it caught her fancy instantly:

> Mid the sharp, short emerald wheat, scarce risen three fingers well,
> The wild tulip, at end of its tube, blows out its great red bell
> Like a thin, clear bubble of blood....[149]

It had to be read over and over again, doctor or no doctor.

Cheered and strengthened, Katherine, with a tremor at the heart but a kind of resolute courtesy, consented to receive Canon Tusher. He wheezed his way in, the good man, carrying a large umbrella and talked kindly for some minutes before suggesting that he should say a prayer. Before performing this exercise, he stood the umbrella carefully upright in a corner. This tickled Katherine into an acquiescent mood; though, to be sure, it would have been better fun to see

> our Lady borne smiling and smart
> With a pink gauze gown all spangles, and seven swords stuck in her
> heart![150]

Recovered at length, she was taken home to recuperate, after treating the nurses to a fine dramatic rendering of the dream-scene from *Richard III*, in which the performer's unfortunate and persistent shortness of breath assorted not too badly with the agitated state of mind of the character.

[The manuscript of this section breaks off here]

149 A poem by Robert Browning, stanza 5, lines 3–5.
150 Ibid., stanza 9, lines 14–15.

BOOK THREE

I

Katherine's dominating sensation, as soon as the existence of the baby had been duly confirmed by the doctor, was one of triumph, mingled with surprise. She was so unaccustomed to success in any physical undertaking, that she fully expected to have to go through life making excuses for the non-appearance of a baby. She had determined to say, with perfect truth, that she disliked children, and leave it to be inferred that she had selfishly refused to have one. That, to be sure, would have displayed her in an unamiable light, but it was better to be misjudged than to be pitied. Now, however, it seemed that this particular awkwardness was to be spared her. She was going to have a baby, exactly like everybody else. She was pleased with her body. It was behaving as a good servant. It might not be able to

"Katherine Lammas" as an adult

play hockey or tennis, but in this important particular it had not let her down. Katherine Lammas had been a speckled bird, but Katherine Somers could fly with the rest of the flock.

It was some little time before she could nerve herself to announce the tidings to Mrs Lammas. She dreaded an outbreak of solicitude. Not to make the announcement would, of course, be unkind. What she would really have liked to do would have been to conceal the whole business from the world till it was over – to write to her mother one day and say: "By the way, I had a baby last night." Unhappily, the physical and social structure of things made this procedure impractical. She must tell Mrs Lammas, and tell her at once – that was only fair. She wrote accordingly:

> We were thinking of going to Italy this summer,[152] but apparently I'm due to have a baby in July, so we shall have to change our plans. It *would* happen just then, wouldn't it? However, Geoffrey seems very pleased about it and doesn't mind having his holiday upset! Please don't worry, will you – because I never felt better in my life.

Mrs Lammas replied with a kind of paean of delight which rather affront-ed Katherine. It seemed to echo her own surprise rather too much – in spite of the fact that Mrs Lammas mentioned that she had been expecting the news. There seemed to be no privacy about anything. Everybody, apparently, had been sitting round wondering and calculating, for the next day brought a letter from Aunt Emily, to whom Mrs Lammas must have instantly written. Aunt Emily said that they had all been hoping for this and that she had thoughtfully pushed the news onto the other aunts and uncles – "as I am sure, dear, you will have so *many* letters to write and they will be so *anxious* to hear the news. We shall all be thinking about you." Confound them, thought Katherine, have they nothing better to think about?

Geoffrey felt that this interest was all very proper, and said that Mrs Lammas must be asked down to Ridings. Katherine agreed and sent the invitation. It was quite right, of course. This was an occasion in which a woman needed her mother. Mrs Duberly, in whom Geoffrey had appar-ently confided, said as much:

"I'm so glad, dear, your mother's coming. It will be nice for you to have her. There's nobody like one's mother, is there, especially when it's the first."

"No, of course not", said Katherine; and told herself that, whatever she felt, she must try and be very nice to her mother.

Mrs Lammas, when she arrived, was excited and anxious, but was obvi-ously doing her best to be tactful. The real trouble was the old trouble –

---

152 An example of the vacillation of the date. No plans for going to Italy on holiday could have been made during World War I. See Introduction, p. xxiv

that she did not really like the business of sex and babies and that her natural tendency was to cross her bridges before she came to them. She fussed.
There was no denying that. She did fuss; and her determination to be
cheerful and encouraging was in constant conflict with her underlying feeling that all this was too much for Katherine and that the whole baby business was very unfair. She kept on telling Geoffrey that Katherine must not
over-exert herself and must be given every consideration. Dr Spooner, on
the other hand, told Katherine to do exactly as she liked and pay no attention to the baby, beyond a reasonable care for her own strength. Geoffrey,
attacked on one side by his mother-in-law and on the other by the doctor,
became distracted and irritable.

"I do wish I could go through it for you, darling", said Mrs Lammas, one
morning when Katherine was not feeling up to much.

"Dash it all", said Katherine, "why should you? It's all right. I've only
got a bit of headache."

Mrs Lammas said, rather mournfully, that Katherine must expect
headaches, and worse things.

"I know, Mother", said Katherine. She had read up the subject and
knew it by this time from A to Z. Nobody could ever understand that she
disliked being told by word of mouth what she could discover more rapidly and impersonally from the printed page.

Dr Spooner was her great ally.

"Don't you let them talk you into feeling ill", he said. "Seventy per
cent of all this morning sickness stuff is nervousness and twenty per cent
indigestion."

"I thought it was due to chemical changes in the blood", said Katherine.

"That's the other ten per cent", said Dr Spooner, cheerfully. "It won't
hurt you if you do get it and it won't last long. Never mind what people tell
you – I believe most of them revel in illness. You follow the example of your
cat there – you won't find her sticking her feet up on a sofa and worrying
about the future."

Katherine looked at Pasht and grinned.

"All right", she said, "I *won't* be sick."

She was not sick.

Next to the doctor, the most helpful person was Great-aunt Agatha.

"Dear Katherine", she wrote in her old-fashioned running hand, now
becoming rather shaky:

> That chattering magpie Emily has written *in haste*, as she says, to tell me
> you are going to have a baby. I don't know what business it is of hers. I
> expect you are being fussed to death. If you find them all getting too
> much for you, come and pay me a visit. I should like to have somebody
> intelligent to talk to for a change. I am so tired of these young women
> who seem to be running the War. It is a mercy that Geoffrey is out of it

for good, otherwise you would be worrying your head off about *him*.
Don't let your mother get on your nerves, and don't let her stuff you up
with her medicines. You never were constipated, thank goodness, and if
Margaret had not bullied her inside with aperients, she would not have
had such a bad time with *you*, my dear. Look after your bowels and the
baby will look after itself. They are much tougher than most people
think, and all you need is plenty of green stuff, *not* pills. People in my
day ate far too much starch. It is a nuisance that fruit is so difficult to get
now, but you will be all right with that big garden at Ridings. I expect
you think I am just as fussy as the rest of them, so I won't say any more
about that, only that I shall be very glad to see you any time. My sight is
not as good as it was, and when you come you can read me some of the
new books, if there are any good ones. Most of the novels I have had
from the library lately have been simply drivel. What nonsense it is to
say that wars bring out the best in a nation. If you ask me, they only stir
up all the mud and rubbish from the bottom. Did you hear that poor
little Pettigrew had been suspected of being *a spy* because he went out
into his garden last week with an electric torch and was seen by some
fool or other who thought he was signalling to Zeppelins? It turned out
that he had thrown a bedroom slipper at a tom-cat, and his teeth fell
out into the garden and he had to go down and look for them.
Fortunately the policeman was quite sensible and found the teeth with
his bull's eye lantern, but it caused quite an excitement in Rye, so
Marcella tells me. Well, my dear, you have my best wishes and congrat-
ulations on being so clever. I suppose Geoffrey takes all the credit. Give
him my love and say I hope his leg is keeping pretty well.

> Your affectionate Great-aunt Agatha.
> P.S. I suppose I shall now be a great-great-aunt, if that is the
> proper word. The young man or woman or whatever it is had
> better learn to call me Ancestress, though that is rather a mouthful.

Katherine did not show this letter to her mother, nor yet to Geoffrey, who
never liked Great-aunt Agatha's allusions to her bowels. The day after she
had received it, Mrs Lammas happened to advise the taking of an occasional "little pill", with the result that Katherine got a fit of the giggles.

"She's a little hysterical", said her mother. "One must expect it at these
times."

"Oh, yes, quite", said Geoffrey.

"Take no notice", said Mrs Lammas.

"No, no", said Geoffrey. "I met Anderson today", he added laboriously,
"and he told me that French…."

At this point Katherine became so convulsed that Geoffrey grew quite
alarmed and – remembering what he had read about the proper treatment
of hysteria – said sharply:

"Come, Katherine, this won't do. Pull yourself together."

"She'll be all right", said Mrs Lammas. "Leave her to me. Now Kitty – "

"Oh, *don't* be such asses!" said Katherine, her amusement vanishing in the old sense of irritation at being ordered about. "Do for goodness' sake leave me alone. I was only laughing… Why shouldn't I laugh? If you only knew how comic you are. You're exactly like people in a book… Pills, my dear! Pills!"

"Come along, old girl", said Geoffrey. "You're a bit upset. It's all right. Just simmer down and take it quietly."

"Put your feet up on the sofa, dear", suggested Mrs Lammas.

"Sofa be damned!" said Katherine, bouncing to her feet. And remembering Dr Spooner, she began to giggle again. "You don't find Pasht putting her feet up on the sofa."

"Pasht?" said Geoffrey, beginning to think his wife was really a little light-headed.

"Or taking pills, either", said Katherine. "Come along, Geoff, don't look so dazed. Come along to the billiard-room and knock the balls about."

"My dear", said Mrs Lammas.

"And if you", said Katherine, "hadn't bullied your inside with aperients, you wouldn't – oh, sorry, Doctor! Did I hurt you? You spoilt my exit."

"Did I?" said Dr Spooner. He had been standing on the threshold when Katherine had rather suddenly opened the door and trodden on his toes. "That's a pity. Couldn't you do it over again for my benefit?"

Larkins, seeing that no announcement was required, flitted away through the hall.

"I was accused of being hysterical", said Katherine, solemnly. "I'm glad you came to vindicate my character."

"Hysterical? Nonsense. Least hysterical woman I ever saw. What's it all about?"

"Bowels", said Katherine. "Did you come to see me, or did you only drop in friendly-like?"

"Well, I really came about the books for the hospital, but if anybody's bowels want attending to, I'm your man. Whose bowels? What's wrong with 'em?"

Nobody seemed eager to answer this question. Geoffrey said:

"Well, well. I think I'll just go and – er – See you later, Spooner. You'll like to have a talk with Katherine about – books and all that."

"Coward!" said Katherine.

"Well", said Dr Spooner, "let's all sit down, and have a nice talk about bowels. Begin from the beginning."

"I think", said Katherine, wickedly, "Mother would like to tell you about it with me out of the room. I shall go and play billiards by myself. You'll know where to find me."

She was executing a long and successful break and humming gently to herself when Dr Spooner entered the billiard-room ten minutes later, grinning broadly.

"Now then, Mrs Somers", he said, "what was the joke?"

"Great-aunt Agatha", said Katherine. "I've been dying to show it to somebody."

Geoffrey, anxiously pacing past the billiard-room window in the dusk, under a transparent pretext of fetching something or other from the end of the verandah, glanced in, to see his wife and Dr Spooner in ecstasies of merriment. He walked round by the garden-door and came casually in upon them.

"Hullo!" said Geoffrey, "you in here?"

"Look here, Somers", said Dr Spooner, "you really must protect your wife from pills and potions and kindly attentions. Otherwise she'll die of laughing or something and I shall lose two patients. There's nothing whatever the matter with her, but don't you give way to hysteria."

"Me?" said Geoffrey, indignantly.

"There", said the doctor. "You don't like to be accused of it. Nobody does."

"I'll get those books for you", said Katherine.

"Oh, thanks awfully, Mrs Somers. Now, see here, old man. Don't you let any of these silly women stuff you up with stories about young mothers being unbalanced or any of that rot. Your wife's the most level-headed woman I know, only she's got a highly-developed sense of humour. Treat her as an ordinary human being, can't you? She knows what's good for her a great deal better than you do, or her mother either. And if she says she doesn't want dosing or fussing over, back her up like a sensible man."

"Well, how am I to know?" said Geoffrey. "Women – and all that – "

"Mumbo-jumbo", said Dr Spooner. "Mumbo-jumbo. Fills up half the hospitals. All very good for my trade, but I don't want extra work just now."

Geoffrey shook his head.

"Well", he said, "I don't know, I'm sure. Her mother says I ought to use my influence to get Katherine to give up her work at the Clothing Centre."

"Don't you start using influence", said Dr Spooner, irascibly. "Influence is the biggest home-breaker I know. Your wife's not a child. Why can't you leave it to her?"

*

"But there it is", said Mrs Halliday with a sigh, brushing the cake-crumbs from her knee and accepting a Turkish cigarette. "You give up the best years of your life to your husband and children, and then, when you get to be my age, you find out that you're not wanted any longer."

"I don't understand", said Katherine. "What do you mean exactly by 'given up the best years of your life'?"

Mrs Halliday looked blank, as people do when their fundamental assumptions are challenged.

"I mean", said Katherine, "you'd have had to do *something* with those years, wouldn't you, even if you hadn't married and had children? It's not like giving away money. That is depriving yourself of something, because, if you hadn't given it away, you'd still have it to spend. But you can't save up your youth to spend later, can you?"

"No – it's a pity one can't", said Mrs Halliday. "It's so dreadful to think of getting old and losing one's teeth. You're slim, that's a great thing to be thankful for. Do you know, I've put on seven pounds since April, even though I'm terribly careful what I eat and do my exercises every morning. You'd think Kim would have some sympathy, but he says I'm a fool to bother. As if it wasn't for his sake that I try to look young."

"If he doesn't appreciate the effort, I shouldn't bother", said Katherine. "Why not take him at his word?"

"Ah, my dear, that's easy to say. But whatever he may *say*, he'll soon start grumbling if I let myself go. One's got to look young these days. Besides, I don't want the children to be ashamed of their mother."

"I didn't realise that it was all done on their account."

"Oh, yes. That's what I mean. You don't know what I've sacrificed for them one way and another. I've simply slaved for them. Why, I was married at twenty, and Jim wasn't in anything like such a good position then, you know. We started in quite a little house with one servant and I always made it such a point that Jim should have everything nice in his home to bring his friends to. Friends are *so* important to anybody in business. I really had to work hard, my dear, to keep myself and the house always looking bright and pretty; but I said to myself, the very day we were married, 'Jim's career must come first', and I've always stuck to that."

"Before your own career, do you mean?"

"Before everything", said Mrs Halliday simply.

"But if you hadn't married Mr Halliday, what should you have done?"

"Well, of course there was Walter Grimby", said Mrs Halliday, thoughtfully. "But he was quite dreadfully poor and my people wouldn't hear of it. Though he did very well afterwards, till he was killed in the War, poor fellow."

"Well, it would have been the same thing with him, then", said Katherine.

"Oh, yes, of course. After all, that's a woman's job, isn't it? My mother used to say, wherever you see a successful man you'll find there's been a woman behind him. A mother or a wife, you know, helping him to get on."

"Well then", said Katherine, pertinaciously – not stopping to dispute this pronouncement – "if you think that sort of thing was your job, I don't see what you gave up. Or would you have had a happier life if you hadn't married at all?"

"Oh, no", said Mrs Halliday, shocked. "A woman can't be really happy without a husband and babies. I know some of them pretend to like being old maids, but it's sour grapes, really, isn't it?"

"I don't know", said Katherine. "I think some of them are genuinely devoted to their jobs. If *they* marry, they *do* give up something. But you didn't want to be an artist, or a musician or a business woman or anything, did you?"

"Oh, no. I was never what you would call brainy, though I've often told Jim I've more common sense in my little finger than he has in his whole body. I always think that women are so much more sensible than men, don't you?"

Katherine said: "Some are more sensible than others", and then wondered if this sounded rude. But Mrs Halliday obviously took it as a compliment.

"Well, that's true. My sister Phyllis was always a scatterbrain. Mother used to say, 'What will you do when you're married, Phyllis, if you go on being so dreamy and forgetful?' But she never did get married, poor dear. She breeds cats, of all things, and I'm sure" – here Mrs Halliday lowered her voice and laughed a little – "I'm sure it's a wonder to me that she ever remembers to – well, you know – to marry her pets properly. I mean, you have to keep an eye on things, you know, they're such active little things, always clambering about, and Phyllis is so vague, it's amazing that she doesn't get more misalliances. But I believe she does quite well", admitted Mrs Halliday, with obvious surprise at this contradictory state of things, "and gets big prizes for her kittens."

"I expect she just happened to be interested in cats", said Katherine.

"It seems unnatural", said Mrs Halliday, "giving up the best years of one's life to cats."

"But that's just what I mean. One must give up one's years to something. If it isn't a husband and children, it's cats, or painting, or writing books, or keeping accounts. And I don't suppose either the cats or the account-books are particularly grateful for it – so why should one's husband and children be?"

"Ah!" said Mrs Halliday, "you're so clever, dear Mrs Somers. But when you're my age, you'll understand what I mean. Just at present, of course, you're all in all to your children; you must be very happy. I think that's the happiest time of one's life when they are still dependent on their mother for everything. On their father too, of course, but that's not quite the same thing, is it?"

"I shouldn't like to think they were entirely dependent on one for everything", said Katherine, disputatiously. "I want them to be able to stand up for themselves. Supposing I was to die tomorrow."

"My dear Mrs Somers, you mustn't talk like that. It's quite morbid. I always envy you your splendid health."

"Still, I might be knocked down by a car or something. This road's full of careless drivers."

"Yes, isn't it? Too dreadfully reckless and wicked. That's exactly what I'm always saying. They go dashing about, killing people and never stop to think about the poor children who may be crippled for life or lose their parents. You really ought to be careful. I do hope that chauffeur of yours is a steady, reliable kind of man. I often think when I see him going along so fast, what a frightful thing it would be if there was an accident, and poor Mr Somers away in town all day."

"Perhaps it's as well he is," said Katherine flippantly. "Then the children would have *one* parent left at any rate."

"It's nothing to joke about. With all the traffic in London, it's a miracle that anybody gets home safe and sound. I think that all this fast driving ought to be put a stop to. Parkins has his orders *never* to go faster than twenty-five miles an hour under any circumstances. If everybody did the same we shouldn't have all these terrible accidents."

"I'm afraid we should never get anywhere. The roads would be jammed solid from end to end."

"Would they?" said Mrs Halliday, doubtfully. "That's what Jim says, and he and you are both so clever. I suppose you must be right. But it does seem wrong that we should be obliged to go so fast and kill all these people."

II

"Well, I suppose I shall have to behave like a perfect gentleman and divorce you." Geoffrey's face cleared. It was evident that this was the point to which he had been deviously working up, and he was transparently grateful that he had not been obliged to make the suggestion himself.

"Hang it all! When you put it like that, it does sound rotten. But it does seem the best way out of it. I've got to think of Lilias, poor kid. It's my fault, getting her into this ghastly mess. You don't know what a swine I feel. But I knew I could trust you to do the decent thing."

"That was very confiding of you", said Katherine, a little acidly.

"You're wonderful", said Geoffrey, not hearing or not noticing the tone of the remark. "You're so different from the ordinary woman. You're broadminded. You always understand. You couldn't let anybody down if you tried. Of course, I'll make it all as easy and simple as possible. It won't be defended of course, and there'll be practically nothing in the papers. C.... will put it all through quietly."

"There's the children, of course", said Katherine.

"Yes, that's the beastly part of it", said Geoffrey. "I've thought about that a devil of a lot. But, after all, they're growing up – and it's quite a common thing nowadays. You'll be able to make them understand – put it to them sensibly – and sympathetically – I know you can do it so well, much better than I could – I should, I mean, it would make me a feel a bit of a fool. And after all, Molly's engaged – almost as good as married, and Stephen's fifteen –

"Oh, Geoffrey!" said Katherine. She began to giggle idiotically. "It was only last holidays you said it was indecent for Stephen to know about Mendelism."

The whole thing began to seem so funny that she laughed and laughed, unable to stop herself.

"Damn it", said Geoffrey, "that's different. I mean to say – ." He fished about in his mind, but the difference, which had seemed so clear and obvious, eluded him.

"Stop laughing!" he shouted, irritably. "You *would* try and be clever about it, just when I'm so upset. That's what's wrong with you, Katherine – you're so inhuman. Just at this important crisis in our lives" (he felt the phrase to be pompous and ridiculous but plunged on angrily) "you try to make me look small by dragging in Mendelism."

"I'm sorry", said Katherine, "but it really is rather comic. But it may make things easier for Stephen. I mean, if he can see it in terms of piebald mice – "

"Piebald mice!"

But Katherine's hysterical humour had got the better of her. She knew she was saying all the wrong things, spoiling Geoffrey's careful, dignified, manly scene of apology, showing him to himself in a humiliating light, but she couldn't help herself. "After all", she thought, "I'm giving him every excuse for his behaviour. I'm justifying him, really."

"Come, Katherine", said Geoffrey, in a kind, sensible tone. ("It's been a shock to her", he thought, "and I'm in the wrong after all.")

"I know I've behaved abominably to you but don't let's lose our tempers. I'm in your hands, absolutely. I – this means a great deal to me, Katherine. It's madness, I dare say, but men do go mad from time to time. If you don't understand, I can't explain. You've been a marvellous wife to me. We've been very happy – at least I know I have and I hope I've made you happy, too. It's not that. I haven't the least fault to find with you. It's only...."

"Only that you've fallen in love with Lilias."

"Well, yes, that's what it comes to."

"Just one of those overwhelming things that you can't argue about?"

"That's just it. You can't. We just fell for one another. One can't explain these things."

"No. But it seems that I've got to explain them to Molly and Stephen."

"Er – I'm afraid it is going to be a bit awkward. But you'll find a way of doing it."

"I feel like Mother – 'it always falls on me to say the disagreeable things'. Well, I'll try, Geoffrey, if you really mean it."

"That's awfully decent of you." Geoffrey sighed as though a weight had been lifted from his mind, and then was struck with remorse. "I am putting a lot on to your shoulders, old girl, but you're their mother and – er – it'll come better from you. I say, do you suppose they'll mind very much?"

"They won't like it, Geoffrey. No children do – really. And they're at rather a bad age for it."

"Yes, Stephen's at school, and of course – "

"I'm not so much bothered about Stephen. He's not a Hamlet sort of person. I mean, I don't think it'll give him any complexes or anything of that kind. But I'm afraid he may be rather angry about it."

Geoffrey frowned. He never found Stephen easy to get on with, and the thought of encountering those youthful and accusing eyes was not comfortable.

"There must be plenty of other boys in the same position. Dash it, they won't worry him about it. We're not living in the days of *Eric: or Little by Little*."[153]

"Oh, no. I think Stephen can look after himself as far as school is concerned."

"Then what's the trouble?"

Katherine did not like to say, "He'll think you've treated me very badly", though she knew quite well that Stephen would think exactly that. She replied quietly:

"I think Stephen will take it all right. He's more interested in things than in human relationships. But it's going to upset Molly a lot. Julian's people won't like it – and she's very sensitive to what other people think. You know, Geoffrey, I believe you'd have a much better chance if you tackled Molly yourself."

"Me? Good God, Katherine, you can't mean that. I couldn't – dash it! It's indecent! My own daughter – no! That's a woman's job."

"All the tiresome jobs are women's jobs", said Katherine, wearily. "All right. I'll tell Molly – but I won't answer for the consequences. Molly likes things put in a romantic light, and I'm not very good at that. I get on better with the really modern kind of girl. Molly's a throw-back."

"Thank God she is!"

"Yes, but that kind's more difficult to deal with. Molly's rather hard in her way, you know."

153 See Note 59.

"Molly?" exclaimed Geoffrey in amazement. "Molly hard? That's just where you've never understood her. She's a sweet kid. Affectionate. Stephen's as hard as nails, I grant you, but not Molly. I am afraid she may be rather cut up about it, though – feel that the bloom's been knocked off things a bit. It's a blessing she's got Julian to think about."

Katherine groaned. Julian was going to be a definite snag – Julian, with his perfect clothes and manners and his career opening so neatly out in front of him, like a set of railway lines, as he advanced. Julian would very much dislike being drawn into a family complication. And Molly would tackle each of her parents in turn and nag at them in her soft, insistent way – Katherine was suddenly rather sorry for Julian, and then was seized with a pang of self-reproach. How could she possibly be sorry for anyone who was marrying her charming daughter? A nice mother she was, to be sure.

"My God, Katherine", said Geoffrey. "If you think it's going to wreck Molly's life, perhaps I'd better chuck it. At least I can't very well do that altogether, but we might go on as we have been doing – damn it – I owe a duty to you and the children. I could tell Lilias – "

He looked so dismayed at the prospect that Katherine began to laugh again, to cover, even from herself, a curious sensation of nausea. She had already adjusted herself to the idea of a divorce. It was beastly, but Geoffrey's suggested compromise was a great deal worse.

"You idiot! How could we go on in the same way now that I know?"

"Oh, I don't know. Lots of people manage."

"Well, it must be foul", said Katherine. "I couldn't manage all the pretence. And having to make out I didn't know what people meant when they hinted things. Besides, it would be all dreadfully immoral, and I should look such a fool. You wouldn't like it in my place. I can't see you in the role of *mari complaisant*."

"It's different for a man."

Katherine reflected exasperatedly that Geoffrey had been making this remark for eighteen years, without ever realising that it cut no ice with her. It was not only that it was an assertion, not an argument. She disliked its bland assumption that a woman had no feelings, or that if she had they did not count. After all, she ought to know best what her own feelings were. But she wouldn't go into that now.

"Perhaps it is different. The husband is supposed to be funny and the wife to be rather piteous. But I absolutely refuse to be piteous. It's a thing I dislike very much."

"Anybody would think you *wanted* to divorce me", grumbled Geoffrey. The interview, which had begun so well, was taking an unsatisfactory turn.

"Of course I don't want to divorce you. But I'd rather do it and have done with it than go on like Brer Tarrypin, loungin' round and sufferin' ".

Brer Tarrypin! Now what had put that into her head? She was back in the old Oxford nursery, sitting on her father's knee.[154] Poor Mr Lammas! Whatever would he have said if he could have heard his daughter arranging to divorce a faithless husband! How pained he would have been! And Mrs Lammas would have bristled like a hedge-hog at the thought that any man could deal – oh dear!

Geoffrey grinned rather sheepishly.

"No, you're quite right. It wouldn't do at all. It would be horrible. Besides…." He stared vaguely out of the window. Katherine knew quite well what that look meant. It was the look with which he faced the necessity of sacking the gardener or having a row with a taxi-driver. He was mentally picturing the interview with Lilias when he told her he had decided against a divorce.

"Poor old Geoffrey!" thought Katherine, with a sudden pang. "He's very much in love and she's much too young to be considerate. I wonder if I ought to be beastly in his own interests."

"Geoffrey," she said suddenly, "what's Lilias like? You haven't told me."

He started.

"I didn't think you'd want to know. She – she's only a kid, you know. She's – well, dash it! She's fair and slight and – well, I don't know quite what to say. She makes you think of a – of a water-lily."

"Peroxide kitten – with claws", was Katherine's mental translation.

"She's horribly inexperienced. I don't suppose she's ever been really up against things before. That's why – damn it, Katherine, you really can't expect me to go into all that."

"Oh, gosh!" thought Katherine. Aloud she said:

"Yes, I see. Are you sure you're not – well, a little bit mature for her?"

"She doesn't seem to think so", said Geoffrey, with a fatuous smirk, which was somehow rather pathetic. "It does sound ghastly and all that, but she seems to think I'm – well – something rather wonderful. I can't help it, but she does. I suppose, taking it altogether, she was a bit overwhelmed and – all that."

"Geoffrey! I'm not quite clear about this. Who is she, actually?"

"Well, she's a – she's a secretary – a private secretary – up at our place. Not a typist. I mean, she can type, of course, but she's not just an ordinary typist or anything like that. She's – well, you know what I mean. Her people are quite all right and all that. She took it up because she didn't want to be just doing nothing at home. Her father's in the City – quite a decent chap."

"Yes, I see", said Katherine again. "And you just carried her off her feet.

154 See *My Edwardian Childhood*, Note 29.

Has – forgive my asking but I shall have to know, shan't I? Has the worst happened?"

"I don't know what you mean by the worst. There's no baby arriving, if that's what you're thinking – at least not that I know of."

"That gives us a bit more time, then. I gather that everything else has happened."

"Why, yes. I thought I'd made that plain."

"You weren't exactly plain about it. Well, we shall have to think. What would you like me to do? I suppose I'd better go away on a visit or something. I'm not sure of the proper procedure. By the way, how long will it take you to provide your evidence?"

"Evidence?" said Geoffrey vaguely.

Katherine clicked her tongue. It was tiresome of him to be so stupid and leave all the thinking to her, especially as, with the curious cold feeling at the pit of the stomach, she didn't feel so clear-headed as she ought to be.

"Well – I imagine you don't want her – the Water-lily's – name brought up in court."

"Good God, no! Curse it. Yes, I see. I hadn't thought of that. What beastly things our laws are. I shall have to fix up something."

"Be careful about it. You remember that book of A. P. Herbert's.[155] We don't want all that bother, and then to have it upset and start all over again."

(That was the dream, of course. Grannie was not really dead – nobody really dead – all the funeral rites over again.)

"Oh, I'll be careful. Really", said Geoffrey, with a vexed sort of laugh, "you're being dashed helpful. Who's running this, you or me?"

"I'm sorry", said Katherine. "It must be the Lammas bossiness coming out in me."

"You're quite right, though. I promise you it shan't be a mess-up. I'll see to that. It would be awful to let you in for anything more than absolutely necessary."

"It's a pity it's got to be necessary at all."

"I know, old girl. It's damnable, and you're a brick. And we've had such a hell of a good time together. It's all my fault. It's just that – things happen. I didn't mean it. It happened."

"It happens to quite a lot of people just about your age", said Katherine thoughtfully.

"Oh, that. But this wasn't like that. It's quite different. It's the real thing."

"I expect it always is. Well, it's not much good keeping on about it. I

---

155 *Holy Deadlock*, a novel by A. P. Herbert, published in April 1934. See Introduction, p. xxv.

think I'd better go and pay Great-aunt Agatha a visit. Stephen will be all right till the end of term, and then I can take him to the sea or somewhere."

"And Molly?"

"Yes, that's more awkward. I think Molly had better be told, and make her own arrangements. She's seventeen. She's old enough to decide for herself."

"There's no frightful hurry, Katherine. And I'm the one that ought to go away. Why should you do all the work?"

"We shall both have to stay over next week-end, because the Fosters are coming down. But there's nothing after that and I think I'd rather not have to sit here and make polite conversation to the neighbours, if you don't mind – all about my husband's career. I'm not a very good actress. Besides, I should rather like to see Great-aunt Agatha. She's a sensible old thing and doesn't ask silly questions."

"Oh, all right", said Geoffrey.

"Shall you stay on here, or shall you go away too? I mean, I shall have to arrange about the house and the servants."

"Must we go into all this now?"

"Eventually, why not now?"

"Surely these details can arrange themselves?"

"Details never arrange themselves. That's what makes life so tiresome."

Geoffrey was beginning to look a lot older, she thought. She was very sorry for him. All for love and the world well lost was a good phrase; but the world refused to get lost. It kept cropping up in all kinds of foolish ways – servants' wages; does this *famille rose* jar[156] belong to you or me? Where shall I store all these books? We shall have to put off the Robinsons; there's a parcel coming from Harridges[157] – will you open it and take out your shaving-mirror and send me on the other things; you had better counter-mand that order for the curtains, you may want another colour-scheme; I promised Mrs Finch a cutting from the Mermaid rose – will you see that she gets it? Don't forget to see the Bank manager about the signatures for the joint account; I'd better leave my big trunk here and send for it when I want it; we need the sweep in the dining-room…everything so complicat-ed and tiresome. Quite little things came thrusting into her mind. Another woman coming here. What would she think about that drawing-room car-pet? The table-linen really needed renewing. Would she think she had been a bad manager? Would she remember that his income wasn't elastic? Would Geoffrey remember it? Would the servants stay on? And if not, would anybody see that the new cook did steaks as Geoffrey liked them? Then there was Perkins. Perkins would personally object very much to a

---

156   D. L. S. possessed a *famille rose* jar in her house in Witham.
157   A fictitious name formed from Harrods and Selfridges.

new mistress but Katherine certainly wouldn't be able to keep her on, and she was rather old to be looking out for a new job. Perhaps Mrs Finch....

She came out of this calculation to find that Geoffrey was muttering something about alimony.

"No!" she said. "There I draw the line. I won't take any money from you, Geoffrey. I've always thought that was a beastly idea. I can manage on my own, and I will."

"You'll do nothing of the kind. That's ridiculous."

"But I shall, and you can't prevent it. Stephen's your job for another year, of course, legally, and you'll want to see him through Cambridge. And you can make Molly an allowance. There's nothing wrong with that. But you're not going to pay for me. For one thing, you'll have plenty to do to run this place – and possibly another family. And for another, I wouldn't take the money if you were a millionaire."

"Damn it, Katherine! I'm not going to have it said that my wife – "

"I shan't be your wife, Geoffrey. And I'm not going to have it said that an able-bodied, educated woman of forty-two couldn't keep herself without depending on a man who'd got tired of her."

"Don't put it that way. It makes me sound such an awful sweep. Hang it all! I've got to do the proper thing. You've no right to put me in such a position."

"I'm sorry. I'm afraid you'll have to pocket your pride. No alimony or no divorce. Those are the conditions. Take it or leave it."

"I've told you before, I don't approve of these modern ideas."

"But I shan't need your approval in future, Geoffrey."

This idea seemed to stagger Geoffrey. It was obviously distressful.

"I suppose not. You sound as though you'd be dashed glad to do without it."

"No - o", said Katherine. "If one's living with a person, it's easier and nicer to be approved. I like being approved. But it would be rather a nuisance to have to go on being approved by somebody one wasn't living with."

"I suppose you want to go and turn into a sort of Bloomsbury frump with all your Museum friends."

This, leaving out the frump part of it, was more or less what Katherine had been thinking of doing.

"Well, I thought I might go back to some of my historical work, if I haven't lost touch too much. Professor King could probably give me some work on her Elizabethan Lives."[158]

"Look here", said Geoffrey, "have you been thinking about this before?"

---

158 A reference to work on the lives of the Tudors by her friend Muriel St Clare Byrne, which was then in progress.

"Only since it became rather obvious that you were working up to something."

"Well I'm dashed! Of all the cold-blooded....Was I so very obvious?"

"Rather obvious, I'm afraid."

"I didn't mean to be. Have you been going through a very rotten time?"

"It wasn't very jolly. I'm rather glad it's all come out into the open now. One knows where one is. But in any case, it's the plain course for me to take. History's my job, and it's natural to go back to it. I've got to occupy myself somehow. You didn't think I should take a cottage and grow tulips? Or drift round boarding-houses at watering-places?"

"No, I can't see you doing that. I don't know that I thought about it. I'm a selfish beast", confessed Geoffrey. "Anyway", he added, cheering up a little, "it'll only be for a short time. When Stephen's older – "

"I can live on him! Is that your idea? Not bloody likely!"

"Katherine!"

"Quotation from Mr Shaw.[159] And I shan't go and live with Molly either. That would be frightfully respectable, but it would be hard on Molly. And very dull for me."

"I don't believe you care a bit for Molly."

"Of course I do. She's –"

Katherine found she was suddenly short of words. Not care for one's own child? That couldn't possibly be true. It would be positively wicked. If anything happened to Molly, she would fly to her assistance. But if it came to that, she would fly to the assistance of any friend. The trouble with Molly was that they had really nothing in common. They couldn't discuss anything of importance. But all the same, she loved Molly – she was her mother. All mothers loved their children.

Pasht, becoming bored with the conversation, got down suddenly from her chair, stretched herself elaborately and walked to the door with her tail erect.

"Oh, Geoffrey, Pasht wants to go out."

Geoffrey opened the door. There was a scuffle in the hall and a noise of human interference.

"It's only Tigleth-Piloser", said Geoffrey. "Pasht gave him one for himself."

Pasht seemed to have no inhibitions about getting bored with her kittens. However –

"Molly's a darling. But it doesn't do for mothers-in-law to foist themselves on newly-married daughters."

(And suppose this wretched business upset Molly's marriage. That *would* be a mess-up.)

"Well, you must do as you like", said Geoffrey, who had apparently

159 A reference to the exclamation of Eliza Doolittle in G. B. Shaw's play *Pygmalion*.

recovered his temper. "I won't interfere. I owe you that much. But as regards the alimony – "

"All right", said Katherine, suddenly exhausted. "We'll talk it over again tomorrow."

"Yes, that's the idea." She realised that he was longing to get the conversation over. "It's getting late and we're both a bit worked up. You trot up to bed. I'll be up in ten minutes."

"You'll find it all right in the dressing-room", said Katherine. "That bed's always kept aired."

"In the – ? Yes, of course. I say, Katherine – you've taken this so wonderfully. Is there anything I can say – anything I can – ?"

"No", said Katherine, avoiding his outstretched arm as she passed him on her way to the door. "I don't think there's anything. Please don't go all goofy. I reallly couldn't stand it."

"Right you are", said Geoffrey. "Good night."

"Good night."

III

"Well, well", said the Professor, a little impatiently, "at any rate she does seem to know what an authority is and what it is not. That's something. The wretched Miss P…. seemed to put the….on the same level as the…. Send your Mrs [Somers] [160] along. She might do."

Katherine waited quietly while he turned over the leaves of the manuscript. She felt no serious anxiety, knowing that he could have no serious fault to find either with the argument or its arrangement. She was only nervous lest some slip or omission might show her to have lost touch with the more recent authorities on the subject.

The Professor's first words seemed to confirm this anxiety.

"You have not mentioned Dr R's article in *Romania*", he said, peevishly, and scrawling a mark on the margin. "Didn't you see it? You must have seen it. It only came out last September."

Without troubling to mention that last September had found her in the throes of obtaining a decree nisi,[161] Katherine merely said she had overlooked it, and was sorry.

"It is the most important thing that has been published on the subject in the last five years", said the Professor. "It throws completely new light on the morphology of the unaccented A.[162] I see you take J's views of…. You don't accept F….?"

160 D. L. S. had not then chosen Katherine's married name.
161 See Introduction, p. xxv.
162 At this stage D. L. S. had decided to make Katherine a scholar in Romance philology. She later changed her to a historian.

Katherine said she did not accept F….and stated her reasons.

"Well, I am inclined to agree with you", said the Professor, rather unexpectedly. "Your last example is new – where did you get it?"

"I don't think I've found it anywhere else", said Katherine, "but it seems sound. Do you see anything against it?"

"No", said the Professor. "It had not occurred to me, but I shouldn't wonder if you are right. I will look into it." He grunted and made a note on his blotting-paper and continued to thumb through the manuscript, making a sharp comment or revision here and there.

"I like your work", he said abruptly, pushing his spectacles up on his forehead and turning round to stare at Katherine. "You have the mind of a scholar. But there are lacunae in your reading. How old are you? Forty-five? Why have you been wasting so much time? Domestic interests? Yes, of course. Pity, pity. But you can easily make it up. Too late? Of course not. It's never too late, if the habit hasn't been lost. It's the mind that matters. You can't give people new minds at 45 – or at any age. I say you have the scholar's mind."

Katherine was silent. Twenty-five years ago, Miss K….[163] had said the same thing, and it seemed to her now that through that long interval she had only been waiting to have it said again. It was as though he had thrown a searchlight back over her life. She saw now that there had been only one aim that she had ever pursued, without misgiving, without interruption or turning back. She remembered Aunt Agatha too. Of all the people who had pressed advice and criticism upon her, that eccentric and ill-educated spinster had spoken the only true words: "My dear, if you want a thing *enough* you will always get it. Your trouble about happiness has been that you have never really wanted it."

She had never been conscious of wanting scholarship. She had never been conscious of making any sacrifice to obtain it, and she knew now that her very unconsciousness was the measure of her devotion. It had come without agonising, because it was as natural and necessary as breathing. She had thought of it as a relaxation, and now she knew that it was her life, and that it would be her whole life henceforward. She had wasted some time, but not much, because the gift had never ceased to mature. She had never wholly ceased to live.

The assurance came to her so quietly that it scarcely disturbed her. The illumination had come and gone in a moment. She said: "Oh, thank you, Professor. I'm glad you think it'll do. Shall I – ? Are you – ?"

"Oh, yes", he said. "You can do my work very well, I think. How about terms?"

163 A reference to Professor M. K. Pope, D. L. S.'s tutor at Somerville College, who had said the same to her.

IV

Sir Philip received the news with cheerful complacence.

"Do his job? Well, of course you can do his job. I know enough about your brains to be sure of that. I don't suppose you will have to do it for long, but you will probably enjoy it for a change, as long as you don't overwork. It's not right that you should have to be starting work again at all."

"But I really like it. It's the thing I do best. I couldn't sit still and do nothing."

"Of course not. There's nothing like a little mental occupation to keep one from brooding over things. It'll do you no end of good – help you over the bad time. Nobody understands that better than I do."

Katherine did not think he understood at all. She tried to explain her enthusiasm.

"I know, I know", he said. "But you mustn't let your enthusiasm carry you away. After all, Kitty, we must look facts in the face. At the present moment, with your eyes shining like that, you don't look a day over 30, but you're 45, my dear, and I'm an old fogey of 50. We've got to begin to take things easy."

"Too old at 45", said Katherine, trying to smile. "It's like a headline in the *Daily Express*."

"Not too old to be the most delightful woman in the world", said Sir Philip gallantly, "but too old to tear yourself to pieces doing other people's jobs for them. You've lived for other people all your life – it's time now to think about yourself."

"I am thinking about myself."

"In a sense", said Sir Philip. "You've got this idea about independence – but you're really thinking of Geoffrey all the time and it's far more than he deserves."

Katherine realised with a shock that she had not been thinking about Geoffrey at all, and tried to say so.

"That's right", said Sir Philip. "Try to put him out of your mind. It's hard, I know."

The old sense of guilt came over Katherine again. It was not hard. It was easy. She realised that she had not given Geoffrey a thought for the last three weeks. There must be something wrong with a woman who could forget the greatest thing in her life as easily as all that.

"Your pride – your wonderful, splendid pride, is sustaining you", went on Sir Philip, "but I'm so afraid the relapse will come. Kitty, my dear – when it does come – you'll remember that I am always there, won't you? I haven't said much about myself, but I think you know what I mean. We're neither of us children. Let me tell you, now –"

It was there again – the old soft, clinging grip of other people's feelings and her own emotions.

Appendices

ᏨᎵᏨᎵᏨᎵ

APPENDIX A: EXPLANATION OF EUCLID'S TENNIS COURT

The solution depends upon the principle that all points of the circumference of a circle are equidistant from the centre. Mr Lammas having found the first post-hole by trial and error, on Mrs Lammas' supplying the dimensions of a tennis court "from some drawer", he attempts to locate a corner-iron by pacing the appropriate distance from post to corner and, failing to find it, walks *in a straight line*, presumably parallel to where he thinks the net would be. Katherine sees the error: in order to find the corner of a certain distance from the post-hole, one must inscribe a *circle*. This she does by placing a peg, to which a length of string equal to half the long side of the court is attached, in the post-hole and then prodding along the arc of the circle traced by the end of the piece of string. Meanwhile Mrs Lammas has found the second post-hole by trial and error, so the second corner can be located more expeditiously by employing the first and a second piece of string (equal in length to the width of the court), inscribing arcs centred on the second post-hole and the first corner respectively. The corner is found where the two arcs intersect. The process can then be repeated to find the last two corners.

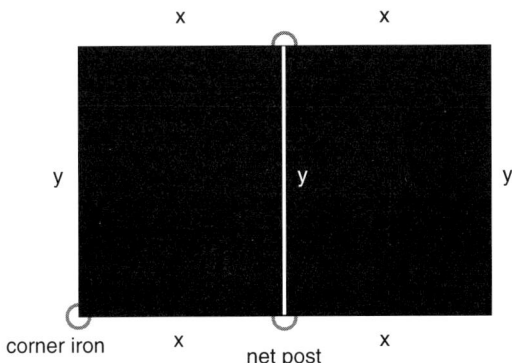

corner iron   x   net post   x

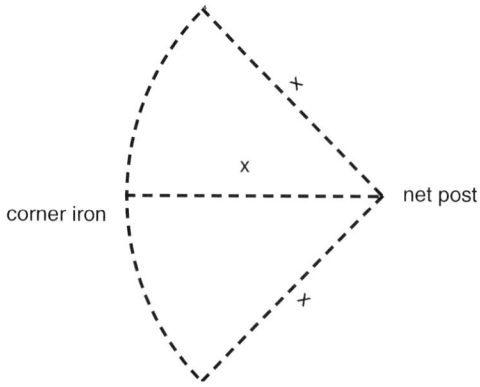

corner iron   x   net post

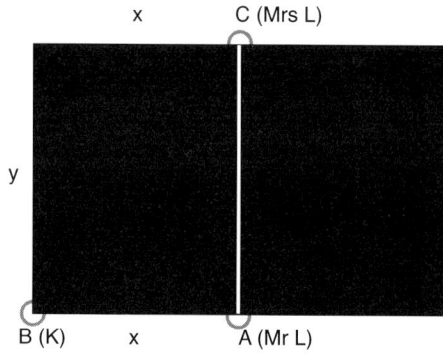

x   C (Mrs L)

y

B (K)   x   A (Mr L)

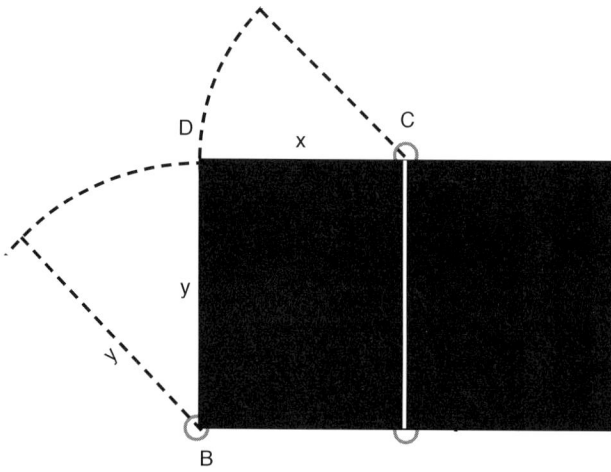

D   x   C

y

y

B

APPENDIX B: TRANSLATION OF FRENCH

"Porthos, old friend, we will never forget the fair days of our youth."

"No, no, my dear comrade. You will write to me?"

"Of course, I will write to you. To think we shall never see each other again – it's sad, isn't it?"

"It's sad, yes. But we'll always have the memory."

"Ah, yes, indeed. And perhaps you will come to visit us."

"That would be lovely. Thank you, dear Athos. Look, don't be too sad. You will find other friends."

"It's not the same thing. It won't ever be the musketeers. Let us never forget our oath. All for one and one for all."

"Of course not!"

"Faithful unto death."

"Faithful unto the tomb."

APPENDIX C: TRANSLATION OF FRENCH

"Good morning."

"Good morning, Mademoiselle."

"Today we are going to talk about Molière."

"Can you tell me who Molière was?"

"Let us see. You have heard of Molière. Who was he?…No?…Nobody knows anything about Molière?"

"Ah! It's Kitty Lammas, isn't it? Well, Kitty. Can you tell us something about Molière?"

"Molière is the greatest comic writer of France; perhaps one of the greatest who have ever lived."

"Ah! Very good. And what did he write?"

"Plays, of which the most important are: *Tartuffe*, *The Feast of Peter*, *The Miser*, *The School for Women*, *The Learned Women* and above all *The Misanthropist*, which is his masterpiece."

"And in which century did he live?"

"In the seventeenth century, at the court of Louis XIV, for whom he wrote the majority of his comedies."

"Good."

"We are going to read *L'avare*. What does *L'avare* mean? Good".

APPENDIX D: GENEALOGICAL TREE

(Overleaf)

Barnabye Barnabas Leigh = Grace Lyte

Barnaby = Mabel Dingley

Sir John Leigh = Elizabeth Dingley
d 1628   of North Court I.O.W.

(1566–1625)

Benjamin
d.1676

Benjamin
1646–1709

Benjamin
1690–1754

Benjamin
1725–17?

Barnabas
1751–1807

Leonard
1773–1848

Frederick
1817–1886

Helen Mary = Henry Sayers
1856–1929   1854–1928

Barnaby

Richard Beckford
of Maidenhead

Peter (to Jamaica)

Sir John
1596–1666

John
1650–1688

John

Col. Peter (Lt. Governor
of Jamaica)
d1710

Peter

Francis ─ William

William
(Author of Vathek)

John = Amelia

Amelia Catherine Elizabeth Mary

Edward Lloyd
1615–1695 From Wales
to Virginia

Philomen
1646–1685

Edward
1670–1718

Edward
1711–1770

JOHANNA
1758–1814

FRANCIS LOVE BECKFORD
1764–1838

m 1788

Francis William John Carleton Ann Charles Thomas
Love
1783–1867 b1789 b1790 b1791 b1793 b1795 1798–1884 1799–1814

RICHARD BENNETT LLOYD
1750–1787

m 1775

Henry Emily
d.1789

Edward Richard
1779–1834

APPENDIX E: EDITORIAL NOTE

The manuscript of *My Edwardian Childhood* consists of 36 pages of lined A4 paper taken from a writing pad. The handwriting is unhurried and there are very few alterations. The manuscript of *Cat O' Mary* consists of 210 pages on similar paper, written in a more hurried handwriting but still with few alterations. It is followed by another 35 pages which appear to be a first draft of sections of a continuation. These items are in the possession of the Marion E. Wade Center.

Another item, in private possession, consists of a small notebook, about six inches square, containing, among other things, jottings for the further continuation of *Cat O' Mary*.